my BIGGEST MISTAKE ...

AND HOW I FIXED IT

my BIGGEST MISTAKE ...
AND HOW I FIXED IT

LESSONS FROM THE
ENTREPRENEURIAL FRONT LINES

by Marcia Pledger

ORANGE FRAZER PRESS
Wilmington, Ohio

Additional copies of *My Biggest Mistake...and How I Fixed It* may be ordered directly from:
Orange Frazer Press
P.O. Box 214
Wilmington OH 45177

Telephone 1.800.852.9332 for price and shipping information
Website: www.orangefrazer.com

Cover design: Jeff Fulwiler
Book design: Chad DeBoard

Library of Congress Cataloging-in-Publication Data
Pledger, Marcia, 1965-
My biggest mistake-- and how I fixed it : hard won lessons from the entrepreneurial front lines / by Marcia Pledger.
p. cm.
ISBN 978-1-933197-50-0
1. New business enterprises--Management. 2. Business planning. 3. Entrepreneurship. I. Title.
HD62.5.P575 2008
658.1'1--dc22
2008029863

ACKNOWLEDGEMENTS

FIRST AND FOREMOST, thank you to every business owner who shared their mistakes and triumphs. I want to thank my current editors at *The Plain Dealer* for their daily guidance and my former editors for their early encouragement of the concept. A special acknowledgement to Marcy Hawley at Orange Frazer Press, who shaped the idea for reaching a broader audience.

To Derrick Pledger, my husband, who gives me a first hand view of entrepreneurship and to my inner circle of friends who all possess the entrepreneurial spirit. To Sharon Christal, for encouraging me to stretch and grow, but mostly for sharing so many personal, and often funny stories about perseverance and risk-taking.

To my mother, a single parent and educator, who first instilled the importance of higher learning, and to my brother who is always on my side.

There are many people who knowingly and unknowingly contributed to this book, including small business advocates in the greater Cleveland area. To all of you, and to aspiring entrepreneurs, I hope you find it useful.

TABLE OF CONTENTS

PREFACE

PEOPLE GO INTO BUSINESS FOR DIFFERENT REASONS. They want to make money. They want to create and sell a better product or service than competitors. Or, maybe they just want to work for themselves doing something that they enjoy.

Nobody goes into business with plans to make mistakes—but problems are a regular part of business life.

This is a small business book that's filled with humble entrepreneurs who share mistakes they made. Most important, they offer tips and practical hints that you can use immediately, whether you're considering starting a business or you're already in business.

In the last five years, I've had the opportunity to interview more than 300 entrepreneurs. Participants range from retail and service businesses to manufacturing and technology firms. They've ranged from sole proprietors and home-based businesses to companies as large as about 150 people. This book includes many of their stories.

Mistakes run the gamut. In these trying economic times, they include cash flow problems, not managing money right or recognizing the importance of a line of credit—until it's too late. But they also stem from being too lax. Maybe they've gone into business with a best friend, or sometimes even worse—family. And sometimes mistakes occur because the company took so long to find a niche, trying to be everything to everybody.

Mistakes tend to take place in different cycles of a business. They occur in the start-up phase, initial growth, high growth and even in a declining stage, due to changes in the economy, society or market conditions. The biggest issue then is how long a business can sustain a significant drop in cash flow.

I've also noticed patterns like trusting people too much, when it comes to dealing with partners or contracts. Sometimes they don't trust people enough. Entrepreneurs often treat their businesses like they are their babies, so it's difficult for them to trust employees or contractor's capabilities.

Lack of effective planning is another pattern that's woven throughout the book. Planning issues include selecting a location, not reaching out for help, or even not dressing appropriately for one of the many roles that entrepreneurs play each day.

This book is designed to be read sequentially, if you're so inclined. Or you can go directly to topics that are immediately of interest to you and your company.

Either way, prepare to learn. Forget statistics or step-by-step instructions on how to run a successful business. In my opinion, there's no better person to learn from than a determined entrepreneur who has overcome an issue and moved forward.

Remember, every problem has an opportunity if you're flexible and willing to make changes.

FOREWORD

There are no magic formulas to make a business successful. Reality is: success requires laser focus, sustained hard work, a bit of luck and a hefty dose of knowledge. For the knowledge portion of the equation, this insightful and revealing book, *My Biggest Mistake... And How I Fixed It,* provides valuable perspectives on what not to do and why. As history has taught us pioneers were too often found face down in the mud with arrows in their backs. The advantage of this book is that it can reduce the "pioneering phase" of the learning curve and help eliminate the dire consequences of those painful arrows. The reader will learn from and be inspired by those who have made sometimes near-fatal mistakes and survived to tell about them.

In her book, Ms. Pledger reveals to readers the critical steps to success beginning with the startup phase through high-growth expansion, including tricky vital marketing and finance strategies. She also illustrates in this lively narrative the sometimes less-than-obvious ramifications of errors of omission and commission. These range from dealing with the delicate issue of family members in the business, satisfying the most recalcitrant customers, and techniques on how to nurture that burning in the belly passion that is a ubiquitous ingredient for every successful business owner and operator. As the founder of a Fortune 500 company that grew from one store to an international chain with almost 1,100 locations, I quickly learned some of my most valuable lessons by trial and sometimes, seemingly, at least, almost catastrophic errors. This book approaches the learning process chronicling lapses of business judgment and showing how they became a positive knowledge base, providing a "hands on" tutorial that guides the reader through real life solutions and practical tips on what not to do. *My Biggest Mistake* is a must read and will surely find a place as a permanent desktop reference for both aspiring entrepreneurs as well as experienced professionals in either large or small companies.

—*Michael Feuer, co-founder OfficeMax*

my BIGGEST MISTAKE ...
AND HOW I FIXED IT

START-UP

STARTING A COMPANY IS A DREAM many realize, but making a go of it is tough. Only one third of all start-ups ever turn a profit.

Two-thirds of all start-ups survive at least two years, and 44 percent survive at least four years, according to the Small Business Administration.

If you have a hobby, talent or vision for a niche unfulfilled, you can start a business. It's good to be in America. All of those factors are key in launching a company, but so is a well-thought out plan.

Too often, entrepreneurs I've met learn that it would have been nice to have a business plan and access to capital before they opened their doors for business. Sometimes they're confident their drive to hustle for sales and services will be enough to generate cashflow. Sometimes it works. Generally it takes more time than anticipated, and bills don't stop coming. It's the reason one of the first things small business advisors often say is hire a good accountant and lawyer before you start a business.

I'd add, finding a knowledgable mentor or mentors, to the list of must haves before hanging a shingle. Surrounding yourself with people who have your best interest at heart is critical in the start-up phase—especially if you're winging it.

Years ago, my husband left the military and started a tennis shoe business in a Las Vegas swap meet center. I went with him to get his business license from the state of Nevada. He was excited, so he shared his plans with the clerk. The clerk listened intently, not like he'd heard it all before. He granted the license, then flashed a smile. To our surprise he said, "Come see me when you're out of business." It was a horrible comment, especially since he knew nothing about my husband's finance plan that basically entailed maxing out credit cards. He couldn't have known that my husband doesn't even wear tennis shoes.

The clerk was right though. The shoe business didn't make it to three years. Starting and running a business wasn't as simple as he thought it would be. He wasn't prepared for the long hours, dealing with inventory, taxes, sales or haggling with customers. And he definitely wasn't prepared for surprises like a move to another location.

He's not the first and he won't be the last of entrepreneurs who face issues in the start-up phase. There's an old business axiom that says if you can last five years, then there's a good chance you'll make it. That was certainly true with his next business.

In this chapter, entrepreneurs share mistakes that they made in the start-up phase. Some deal with trust and confidence. Others with focus, marketing and locations. And of course finances are a factor. Bad decisions can run amuck when every decision is based on a lack of finances.

When you start a business, it's good to think about the big picture. But not paying attention to details can put you out of business.

Consultant had to practice what he preached

Andy Birol
Title: Owner
Company: Birol Growth Consulting
Founded: 1997
Headquarters: Solon, Ohio

I started my business when I had a defining point of losing my job as vice president of sales and marketing at an information services company. At the same time my 6-month-old baby girl was hospitalized for about a month with a potentially fatal illness. I started my growth consulting business in the hospital when I said to myself and aloud, "Nobody will ever do this to me again."

Now I work exclusively with business owners helping them to either build their businesses faster or return to growth. I also help with transitioning businesses from parents to children or from owners to professional management. I've been the only individual on the Weatherhead 100 list of fastest-growing companies in Northeast Ohio for the last two years. And I know I'll make the list again because I've just completed a record year.

But my business didn't start out this way. Like most entrepreneurs leaving corporate jobs, I relied on family and friends to build my business. One year into the business I was hit with a double whammy. Number one, I ran out of friends and family. Secondly, 92 percent of my business was with one client— that I lost.

My biggest mistake was not doing what I tell my clients to do, which is selling, delivering and developing at the same time. I was spending most of my time selling work and delivering on the work I sold. But I was not developing my business.

An owner would hire me, and I'd spend time interviewing their employees and customers to develop strategies to build their business. But I failed to focus on developing my own business.

I was terrified. I realized I had to start using the same skills and methods I was applying to other businesses to my own. Basically, I had to start running my business like a big company, even though I'm the only person in it.

The first thing I did was invest in technology. I built a web site and loaded it with valuable information. The idea was to give away proof of my expertise. The site started attracting business owners who began to think, what could he do if he focused on my business?

The next thing I did was re-engineer my image around a professionally designed tag line and logo. Then I started a monthly newsletter. I started collecting business cards, asking people if I could e-mail them my newsletter.

The newsletters contain tips about how businesses can grow, and it regularly features case studies about my clients. The key is that it's not promotional.

The more people started reading about my thinking and the local businesses that I helped, the more my business grew. That got me lots of invitations to speak and write. And I self-published a book, called *Focus, Accomplish, Grow*, and I'm in the midst of another.

Another thing that made a difference was asking clients if I could list them on my site with testimonials. Chances are business owners recognize someone.

I've positioned myself as an expert on growth. The stronger my business gets, the more I can help develop my clients' businesses.

I coined the term "best and highest use," which means focusing on what your company likes doing and what it's good at doing. For me it was advising owners, as opposed to working for an owner. Never again will I neglect the "developing" part of the equation to sustained growth.

She wasn't ready for business to begin booming so soon

Lisa Paige Blair
Title: Owner
Company: Pretzables, Inc.
Founded: 2001
Headquarters: Cleveland
Employees: 5—25

I've been in the food business my entire career. My passion for it started as a child watching my grandmother and my mother cook.

I was enamored by their elegant entertaining style.

While attending Ohio State, I did a lot of cooking at my sorority house when our cook was off duty. I've been a private chef, worked in restaurants, and I've owned a restaurant and event catering company. I was fortunate to count Michael Jordan and the prince and princess of Sweden among my clients. I've learned a lot from culinary opportunities I've had such as meeting renowned chefs one-on-one and working with them.

Friends and family encouraged me to start Pretzables a couple of years ago because of my culinary skills and attention to detail.

I sell decadent baked goods and package candy-covered chocolate pretzels, Oreos, and popcorn in everything from sandbuckets to Baccarat crystal.

Today, my customers are corporations, individuals, event companies, and wholesalers.

But it didn't start out that way.

When I started the business, I wanted to target the wholesale market specifically.

But I was not prepared at all.

I didn't know the right questions to ask prospective customers, and I wrongly assumed that vendors I needed would be able to handle massive orders on short notice.

My first contract was with a gourmet food market.

A couple of days later, I got a big order from a gourmet food store in Columbus.

Then within a week I got an appointment with a grocery store chain.

I didn't expect to get an appointment with the grocery store chain so soon, and I definitely never expected them to order thousands of chocolate-covered pretzels and Oreos and hundreds of pounds of chocolate-covered popcorn.

I left the meeting saying, "Thank you for the order."

But I was thinking, "Where do I start? Now I have to deliver, and I have one employee."

My packaging is designed for all seasons, holidays and special occasions, and this order was for St. Patrick's Day and Easter.

The problem was that the ribbons—which come from France—and the plastic packaging that comes from different parts of Europe, had to be overnighted.

It was already midseason, and I didn't expect vendors to be short on products.

That meant I had to buy from several vendors.

A dear friend had to drive Easter baskets in from Indiana.

I didn't realize that thousands of those products equated to hundreds of boxes.

Therefore I couldn't pull my sport-utility vehicle up to the loading dock. I had to rent a semitrailer and hire many employees.

We delivered on time—with a minute to spare before the dock closed. The grocery chain reordered, and we delivered again in a semitrailer.

I learned a lot from this stressful but incredible experience.

I allow enough lead time to fill all orders. But in this case, I stayed up four days straight in order to deliver on time.

A lot has changed since then—including my ordering of the packaging materials seasons in advance.

I have relationships with confection and packaging vendors, and I meet with them at trade shows in New York, San Francisco and Chicago.

My passion for food and design is stronger than ever before, but this experience helped me to become a better business woman.

The proper attire is always required

Steven Lovelace
Title: Vice president/CFO
Company: HSI Hemodialysis Services Inc.
Founded: 1992
Headquarters: Beachwood
Employees: 43

We operate a health-care organization that specializes in providing hemodialysis services at 20 facilities in Northeast Ohio. Hemodialysis is the process of removing toxins from blood for people suffering from acute or chronic kidney failure.

We provide emergency services 24 hours a day, seven days a week. My partner, Charles Wilson, and I collectively have worked in the dialysis industry for about 50 years.

We've worked hard to build the business. We're proud of being recognized by Case Western Reserve University's Weatherhead School of Management last month; we were ranked 28th out of the 100 fastest-growing companies in Northeast Ohio.

Most small-business owners know that building your business means wearing a lot of hats. One of the biggest mistakes that we made was not dressing like business owners when we were trying to secure a new account.

About five years after we started the business, when we had just seven employees, we were especially hands-on in every facet of the business. That means we were fixing and delivering equipment, providing patient care, meeting with administrators and doing billing and payroll.

Around that time, we submitted a proposal for a new contract at a hospital. They contacted us and asked how soon we could come over to discuss terms. Since we were in the area delivering equipment and supplies, they asked us to come right over.

We considered changing clothes, but didn't—big mistake. When we first pitched the business we were dressed appropriately in suits and ties. But when we went to talk about the proposal, I was wearing khakis and a polo-type shirt, and my partner was also dressed casually. Our clothes were wrinkled because we had been repairing floor equipment.

The hospital administrator looked at us differently. I can still remember her words. She said, "If I knew you guys were going to come like this I wouldn't have put my jacket on." I apologized for our attire, but the damage was done. The course of our negotiations changed, and we didn't get the contract.

We believed that the administrator didn't think that we were as professional as we should have been. I don't think she thought that we could deliver after seeing us.

Now, I don't go out anywhere unless I am appropriately dressed, even if we have already secured a contract. We're good guys. Our company is solid, and we've always been able to make sales and build relationships.

Right or wrong, I learned that judgments are made based on first impressions. They see you before they hear you, so I always dress for success.

Having the wrong support hinders business

Tracey Mc Hale
Title: Co-Owner
Company: Lush Boutique
Headquarters: Lyndhurst
Founded: 2001
Employees: 6

I started Lush Boutique with my sister Kathleen. We opened our business in Shaker Square nearly three years ago and moved to Legacy Village in October.

We sell fashion-forward lines often found in small boutiques in other major cities such as New York, Los Angeles and Chicago. We specialize in contemporary and novelty pieces and offer a wide range of clothing lines.

Before we opened the business, my sister gained retail experience in New York buying for Saks Fifth Avenue and as a merchandise coordinator with Nautica Apparel. My background is in marketing, public relations and recruiting.

Together our experience made us perfectly suited to open an upscale women's clothing boutique. At least that's what we thought. Our biggest mistake when we started the business was not having the right support network of consultants who understand retail.

We used different accountants and attorneys for basic jobs such as incorporating our business and filing taxes. But we needed consultants who would make sure that we paid attention to details that are vital to our future.

We found our latest attorney and financial consultant about a year and a half ago. We used a different attorney for our start-up needs, and we went through a couple of accountants. We asked around for referrals when we realized that our business had special needs. It's a seasonal business that requires forecasting, and we needed consultants who could help us with our financial planning. Luckily, our lawyer knew an accountant who also specialized in small businesses, including retail.

It would have saved us a lot of headaches and money if we had found them sooner. Some people might think that getting a specialist in your corner is more expensive. But actually it saves money because in our case we were often paying people to research information. A specialist will have answers to your questions off the top of his head.

Our focus should be on sales, stocking our store with the best products and developing and keeping clients—not on financial and legal issues.

We want to get into e-commerce in the near future and expand our business down the road. That takes a lot of planning and money. Good financial and legal consultants can help you minimize operating expenses and make sure that you're not wasting money.

When we moved to this location last year, we doubled our square footage and our inventory. We also had to plan for build-out expenses.

But long before we made this move, our attorney knew exactly what we could afford based on our square-footage and sales projections.

You should never be in a space too big for sales. That's how businesses lose money.

For the first time, we feel confident that we have people behind us who have our best interests at heart.

They're knowledgeable. They work well together.

And they have faith in what we're doing.

Slow paying customer put venture at risk

Ingrid Rodriguez-Reichert
Title: Chairman/CEO
Company: PS Promotions
Founded: 1992
Headquarters: South Euclid
Employees: 2

I always knew I wanted to own a business one day. I grew up hearing about orders and the language of business from watching my father run an injection molding business in the Dominican Republic.

He started his business from our apartment, in our living room, with a machine the size of a car that made bobby pins. I still remember that awful, loud noise. I watched the business grow with products ranging from hair rollers to chalk.

After I graduated from college, I worked for a company that imported casket frames from Mexico. I finally got the push to start a business when the company moved out of state. I knew running a business would take a lot of hard work, but I also knew it would give me the flexibility I craved to spend more time with my kids.

I started a promotional products company because I spent a lot of years observing how different trinkets helped businesses stay on the top of their customers' minds. I remember hotels calling my father asking him to personalize pencils and other products.

I ran my business from home for the first 11 years, but business has doubled since I created a showroom in an office building in South Euclid and a web site.

My first order came from Motorcars. I approached the

president and asked him if he would do business with me if I could save him 10 cents for each personalized car plate frame.

Today, my customers vary considerably from small and large corporations to the government, and my products are just as diverse. We sell everything from typical promotional magnets and rulers to specialized products like hand-woven bags from Guatemala.

My biggest mistake was not getting money up front for an order from another country. Luckily, I learned this lesson 14 years ago, soon after I started the business. It was a lesson that I learned the hard way. I thought I would be put out of business just four months after I started.

Since that experience, I have insisted on getting half of the money up front, or at least a letter of credit that ensures I'll be paid by the bank once an order is delivered.

I sent catalogs to every company I was familiar with.

So when a major rum company in the Dominican Republic inquired about ordering coolers, I was excited. The company ordered about 1,500 coolers at $10 each.

I asked for payment in advance, but I was told a company that size does not operate that way. I started the business with money from my husband and a $10,000 loan from my father. But I didn't want my company to look as small as it was, so I accepted the order and took out a bank loan to produce the coolers.

After I shipped the order, I immediately invoiced the company. Three weeks later, I inquired about payment and was told the paperwork was in accounting. Forty-five days later, the paperwork was supposedly being approved. At 60 days, I was told it was on the vice president's desk waiting to be signed. And at 90 days, it was at the president's desk.

I couldn't believe it. I was starting out in the hole. After four months had passed, I decided to buy a plane ticket to the Dominican Republic. I was determined that I was not going to leave that company without my check. I ended up waiting four hours before I got my money. I didn't make any profit. I was only supposed to make a $1,500 profit and my plane ticket alone cost $600.

But I did learn a valuable lesson. I learned that you shouldn't give credit to any company internationally. I still do business overseas. I have clients in Russia, Puerto Rico and Mexico, but I always get money up front or charge a credit card. Here you're entitled to interest charges if a company doesn't pay in 30 days. In my experience, that's not the case internationally. Some cultures have a very slow payment structure.

You have to protect your company by getting money up front, because you don't have the same rights when you're dealing with another country. Who are you going to turn to for help if you have a problem? It would not be worth the hassle or expense to get a U.S. lawyer to sue a company out of the country. What are you going to do, report the company to the Better Business Bureau?

When I made this mistake, I was a new business owner and I didn't understand my value. For instance, I should have charged a lot more for that job. I didn't just order coolers. I donated my bilingual and creative abilities by creating a tagline in Spanish for coolers that were passed out at resort beach parties.

I learned the value of my products and services and realized I had every right to ask for and expect my money up front.

I still do business with that company. But when I got my first order, I was intimidated by the company's size. They knew I would do my best to service them because I wanted to build my business.

Today, about 75 percent of our customers are mainstream.

But in recent years, the largest part of our growth has been with companies targeting the Hispanic market. We've been doing a lot more work for companies that sell products in South America.

Throughout the years, a lot of things have not changed. I still keep my overhead expenses low in order to keep prices low. And I still love offering my opinions about which products have the best chance of making consumers consider the business.

Luckily for me, one thing did change. I won't put my company at risk for a deal.

Don't give away your services before you are hired

Julius Dorsey
Titile: President
Company: Dorsey & Co.
Founded: 1987
Headquarters: Cleveland
Employees: 2

Companies will always have competitors and finite resources. As marketing consultants, we know that it's not always how much you have, but how you spend it.

I spent 13 years as a marketer at major corporations and advertising agencies before I started Dorsey & Co. My new-product marketing experience started right out of college, when I was an account executive at J. Walter Thompson working on launching Gillette's first disposable shaving system, the Daisy. Throughout the years, my experience has ranged from serving as director of new product marketing at McDonald's Corp. and part owner of Metropolitan Cablevision.

Our team consists of 30 marketers nationwide. We help companies restage existing brands or products, resolve problems in supply chain or respond to unexpected sales performance. We've worked with a lot of different Fortune 1000 clients, including BP, Goodyear, National City, KeyBank, New York Life and McDonald's.

In nearly 20 years, I've written more proposals than I can count. Yet one stands out. My company was just a few years old when I made my biggest mistake: submitting a proposal that included what we thought the problem and solutions were, prior to being hired.

Looking back, I have a lot of sympathy for the new consultant. No matter how much experience they have in their respective fields, they don't have a track record as a consultant. There's a need to gain a meaningful rapport with a potential client, but without examples to give, you start to talk about their business in a specific way.

In my case, we learned a great deal about a regional security brokerage firm in two prospect meetings. We spent time trying to zero in on the scope of work to be addressed and the president's needs, while explaining our approach.

That insight was superficial, though. It was not yet validated. We had not conducted an appropriate marketing analysis of the prospect's market, competition, marketing objective, strategy, budget or tactics for reaching the target audience.

Nonetheless, given our training and experience, we suggested a possible cause and solution for the poor sales performance.

But it's no different than having a physician give a possible diagnosis after listening to a patient describe certain symptoms. It's just an initial diagnosis. Using that same analogy, a physician doesn't prescribe corrective action or medication until X-rays, blood tests or CT scans have been completed.

We returned to the prospect's office for a third meeting, which I believed was scheduled so we could answer any questions and perhaps reach an agreement to do the work. Instead, we got a surprise.

After responding to a few questions, and recognizing that the president agreed with how we intended to proceed, I suggested that we begin working on the first of the month.

Instead, the company's president told us that he believed that we had found the problem and the solution, and that his marketing manager said that she could do the work after reviewing our proposal.

I warned him that our conclusion was preliminary and needed proper marketing analysis and review to verify the problem. Unfortunately, the only thing this prospective client could see was the chance to save the cost of our fee.

It was a big lesson for us. We gave away value that we should have been paid for. Our fee would have just been a tiny fraction of the profit that was available to his firm if it was successful in its quest for new customers.

That was the last time we shared our thoughts about a possible solution with a potential client. Ever since then, we have written only about the process of figuring out the answer in our proposal.

More often than not, it's unwise for both the client and the consultant to put possible answers in a proposal.

Straight talk helps keep clients happy

Greg Harsh
Title: Partner
Company: Concept Services Ltd.
Founded: 2002
Headquarters: Wadsworth
Employees: 21

Just about any company will tell you that sales are an important part of its business. When you get a closer look, you find that the sales structure doesn't reflect that so-called priority.

My brother, Dan, and I run a company that generates business leads for other companies. We deal with all sorts of companies, from small entrepreneurs to Fortune 500s. Whether it's a startup or a 109-year-old company, we have found common threads across all industries—bad practices in sales.

Our employees help our customers find new business. When our people call on potential clients, it's as if they were working for our customers, not for us. When someone expresses an interest in or a need for our customers' products or services, we schedule appointments. However, we found that was not always enough to help our customers succeed.

Our biggest mistake was not having the confidence sooner to tell clients that the contacts we provide will not help them if they don't have the right sales infrastructure to follow up. We feared upsetting customers by critiquing their sales operations. Only about a year ago did we start speaking up.

In the first few years of our business, we cycled through

customers pretty regularly. We were hesitant to address our clients' sales issues. Figuratively speaking, we didn't want them to think that they had to fix the foundation of their house before they could work with us.

The problem was we would do our job and turn over the information. But if those leads did not result in sales, Concept Services lost a customer. We had to continually work on getting new clients.

For instance, the leads we turned over to one company went directly to a sales force that hadn't embraced technology. They weren't using any sales-tracking software to enable them to more efficiently stay in front of a potential customer.

In another case, the feedback from the sales force to a client's president was that the leads were no good. We challenged him to take a closer look at the leads and his staff's sales practices. That customer is now our longest-standing customer, staying for three years.

My brother and I both had careers in sales, even though we took different career paths. I spent years in manufacturing, selling pumps—equipment that you don't replace, you service. He spent most of his career in technology, selling software, hardware and web site design.

Long before we went into business for ourselves, we realized that sales people all have different strengths and weaknesses. Just because you're good at closing in a face-to-face situation doesn't mean that you're good at cold calling.

We believe that sales drive a business—any business. When a company makes sales a priority, it allows the company to focus on what it really wants to do, like being creative or concentrating on services.

When Dan started our company, a year and a half before I came on board, it wasn't growing. His hands were full just managing four employees and taking care of clients.

I left a career with a large firm at a time when I had two children in college. Joining this company meant that not only did I have to invest money, but both of our salaries were slashed in half.

We had to be serious about building sales.

We decided that my only goal would be to concentrate on sales, no matter how tempting it might be to meddle with other parts of the business. Our company grew rapidly as a result.

We don't see companies spending the dollars, investing time or planning a strategy to make sales the priority. What we see are companies being reactive instead of proactive.

Early on, we were performing a task. We were hired to do a task, and we did it. Now, we realize that our task is only as good as the sales structure and the processes that our clients have to support it. Our retention rate has improved as a result. We talk to customers about being set up properly to manage sales.

We're no longer cycling through customers. And it's making our jobs easier as a result. It's difficult to start with a new customer. With a long-term relationship, we learn about a company's culture, products, services and even individuals' personalities .

We're keeping clients longer because we're getting much closer. They start fostering successes and they don't want to leave because we become partners.

Not having an identity hurt growth of a restaurant

Zdenko Zovkic
Title: Proprietor
Company: XO Prime Steaks
Founded: 2003
Headquarters: Cleveland
Employees: 25

XO Prime Steaks is a modern steakhouse with an extraordinary twist on a classic.

It didn't start out that way. We've always been able to serve a superior product in a creative way. But we used to be a little too unusual for a downtown location. The model for the previous XO was serving modern American cuisine with a European twist in a high-energy setting.

Dishes like pork chops with a huckleberry glaze, apple goat cheese and a caramelized onion strudel quickly built us a strong following and base. Word spread fast that we were doing something new and exciting. But a year and a half after we opened, business was at a standstill. We weren't growing. At West Sixth Street and St. Clair Avenue, our location is perfect, but I didn't see the opportunity to get where I wanted to go with the concept.

I started talking to guests more about what they liked and didn't like about the restaurant. I asked them where else they liked to go and how often. I got some feedback about wanting more selection, but identity was clearly the biggest factor, especially in talking to people who most often refer guests from hotels and corporations. People didn't know how to describe and categorize XO.

My biggest mistake was focusing more on a creative cuisine than on the identity and marketability of the restaurant. I'm from Europe, and I always knew that I wanted a downtown location because I like the variety of guests that you get in the city. It gives me a feeling of being connected with other cities. But we were not getting the transient diner or many of the corporate types as I had anticipated.

Why weren't we getting the referrals? People tend to want a themed restaurant. If you're traveling and you want to go out to dinner, you might ask a hotel concierge for a recommendation.

But you'll start out by saying, "I'm in the mood for Italian, seafood, Chinese food or steaks." Even if you would have thoroughly enjoyed our offerings, you're just not going to say, "I want some creative cuisine."

It's human nature. Whether you're talking to your family at home or to friends at work, when you're trying to figure out what you want to eat, the first thing you do is decide what type of food you want. Then you figure out where you want to go.

I changed my entire concept and menu, and it paid off. Sales increased 25 percent in one year. The hard part was figuring out the problem. It was an easy decision to change. My theory is, if you don't make a decision, someone will make it for you.

The first thing I did was look at what was already available at downtown restaurants. I read a lot about restaurant trends in trade publications. A modern steakhouse didn't exist downtown. Once I settled on steaks, I also visited some high-end steakhouses in other states.

After I decided to change the name to XO Prime Steaks, the challenge was figuring out how to maintain a creative edge and keep our loyal base but also add to it.

We had built a reputation for quality, and I didn't want to compromise that. So when we decided to focus on steaks, all of our meat had to be USDA Prime-Aged grade. Only 2 percent of all beef rates at that level, which translates to juicier and more tender steaks. We came up with a menu that includes seafood, pasta and chicken dishes. We also added eight potato dishes and eleven vegetable selections.

We closed the restaurant for five days for training and decorating. We added wood blinds and table lamps to create more of a steakhouse feeling. We changed the bright wall colorings to chocolate brown and golden browns to give the place a warmer and more intimate feeling.

Whatever changes I made with decorations, menu and staff, I knew it would remain a fine-dining establishment. It's the environment where I'm most comfortable.

I started my hospitality career through a three-year apprenticeship program in Germany, where I was raised, at the Intercontinental Hotels in Cologne. I worked my way up from server to manager at a variety of fine-dining restaurants. I've been a beverage director at the Ritz Carlton in Cleveland and in Aspen. I've helped open and manage a downtown Cleveland nightclub and worked in several managerial roles in area restaurants and a country club. I've even co-owned a restaurant in Germany and owned another restaurant in Cleveland.

My goal was to experience hospitality at different types of venues before opening XO. I wanted to find out what works, what doesn't work and why—although there are so many variables to that equation. Something that works in one city might not work in another. Something that works great in a suburb might not do as well in the city.

I learned that you can never be thorough enough in researching your market and demographics. I also learned that you can't hold on too long to something that might not succeed. Don't be afraid to make a change.

Large order with no contract proved to be a large loss

Valerie Allen
Title: Owner
Company: A Desirable Fragrance Bar
Founded: 2004
Headquarters: Bedford
Employees: 1

When people come to the fragrance bar, they come for a unique shopping experience. I enjoy helping people find a blend that makes them happy.

I've always believed that fragrances are an extension of someone's personality. People who like natural scents tend to be people who enjoy life. People who enjoy spices tend to have more bold and fiery personalities. And people who like soft fragrances tend to be more easygoing.

I fell into the fragrance business. As a hobby, I created a fragrance for myself that got so much attention I was persuaded to open a business. Now, my company offers more than 300 fragrances, ranging from familiar scents to custom blends.

The clients I had served during a 25-year career as a makeup artist became my first fragrance customers. Word spread fast. After just a year in business, someone from a national wellness company tried a fragrance and ordered 2,000 bottles.

I was so excited that I accepted a verbal agreement. My biggest mistake was not getting a retainer fee or a written contract before shipping the product.

As a small-business owner and sole proprietor, I was looking at the end result and I didn't pay enough attention to how I would get there—especially with limited capital. I agreed to a $10,000 order and I figured I would do what I needed to do to complete the order, including bringing in family members to help.

I didn't ask for a retainer fee up front because I didn't want to blow the deal. I don't know if it would have been an issue for that company or not. I do know that by not paying attention to details for an order of that size, I got in over my head.

If I had a contract, terms and conditions of doing business with my company would have been outlined and it would have included a retainer fee.

If I had gotten some of the money up front, I would have been able to buy all of the materials needed before I started working on the order, including the teardrop-shaped bottles and satin drawstring bags.

My plan was to ship nearly half the order with payment due upon receipt. That plan fell apart when boxes, soiled from spilled oils, were returned to me with broken bottles. Believe it or not, I didn't have insurance—and more than half the bottles were ruined.

I was devastated. But I quickly regrouped because I knew I had to fill the order in time for a Valentine promotion. I contacted the bottle company to order another 1,500 bottles, only to find that bottle style was sold out.

The wellness company insisted on the bottle design that the first batch was made from. With no contract, things went from bad to worse. The company also decided it no longer wanted the cork caps dipped in wax to create an elegant appearance. It wanted tops that screwed on. And because I couldn't get more satin drawstring bags fast enough, the company changed the price from $5 to $3 a bottle.

It was a nightmare that could have been avoided. The company ended up purchasing only about 400 bottles instead of 2,000, and I took a big loss.

After that experience I decided I needed to focus on creativity and to let a professional handle the details. I hired an attorney. But I also knew that wasn't enough. I had to educate myself.

I started reading financial books and publications and started attending business seminars and workshops. Those seminars are great, but I've learned just as much from other business owners. When you go after a large contract you have to be ready. You want to deliver a product on time, but you also need to protect yourself. Part of being ready means having a contract that details how everything is going to flow, including costs and delivery date.

I still enjoy making people happy at my fragrance bar. It's a competitive field because a lot of people sell fragrances. But it's a business that reminds me of the millions of real estate agents out there. It's the personal touch that makes a difference. I put a part of myself into what I do and I love it.

I learned the hard way that when it comes to doing big orders, it's strictly business and you have to be prepared.

Starting out without a business plan led to painful adjustments

Jane Cibulskas
Title: President/Owner
Company: National Embroidery & Transfer Services Ltd.
Founded: 2004
Headquarters: Berea
Employees: Four

I was facing retirement with nothing to do. I needed a new hobby. Just hanging out with grandkids alone didn't appeal to me. I've raised my kids.

I've sewn all my life, so when my daughter talked me into buying a $6,800 embroidery machine, it sounded like a good idea. For 25 years I was an office manager for an oral surgeon. For 30 years I ran a concession business on weekends with my husband. In the back of my mind, I could see getting really good at embroidery and supplementing my retirement income.

A year later I had put embroidery on baby clothes, towels, sheets, fleece throws, shirts, hats and jackets. I was perfecting this new craft and I was having fun. I could see turning this hobby into a business, so I called a commercial dealer to inquire about upgrading to a better machine.

That's when I got taken in by the hype. He talked about how 1,000 stitches a minute translates into $65 an hour. I could see making $125,000 in that first year alone. Then reality hit me: The $20,000 machine wouldn't fit through my front door.

My biggest mistake was buying a commercial machine and starting a business without a business plan. The reality is, it takes a lot more machines, employees and marketing to make it in this field.

Luckily for me, a longtime friend allowed me to operate for a year in a 10-by-10-foot room in a medical building. I knew I needed help, so I went to a conference run by a top sewing and embroidery company. They painted a better picture of what it takes to be successful in this field. But details were still left out.

For instance, it's not realistic to sew 1,000 stitches a minute because of occasional thread breaks. And the machines sometimes break, too. You have to have another machine while you're waiting for a repair. That's another expenditure. It also takes time, trial and error to figure out ways to stabilize specific products so you don't have thread looping and thread breaks.

It takes time and effort to market a business like this. You start with friends and family, but you run out of them pretty quickly, so you have to start networking with organizations and businesses. It takes time to develop relationships and subcontracting opportunities.

I was in business for two years before I developed a business plan. I tried to follow it because it called for controlled growth.

The last thing I wanted to do was to take on a major order that I couldn't deliver in a timely manner. So I took on all sorts of small orders from school sports teams, bands and small businesses.

Three years had passed and business was growing slowly. The only solution was to spend more money on machines. Costs for new commercial machines can range from $50,000 to $150,000. Fortunately, last summer I found a similar business that was ready to sell at a great price after 21 years. I was most interested in the company's four high-capacity machines. The machines are old, but they're built to last and they work well. The deal also came with a subcontract for the auto industry to embroider emblems on truck rug mats.

Now I can do larger orders faster and more efficiently. If it takes 10 minutes to sew one shirt, now I can do 48 in the same time. That means the cost per piece goes down and makes me more competitive. When I first started, it used to take 31 minutes to sew out a Winnie The Pooh on a child's T-shirt. Now it takes five minutes.

For the first time the business is profitable, with plans to hire more people. We recently expanded into the promotion products business and bought a garment printer.

Buying a machine first and then deciding to go into business is not the way to do it. Start with a realistic business plan. I can't say it enough. Plan. Plan. Plan. Put it into action. Then monitor it and make changes.

Now I'm a believer in the adage, plan your work. Work your plan.

New sign business owners see writing on wall; adjust

Brenda O'Toole
Title: President
Company: Signs PDQ
Founded: 2002
Headquarters: Wickliffe
Employees: Five

My husband, Don, and I were working from home in corporate sales for two different companies when we were both downsized around the same time.

We learned about Signs PDQ through a franchise broker and we bought what he was selling—hook, line and sinker. We liked the idea that we were buying a business opportunity instead of a franchise with lots of restrictions. We loved the huge potential for clients because it's not a business that depends on walk-in traffic. Our customers vary considerably because we do everything from large-format digital printing and retail signs to business printing and vehicle and window graphics.

When you spend your entire career in corporate America, though, with no plans of ever starting a new business, this kind of change is not something you take lightly. We visited similar businesses in New Jersey, Detroit and Columbus. All of them were in strip retail locations, following the parent company's recommendation of starting out in a visible location with walk-in traffic before moving to an industrial site after becoming established.

We were visible in a Willoughby Hills strip center, but not necessarily to the right people. Our biggest mistake was opening our business in a retail location instead of in a light-industrial area.

Our top customers have never been to our shop. They're large and small businesses that have heard about us from referrals or advertising. They place orders by phone or we correspond through e-mail and fax. Our comfort zone has always been the business-to-business market.

Don is our sales manager. But when he was the national account manager for Alberto Culver, his top account was Wal-Mart. One reason he was attracted to the sign business was that he used to make his own PowerPoint presentations. I used to be a local sales representative for Neutrogena.

We spend a good deal of time marketing the business through networking groups, and most of our business has come from referrals. The concept of starting out in a retail location makes sense for this type of business if your goal is reaching single-purchase customers. Some people found us while waiting for Chinese food, or because they were headed to a workout or to the nearby coffee shop. Others stopped by just to visit.

The vast majority of those potential customers were people seeking small jobs like business cards, letterhead or banners for a birthday celebration. We have items for every customer and we take pride in customer service, but with a retail location, many customers had unrealistic price expectations for our quality products.

When we started our business, our target was $1 million in sales by our fifth year in business. The types of customers we were attracting in our retail space made that goal impossible.

Our former 2,000-square-foot location was long and narrow, forcing us to do print jobs in different rooms. The 18-by-120-foot layout didn't promote working together because we didn't have a big, open space. And because it was a retail location, we had to do all vehicle lettering and wraps outside, when weather permitted. Heavy winds, rain or snow prevented us from doing those types of jobs.

We signed a five-year lease, which meant we had to stick it out. But halfway through our lease the owner filed for bankruptcy, voiding our lease. The new owner said our rent would increase by $600 a month, because our former rent of $1,700 was too low. We panicked—for about 10 minutes. Then we realized it was an opportunity to fix our mistake and go after more corporate customers.

We found a great industrial location in Wickliffe with 1,000 square feet more at a lower price. The best part is that we were able to build it out the way we wanted. Besides the office, the front counter and the table used for client consultation, most of the open space is for production. About 25 percent of our space is an enclosed garage that we use to store materials or work on vehicle wrapping.

The new space not only promotes an environment to work together on jobs, it also offers more space for new machines. Our new printer makes it possible to produce spectacular waterproof designs on a variety of materials. Our latest machine engraves all kinds of signs. Our former space couldn't have accommodated that machine.

Eight out of 10 customers have never been here. They're new business owners, consumer products companies, hospitals and construction companies. Most important, they're repeat customers with a variety of needs.

When you start a business, you never know for sure who your customers are going to be, so it's natural to listen to business advisers. It's important to listen to opinions. But it's even more important to know what you want from your business.

Entrepreneur underestimated effect his youth had on possible clients

Scott Snider
Title: Owner and President
Company: M & S Connection Landscaping
Incorporated: 2005
Headquarters: Strongsville
Employees: 13

I borrowed my father's mower and my friend Mike borrowed his dad's Ford Taurus. That's how we started M & S Connection Landscaping six years ago.

Actually we were just 16—so landscaping wasn't part of the name then. We were just cutting grass for family members because we wanted to make some money. We both love the outdoors and we needed flexible schedules so we could play soccer.

A couple of years later, our clientele grew from family and their friends to include our first commercial client, Kemper House nursing home. We invested in a truck and a top-of-the line commercial mower and started expanding services. After my freshman year in college, I no longer wanted a business degree. I changed schools because I wanted to learn as much as I could about plants, trees and grass.

Sales have tripled in the last two years. Our clients used to be 80 percent residential. Now they're 90 percent corporate.

Three years ago, we weren't growing much at all. But it wasn't due to a lack of trying.

I was rejected so much that I did my best to keep myself going. I read a lot. I even went out and bought a motivational poster titled "perseverance," with a photo of a guy hanging off a cliff. It's still on my bedroom wall.

My biggest mistake was underestimating how my youth was a factor in the way prospective corporate clients viewed me.

I have a deep voice and my marketing materials have always looked good, so getting an appointment was never a problem. Things went downhill after they saw me in person.

I've always dressed nicely, wearing a plain button-down shirt, a polo shirt or a dress shirt with a company logo, and slacks. That's not typical in my industry. But I can't do anything about my youthful-looking face.

When I met with one nursing home administrator, I immediately sensed that she was uncomfortable, so I began by talking about my age and experience. I mentioned things like my degree from the Ohio State University Agricultural Technical Institute in Wooster.

When I stopped talking, she came back to my age. She told me that she thought I was 12 when she first saw me. I'll never forget that. I had spent four hours working on a proposal, walking the grounds, tallying up the numbers and making sure it was personalized. I never heard back from her. Follow-up calls were ignored.

One of the first times I met with a hotel general manager, we met in a restaurant at the property. He was hunched over and spent most of his time looking around at his staff. I kept trying to get eye contact as I flipped through charts of my proposal. I did my best to tell him we were all about great service. He wasn't interested. It was horrible.

I was excited before I got there. I got all pumped up and put my game face on. After I left, I felt deflated. It would be like going to a soccer game and having no one care—not your team, the other team or even the crowd. It was such a downer. He might as well have shooed me out of there before I wasted his time. I followed up, but he never returned my calls or e-mails.

Another time I met with a hotel's maintenance manager. He couldn't get past my age or lack of commercial experience. There was no point following up with that guy. Looking back, I guess I shouldn't have been surprised.

When I was 19 and living in a dorm, other students didn't take me seriously. They'd want me to play video games, but I couldn't because I had to bust out a proposal. They didn't understand. Even some family members didn't take me seriously as a business owner. When they saw my truck and equipment, they'd think, OK, I guess he does actually run a business.

One morning, over breakfast, my father asked me how the business was going. I was gearing up for the busy season, I said, but was disappointed that I hadn't lined up any new commercial accounts. Then I shared my experiences and asked him if he would come to one of my presentations.

I kind of needed that gray-hair effect. He's an entrepreneur and has been a chief executive officer and a chief information officer. Just having him present would give prospective clients an open mind about me. He agreed.

I still set up meetings on my own and I make it clear during my presentation that it is my company. I'm the one who works on crews once a week. But having my dad there weighing in on discussions about contracts and services makes a difference.

In the past two years, we've served Marriott Corp., Holiday Inn Express, Royal Oaks Luxury Apartments and Dover Farms Luxury Apartments. Names like that on my marketing materials make it easier to get in the doors of new clients. Doing a great job, networking with associations and focusing on building relationships with monthly visits to my clients helps me keep them.

GROWTH

EVERYBODY GOES INTO BUSINESS with different goals. Some people have no desire to go beyond a home-based business as a sole entrepreneur. Other's envision multiple locations with dozens of employees. Either way, I've never met any small business owners who didn't want to expand their clientele, goods and services.

Have you ever heard of the term, pigs get fat, but hogs get slaughtered? How about the saying, be careful what you ask for, you might just get it? Small business owners who don't prepare properly for expansion can relate. Systems aren't in place. Sales are lost. Customer service and your reputation suffers. Your focus is redirected away from your core strength. Meanwhile leases and bills have to be paid even if the business can't support the expansion.

Sometimes when business is good, seeking new customers and opportunities is the furthest thing from a small business owner's mind. Then, often to no fault of their own, customer relationships end and no other business is in the pipeline.

These entrepreneurs share mistakes they've made with locations, partners and veering off to fields they knew little about.

Whether a business involves multilevel marketing, retail, manufacturing or services, be careful about taking on more than you can handle. When it comes to growing a business, it's good to update a business plan using a pencil topped with a big eraser.

Learn to create order in the midst of chaos

Joan Rosenthal
Title: Owner/President
Company: Marigold Catering
Founded: 1997
Headquarters: Cleveland
Employees: 25

When it comes to catering, does anything ever go completely right?

Our chosen pursuit inherently teeters between controlled crisis and carefully composed chaos. And the days where nothing goes wrong are usually marked by an empty date on the event calendar.

Catering is the ultimate center-ring act under the big tent of the food and beverage industry. It's a team of chefs, planners, servers, bartenders, delivery drivers, florists, food purveyors, rental companies and others balancing on a bicycle on a tight rope under uncertain skies and above a crowd that expects a perfect performance every night for their price of admission.

Sure, we manage. I'm proud of my colleagues and the awards Marigold Catering has received. We were just named among the Weatherhead 100 top Northeast Ohio fastest-growing companies.

I'm probably even more proud of being recognized by Northern Ohio Live as one of the top three caterers for two of the last three years, because it's based on customers' surveys instead of numbers.

But it hasn't been easy.

In the last six months alone, we've wrecked two vans, burned up three hot boxes and one tent wall, and cooked lobster tails and filets outdoors for 150 guests in a torrential downpour that turned our grills into steamers.

My biggest mistake was not figuring out how to create order in the midst of chaos sooner.

When I started this business nine years ago, I really believed I was up for the challenge. But let's just put it like this: If I would have known what my life would be like after starting this company, I would have run.

I've worked in various aspects of the food industry for most of my life for small businesses and major corporations including Hyatt Hotels and Kraft Food Services.

I've done everything from being in charge of concessions in loges at Municipal Stadium when I was in my 20s to holding all sorts of management positions in the food industry, from banquet manager to being in charge of sales and marketing for a four-state region. I've done just about everything except work as a chef.

But none of that experience totally prepared me for running our boutique-style catering company. Except for our corporate menu, we customize all of our menus based on taste, budget or style. For us, the food is the easy part. One thing that sets my company apart is that my chefs come from some of the finest restaurants in Northeast Ohio.

In the early years of my business, I used to panic over major mistakes. It's normal when you're in a business that thrives from repeat business from referrals. I'd think, Oh my God, they're never going to use me again. I'm going to go out of business.

It takes a while to learn that if you stand behind your product and maintain your sense of integrity, clients generally understand. And if you run into a problem that gets to a point where the client actually needs to know about it, honesty is the only policy.

I learned through trial and error, and I'm still learning. But in the early years, when something big went wrong, I used to be devastated. It would become larger than life.

In the last six months alone, we've forgotten things ranging from napkins and utensils to entrees, resulting in a lot of speeding and unnecessary second (or third) trips around town. We've established regular correspondence with the city of Cleveland's parking violations department. And we've been robbed at gunpoint before a pre-dawn breakfast drop-off.

Those are just some things off the top of my head that deal with one part of our business. In the last six months, we had a driver trapped in an elevator for four hours. We had a new server show up dressed, inexplicably, as a cowgirl. And we blew out the fuse in a client's garage a whopping twenty-three times with an electric fryer.

During that same time we've lost $3,000 in rented plates, glasses, utensils and linens. And we set up a luncheon buffet in the wrong building, forcing us to move it before service.

We have the ability to create events from top to finish with flowers and design. Once, fairly recently, one part of an order was misplaced just a few hours before the cocktail reception—the food order. Just three hours before the event, we put together 12 different hors d'ouevres for 85 guests. Now, that was a close one!

I've surrounded myself with talented people and that helps considerably, because you're going to make mistakes. I've learned that what makes a successful caterer is having the ability to react quickly and, whenever possible, calmly in any of the hundreds of unforeseeable situations that tend to arise.

When you run a company like this, you have to be able to make decisions fast and stand by them. You have to do something. You can't just stand there. And you can't be wishy-washy.

Granted, it's years of making mistakes and having to figure out what to do that allows you to make fewer bad decisions and more good decisions.

It also takes time to realize that in relation to the entire event, these mistakes are just a small piece of an event. The key is keeping calm and translating that calm to those around you.

Tile company lost focus on its traditional customers

Jon Kaplan
Title: President and CFO
Company: Stoneworks
Founded: 1988
Headquarters: Bedford Heights
Employees: 47

If you walk into our showroom, you get inspired. You can't help it when you're surrounded by granite, marble, porcelain, glass and metals.

We're in the business of coverings. We fabricate and install granite, quartz and concrete countertops. We sell thousands of tiles for walls, floors, kitchen backsplashes and fireplaces. Our business has grown steadily through the years, thanks to builders, interior designers and contractors.

But when Home Expo moved into the market a couple of years ago, we feared the worst. We saw how the big-box retailer crushed similar businesses in other markets. If we couldn't beat them, we figured we should join them. We had to compete with them for tile sales. But they needed a granite fabricator, and we were able to provide the service because of our advanced machinery.

In the meantime, we stopped a 14-year practice of offering discounts to designers and builders. We changed our business structure to be like this national retailer, focusing our efforts on going directly after the consumer.

Our sales used to be split 50-50 between countertops and tiles. But when Home Expo started selling our fabricated products, 70 percent of our sales started coming from countertops. In the year and 10 months that Home Expo was in this market, our sales nearly doubled.

Then Home Expo closed here and in 15 other midwestern cities, and we were forced to take a good, hard look at our business. It didn't take long for us to realize that we had lost our focus. We alienated a group that had built our company for years, ever since we started out as a tile installation business.

Our biggest mistake was allowing a competitor to change our market focus. We got caught up with our growth.

In three years, we went from 5,000 square feet to a 30,000-square-foot operation. A lot of factors contributed to that. In 2000 and 2001 especially, the Cleveland economy was doing well. A lot more people were spending money on upscale products. We used to cater strictly to this high-end market.

Even though about half of our sales used to come from consumers, many of those customers were sent our way by contractors. For many years we offered designers and builders trade discount pricing. They're the ones who drive this market.

When we analyzed our business, it was clear. We had to win their business back. We were told in April that Expo was leaving this market—not long after we added equipment because the retailer had told us to gear up for more business.

For years we had been known as an upscale supplier.

The first thing that we had to do was expand our offerings to include more lower-cost products.

We used to have a limited selection available to meet more conservative budgets. Now we have thousands of tiles, ranging from $1.25 a square foot to designer tile that can cost as much as $300 a square foot.

Then we talked to a lot of contractors to find out what types of incentives excite them. We put together a new incentive program, and in June we sent out a letter to contractors and designers saying we made a mistake by taking away their discount.

In that letter we offered incentives to help win back their business. And we offered greater incentives than ever before on both products and fabrication. Then we kicked it up a notch to be especially competitive by offering a year end two percent cash-back discount.

In our field, it's all about word-of-mouth marketing. For us, it paid off to be humble and remind builders and designers of our reputation for good customer service.

Each month we started getting more and more contractors signing up for the incentive program. Our service and selection even helped us recently to win business from Northeast Ohio Home Depot stores.

We learned the hard way that you can't lose touch with clients' needs. If you constantly communicate with your clients and provide what they're looking for, you won't fear competition.

Growing too fast led to crisis and then downsizing

John Hansen
Title: President
Company: Suntrol
Founded: 1975
Headquarters: Bedford Heights
Employees: 15

It's sometimes hard for small business owners to move forward when a business is rooted in a passion for a hobby.

In my case, I became intrigued with tinted car windows the first time I saw them during a visit to Florida. I got hooked on glass-enhancing films after I made a profit selling a car that I had fixed up, including tinting the windows.

When I worked in manufacturing, I was tinting windows on the side. When I went into the Navy and reserves, I was tinting windows. So when I bought Suntrol, nearly 30 years ago, I wanted a successful business, but I also wanted to do my part to turn window tinting into a respected trade.

We've done that. About 60 percent of our business is residential customers. Our clientele includes Northeast Ohio's rich and famous, celebrities and sports personalities. The remainder is commercial. We use our glass-enhancing films for security, safety and sun protection at many major corporations, hospitals, museums and financial institutions.

We got out of the auto window tinting business six years ago. It wasn't planned. Looking back, we should have gotten out of the business a few years earlier. I had to downsize to save the business. The company started growing too fast without proper supervision and we almost went bankrupt as a result.

My biggest mistake was focusing on growth without making sure a structure was put in place to hold employees accountable for their actions and customers' needs. At one point I had 28 employees and three locations.

In less than a year, I was forced to close all three auto locations and cut our staff in half. I had to downsize in order to save the business when I found out that some employees were using the company's materials to do jobs on the side. Meanwhile, workmanship was suffering in general.

Soon after I started the business, I was able to buy out a competitor. Within five years I opened three automotive window tinting and accessories locations in Mentor, Bedford Heights and North Olmsted. When we were in a growth mode, I was put in the position to hire quickly. I spent a lot of time traveling to each of the locations and to most of our installations. At the same time, I was trying to build sales. I went from working 12- to 16-hour days, seven days a week, to working 18 to 20 hours many days. It was a rough time in my life.

The hires that I made quickly came back to haunt me. I entrusted and empowered some employees who should not have been in supervisory positions. My hectic schedule did not allow me to manage them properly and the walls came tumbling down.

Our sales had been growing 10 to 20 percent a year. Then margins shrank to below zero, thanks to the use of company materials for side jobs.

Business suffered greatly, because we used to get a lot of leads for the residential part of our business from our automotive locations. Meanwhile, competitors spread rumors that we were going out of business. Even though we were restructuring, closing three stores helped fuel the rumors.

I felt like throwing in the towel. I did a lot of soul-searching and reached out to other business owners and business organizations for help. I decided I wasn't a quitter and fought hard to save and build the business.

Our sales had grown from about $400,000 in 1989 to $1.5 million 10 years later. But we lost a half-million in a year. Meanwhile, I still had to buy and liquidate inventory. I also had to pay for ongoing advertising contracts.

We worked hard to turn the business around. It's taken us six years to get back to where we were, but we've come back strong. Now we're more profitable, with one-third the overhead and half the employees.

We've always been a leader in our industry. We've gotten so many awards from manufacturers and distributors that we've run out of wall space to display them. We won a Cleveland Better Business Bureau Business of Integrity Torch award in 2003 and we recently got an honorable mention.

I still believe that you have to empower your employees. The key is trusting and empowering people who have the company's best interest at heart.

Quick expansion hurt when problems started to pop up

Al Stocking
Title: Chairman
Company: Litehouse Products, Inc.
Founded: 1955
Headquarters: Brunswick
Employees: 200

When I started Litehouse Products it was a home-delivery company for laundry products. I got into the pool business a few years later because we had liquid chlorine, used to make bleach. We started selling it to such clients as country clubs and cities for their pools.

In the mid-1960s we got into other parts of the swimming pool industry, including maintenance. We opened our first retail location in 1968 in Strongsville, in a building we still own.

Today we have about 25 Litehouse stores. We own eight and the balance are owned by licensees. We sell swimming pools, chemicals, pool games, spas, patio furniture, billiard tables, artificial Christmas trees and trim.

My biggest mistake started in the 1970s, when we grew too fast. At the time we kept adding stores because it was easy. We had goods in the warehouse. You get a location and put up some shelves. We got up to 14 stores very quickly. Then in 1980 things started going badly.

First we had a fire in our warehouse in June, early in the pool season. We had to borrow money at prime to build a new warehouse. Meanwhile, interest rates on other debt was sky high. At the same time, the billiard business was adversely affected by new video games that were coming on the market. That killed the billiard business for a while.

Then there was bad management of the company—by yours truly. What specifically I did wrong, I can't tell you. But you've got to give credit where credit is due.

What saved us was that we started licensing stores in new locations like Youngstown, Toledo, Akron, Canton and Sandusky. We kept the stores in the Cleveland area, but we got out of the big hassle of managing remote locations. It was just too hard. If somebody quits 200 miles away, what do you do? It's too far to just send somebody.

We're no longer adding licensees, but the idea at the time was that owner/operators would do a much better job at running a store than employees. It's a fact. It turned our whole company around in two to three years.

If we had not made that move, I'm afraid we might have gone under. For our size, we lost a lot of money in 1981 and 1982. We turned it around the following year. More importantly, it helped us to stabilize and build the business.

Now we're concentrating on growing in other ways. For instance, we're importers of artificial Christmas trees, operating under the name "Santa's Own." We sell trees to high-end retailers and garden centers. We started that business 10 years ago, but we didn't decide to make something out of it until five years ago. We are now looking to buy a similar retailer in another part of the country.

I think most founders will tell you that their primary objective would be to just make a living and stay in business. I feel very fortunate about the way the company has worked out, and I'm confident that the future looks bright for us.

Expanding without proper planning proved to be costly error

Don Stallard
Title: President/CEO
Company: The Reserves Network
Founded: 1984
Headquarters: Fairview Park
Employees: 120

I moved from Houston to become director of human resources for an oil company in Lorain just six months before the company was sold. I had moved a lot throughout the previous 15 years, working at Fortune 500 companies and as an Air Force pilot. It was good to be home. I had no intention of leaving Cleveland again, so I decided to become a small-business owner.

I found some office space in Rocky River, brought along some old furniture I bought from my previous employer and found myself in business in 1984—me and my five desks, credenzas and chairs.

The first challenge was finding people who would work for a start-up for straight commission and no benefits—a recruitment firm that was financed by the owner's savings. For the first two years I took no pay from the company. Household expenses were covered through my earnings as a squadron commander in the Air Force Reserves. My wife also supported us by teaching grade school.

I remember being so proud on Oct. 26, 1987, when we hit $1 million in sales. A couple years later I changed the company's name to The Reserves Network to reflect our expansion into industrial and technical staffing.

We've worked hard to build this business, adding more professional, information technology and medical staffing services through the years.

We have about 120 employees who work in six states. We'll probably place more than 18,000 people in jobs this year. The average temporary assignment may be 11 weeks, but thousands will get temp-to-hire positions. This year we're anticipating $60 million to $70 million in sales with a goal of reaching $100 million in the next few years.

I'm grateful. I have a good management team and two sons who work in the business. But I also know the company could have been much larger if we had not lost our focus a few years ago when we attempted to branch into the training business.

My biggest mistake was expanding to another field without planning properly. We didn't even define a particular segment to focus on. We decided to offer everything from corporate training to government-sponsored training. We tried to be all things to all people and as a result we were ineffective with all of it.

We opened three training locations. One was at our corporate headquarters in Fairview Park, and the others were in North Olmsted and Garfield Heights. We could have muddled through and developed the business over a longer period, but the recession hit us. Our costs started rising, and less money was coming in.

In a recession, not only is staffing cut back but also training is delayed until better times. The business was not doing well, but we had leases to pay, people on the payroll, equipment and capital expenses. We lost a few hundred thousand dollars over two years. That money could have been used to expand our core staffing business.

Getting away from our core business at the wrong time was a misadventure, a misstep and a miscalculation. We were forced to shut down the training business. We had a lot of expenditures at the worst possible time. For instance, we had a five-year lease at one location and we had to pay $5,000 a month for an empty building for a year before we finally found a business to sublease it.

We came out of the recession in good shape. Luckily we had the capital to sustain our core business.

Entrepreneurial people have big egos. They believe that if they're successful in one arena, they tend to be successful in other arenas. It may be true if they take time to plan adequately, hire the right people and have adequate financing in place to get through the start-up period.

Would I do it again? We're a bigger, stronger company now, more capable of taking on ventures outside our core. But I'd be much more selective in determining new business niches. And I'd make sure that we planned thoroughly.

Business lost the family feeling when it opened larger location

Scott Cowan
Title: President
Company: Century Cycles
Founded: 1992
Headquarters: Rocky River
Employees: 30

Is bigger always better? For us, it was not.

Before we opened Century Cycles nearly 15 years ago in a small shop in Medina, we spent six months working on a business plan trying to determine the viability of making it for five years. Five years after we opened, our sales were about $15,000 above my original projections.

Opportunities and good timing were the reasons Lois Moss and I opened stores in Rocky River and Peninsula. By the time we opened our fourth store, in Solon six years ago, we started thinking that expanding would be phenomenal. The store was 7,000 square feet, more than twice the size of our other stores. We thought it would be so hugely successful that our next step would be other markets.

We were a family business—until we opened that fourth store, it seemed. Losing that family business feeling was just one of the problems with having multiple locations.

My biggest mistake was growing too big for what we really wanted to be.

When we opened the first store, I had lost a job in sales and was at a crossroads. I wanted to find something that I was passionate about. I explored doing something with bikes because I was a serious biker and the industry appealed to me for so many reasons.

Just about everybody has had a bike at some point, and people want those same experiences for their children. I believed in the sport from an economical and physical standpoint, and because it's an activity that you can do your entire life. My 73-year-old ex-father-in-law is biking with a group across the country right now.

But when we opened our fourth location, everything got complicated. With three stores, our model worked well. With four stores, our model was being patched together, from the computer system to deliveries. All of our bikes were shipped to the largest location because we didn't have a warehouse. It became difficult to get bikes to other locations in a timely manner.

There are a million reasons why a store doesn't do well. In our case, the strip shopping center we moved into in Solon soon lost several retailers, including the anchor grocery store, a big Hallmark store and a 10,000-square-foot clothing store.

We lost seasoned employees who bought out our competition. And even though people had been telling us for years that we should open on the East Side and the area's demographics were right for our business, traffic flow was never up to par.

For a bicycle store, 7,000 square feet was big. It felt like a big-box retail store. It didn't have that warm, fuzzy feeling. Despite its size, it was never our best-performing store in the five years we had it before closing it last year. The company started feeling corporate, and I was having trouble getting to all four stores each week.

Things were not going as planned. But it took a lot of soul searching before we decided to close the store. It's a difficult decision.

When you decide to close a location, you have to think about how a company will be perceived by employees, customers and onlookers. We're a pretty big dealer in the bike industry locally and nationally. We're one of the top 10 Raleigh dealers in the country and we wanted to make sure the industry knew it was still a viable business. We did that by taking 17 employees to our national convention last year.

On the local level, we worried about our employees. My former business partner, Lois Moss, and I had decided to end our marriage, so employees were already wondering what that meant for the business.

Together we went to all of the stores to tell employees that we had made a mistake and we had decided to close the Solon store. We also wanted them to know that they had a future in our company. Fortunately for us, everybody remained with the company.

Then we mailed coupons and letters to customers urging them to shop at our other locations. We were able to track the results. Sales at our Peninsula location, the closest store to the one that we closed, are up 25 percent for the year.

Stress levels are down. We're making better buying decisions. And I'm back to visiting all three stores every week. It's fun again.

We're a much stronger company now and we're committed to the future of biking in Cleveland.

FINANCES

GO TO ANY LENDING INSTITUTION in America and you can be sure that the people or staff will want to know about your sales and profits. A great personality and enthusiasm for your product or services will be noted, but that's about it. Success in business is generally equated with revenues.

Whether it's a start-up business or a large scale firm, bad financial decisions can kill a company quicker than anything. It's hard to concentrate on your business when you're worried about paying bills and employees. Great financial decisions clears your mind to create and expand.

A lot of mistakes small business owners make involve finances. They fall out with partners because of money. They sign bad contracts or don't watch expenditures when business is good. They lose sight of the fact that profit is more important than sales. Sometimes money goes out faster than it's coming in. That's when landlords and the IRS start feeling more like pimps. Still, other times money isn't coming in because their entire business strategy needs to be updated, due to shifts in the market or economy.

Entrepreneurs share experiences that range from the classic tale of starting a business undercapitalized to seasoned entrepreneurs who underestimate how much effort it takes to find venture capital. One entrepreneur found it's best to spend venture capital on top managers who can help build the company, instead of being overcautious about allocating funds.

Too often business owners don't try to create or enhance relationships with banks and other lenders, until they're in a bind. Remember, banks need you as much as you need them. They're not interested in paying you interest, they want to charge you interest. One start-up entrepreneur learned the hard way that putting all of the money back into the business and not taking a paycheck, doesn't look good to banks. You have to have a paper trail. Besides, getting paid builds self-confidence.

Every day, small business owners learn lessons about juggling money. Sometimes they tap home equity lines, family, friends or credit cards. When it works out, they pay them off as fast as they can. Other times they face bankruptcy, before they find a way to turn things around.

Unlike other types of mistakes, when they involve finances, it's rare to see small business owners make the same mistake twice. Generally they make drastic changes in order to return or reach profitability for the first time.

Not paying himself first left entrepreneur coming in last

Evon Gocan
Title: President and CEO
Company: EG Enterprise Services Inc.
Founded: 1993
Headquarters: Cleveland
Employees: 7

Don't go too far from what you know. That's what account executives were told about quality issues when I worked for Xerox. So when I decided, a couple of years before I left Xerox, that I was going to start my own business, I knew I would open a graphics print and design company.

I always wanted to start a business, but I wanted to work in corporate America first to gain a wide range of experiences. I worked in labor relations consulting for a law firm, telemarketing and sales before I started my own business 11 years ago. We do everything from designing brochures, newsletters, annual reports and manuals to laying them out, printing and mailing them.

We work with small businesses and associations, and larger clients including the city of Cleveland, Metropolitan Housing Authority, Playhouse Square and Parker Hannifin.

When I started the business, I didn't have much money. I took money from my 401(k), and I didn't have a bank loan. I worked hard to build the company, and everything I made went right back into the business. A big mistake I made early on was not paying myself first.

My accountant advised me to pay myself soon after I started the company. But I didn't take his advice until about three years later. My immediate concern was taking care of employees and vendors and acquiring new customers.

As the business started growing I started adding employees. But I was not taking a paycheck. I was subsidized by my wife's paycheck, and it makes it hard to focus on running a business when your personal needs are not being met. More important, as far as banks are concerned you're not creditworthy because you don't have an income.

A couple of years into the business, I applied for a loan and was turned down. Sales had doubled from the first year, but I couldn't get a loan because on paper I wasn't well-rounded. All of my free labor should have been documented.

Financial institutions look at your financial makeup all the way around—your business and your personal accounts. When you don't pay yourself, you're considered a poor business owner. How can you personally guarantee a loan if you have no personal assets? Back then I didn't have enough assets. I had not even purchased a house before I started the business.

When business owners use their own money to build the

business, they don't generally itemize the labor they donate and all the other little expenses. That means they can't recoup any money because it's not documented. There's no paper trail.

I get a paycheck now, but I may not cash it if times are lean. That's the time to redirect money back into the business. I cash the checks when there's more cash flow. From a mental perspective, seeing a check physically is important. It motivates me because I'm touching and feeling a check. The adrenaline starts to flow.

You have to understand that you're not being a good business owner if you don't put yourself into the budget. It's important in order to focus and grow your business.

Big-business woes put new business of local inventor onto thin ice

Pam Moore
Title: President
Company: Ice Tubes, Inc.
Founded: 1997
Headquarters: Tallmadge
Employees: 4

I started Ice Tubes six years ago after trying to melt ice cubes to fit into my son's water bottle at a soccer game. My product is an ice tray that makes ice for bottled beverages—bottled water, bottled pop or sports bottles.

We've sold almost 2 million ice trays. We're shipping nationally with Wal-Mart and internationally with other stores. We're rolling out our second product, Ice Singles, nationally. But it hasn't been easy.

I had purchase orders for more than 50,000 trays before I had one to sell. I really thought that I would be a millionaire within a year. Instead I had all sorts of product development and production problems.

I didn't make any money the first two years. When I got the largest order that I had ever had, three years ago, Lechters filed for bankruptcy protection before I could collect any money for the order.

One of my biggest mistakes was thinking that I was safe by dealing with a huge, reputable business that had been around for a long time. I thought big businesses were invincible, and Lechters was a housewares retailer that had over 600 stores.

I had been doing business with them for more than a year when they doubled their average order with me to $100,000.

I gave them unlimited credit with 30 days to pay. It was a big step for me, but I did it because it was a big, reputable retailer.

One month to the day after my payment was due, I got a notice by e-mail saying that they were filing for Chapter 11 protection.

The note said that any purchase orders placed before that date would not be covered. But they had secured money to cover any purchase orders placed after that date. I was devastated. I cried for three days.

I still had to pay for the product and all the expenses that went along with it.

But then you have to suck it up and move forward. I tried to get my products back, but I found out that they were within the law to keep them and sell them, and keep all the money.

I was advised to try to work with the company for future orders while they reorganized.

But since they didn't want to prepay for a shipment, I didn't send any more merchandise. I made the right decision, because they went out of business a year later.

The experience taught me to check out companies to see how they pay their bills, no matter how big they are. We have implemented stronger credit-check and accounts-receivable procedures.

About the same time as the Lechters incident, I was negotiating a national purchase order with Kmart that could have been up to $1 million.

This time we did some credit checking. Much to my surprise, the company wasn't paying its bills on time. I walked away from the whole deal. Two months later, Kmart filed for Chapter 11 bankruptcy protection.

At that point, Ice Tubes could not have absorbed that kind of loss. Since then we've walked away from some big accounts. But in business today, it's better to be safe than to be sorry.

Buying on faith was a $30,000 error

Patricia Snowbrick
Title: President
Company: Stat-Expeditors Inc.
Founded: 1980
Headquarters: Columbia Station
Employees: 57

My courier company has come a long way. We deliver medical supplies to more than 500 nursing homes in the Eastern quadrant of Ohio. We work for institutional pharmacies and pharmacy management groups.

But we're no longer just a medical courier company. About three years ago, we branched out and started delivering paperwork for attorneys and payroll services companies. We also have a United States postal route in Olmsted Township. I'm proud to have been recognized among the Top 10 female business owners in Northeast Ohio in 2002 by the local chapter of the National Association of Women Business Owners.

My husband and I started this company in 1980. Three years later, he passed away. At the time it was called Progressive Truck Lines, and we hauled steel for local companies and newspaper ink for *The Plain Dealer* and other Ohio newspapers. Before we launched the business, he was a truck driver and I had spent my career in the steel industry—my last job as a controller.

Several months after my husband died, I was approached by his longtime friend, who said he was moving to Florida and asked me to buy part of his hauling company. I thought it would be a good way to expand my business.

I was supposed to be buying an excellent money-making customer list of steel businesses—accounts he claimed he had had for years. I didn't know that his company was going under.

Nor did I realize that he didn't do much business with companies named on his so-called prized customer list. I was naive. I took him at his word. I was supposed to be getting $10,000 a month in billings. He told me that I would recoup my $30,000 investment from profits in about eight months.

It took only about a month before I realized that I'd been taken.

I had signed a contract to pay $30,000 for basically a list of about 15 steel companies, including LTV Corp. and Olympic Steel.

Nothing at all was tangible.

It was not an intelligent decision, but I learned a great deal from that experience.

I was supposed to pay my late husband's friend $2,500 a month. I didn't want to pay anything.

But my attorney told me that it was a binding contract and I had to make payments.

He said, "You were gullible, and you didn't investigate the company." I dragged it out and paid $1,000 a month, but I still paid the entire $30,000.

In 1990, I sold the trucking and warehousing division of my company and changed the name to Stat-Expeditors.

Later I bought out a woman who owned a small medical courier service. But before I completed the deal, I surveyed every one of her customers.

I asked them, "If we merge, would you do business with me?" Then I solidified contracts from those customers, and we were in business.

The woman from whom I bought the business told me that she had never met anyone so thorough.

She didn't know about what had happened to me before. I just wish I had been that thorough the first time.

Once you've been beaten, you had better not make the same mistake twice. I'm meticulous now. I dot every "i" and cross every "t." Sometimes you learn about business the hard way. So surround yourself with good people and be thorough.

Not adding up project elements had held back paint business

Brendan McGarry
Title: VP of Operations
Company: Mike McGarry & Sons Inc.
Founded: 1946
Headquarters: Cleveland
Employees: 75

My grandfather, Mike McGarry, started working in the paint business in the 1920s, and he opened our business in 1946. Years later he sold the company to one of his nine children. Then his brothers got involved and made the business grow to what it is today.

We provide and apply painting and wall covering for industrial, commercial and restoration projects. Our customers are small to large businesses that range from professional offices to large industrial facilities generally located within a two-hour radius. Some of the projects we've worked on include the Old Stone Church, Severance Hall, the Botanical Gardens in Cleveland and the Heinz Loft restoration project in Pittsburgh.

Work in our industry is sporadic, so we generally have 50 to 90 employees each year, depending on the season and the economy.

As operations manager, my biggest mistake was not measuring projects in a quantifiable way until about five years ago. On large jobs we'd frequently find that we were overbudgeted, and we didn't earn what we had expected.

It's easy to keep track of small jobs. But large jobs can take weeks to as long as a couple of years. We kept getting to the ends of jobs before we figured out that they hadn't performed the way we wanted. Worse yet, there was nothing we could do at that point.

The only time we really knew where we stood on a job was at the beginning and at the end, when we'd find that we didn't make enough money or, in some cases, any money on a project. We started involving our foremen with weekly progress reports, and business immediately started changing for the better.

Until then, we had not adequately communicated with our painters what was expected of them. Our people always did a good job. The problem was, they did a good job no matter what the cost was to the business.

In other words, painters were forced to go with the flow until management started paying more attention to details that affected our bottom line. For instance, before the change, another contractor might come in and put a drop ceiling in an area before we were able to paint with a sprayer. As a result, our guy would be forced to paint with a brush.

That one move would cause significantly more work, delay the project completion date and cut into our profits.

Basically you can't manage anything you don't measure. If you want something to improve, you start measuring. When people know that something is being watched, it automatically improves.

Shopping center purchase highlights importance of hiring consultants

Donna Hom
Title: Owner
Company: Hom's Properties Management
Founded: 1973
Headquarters: Cleveland
Employees: 80

I was a waitress for many years, and my customers always looked for me. They thought I was the boss. They said I knew how to take care of people, and they encouraged me to open my own restaurant.

I told them I didn't have the money. Some customers lent me $5,000 to help me get started, and they told me they would become my customers. It wasn't easy, though. I asked five banks for $5,000 and nobody would lend me money. Finally, a banker gave me a chance. All I needed was a chance.

I've had some success in business. I've had the King Wah restaurant in Rocky River for 32 years and the Ho Wah restaurant in LaPlace in Beachwood for 25 years.

I also have a strip shopping center in Rocky River and several residential rental properties.

I never had a formal education. I'm a good judge of character, and I try to use common sense in making business decisions. I made my biggest mistake about 20 years ago, when I bought Mill Creek Commons in North Ridgeville. I didn't do my due diligence in financing and analyzing the property before I bought it.

The deal included selling a home I owned in South Euclid and adding some equity for the shopping center. It was a land contract deal that involved financing from the owners.

They convinced me that they could provide the financing and I would save money on points, appraisal fees and even attorney fees. I didn't get a lawyer to review the leases. I didn't discuss it with anyone other than the real estate broker. He was actually the manager of the property.

He had sold me other properties, so I trusted him. But I got in all sorts of trouble. I did talk to the tenants before I bought the shopping center. They said, "We love it here. We've been here a long time. Don't worry."

But they didn't stay long after we took over. Those same tenants left about three months later. One by one they moved out. When I bought it there were eight tenants, and it was nearly fully occupied. Plus about half of the office space upstairs was rented.

When people started breaking their leases, I was paying the mortgage for empty spaces. Luckily for me, I had enough assets to cover my losses. Otherwise, I would have had to file for bankruptcy.

The building was also a problem. The main waterline was plastic, and the pipes burst. Before I knew it, water bills went from $200 a month to about $2,500 a month. I spent thousands to make repairs and to change the waterlines to copper. I spent another $10,000 to replace the roof.

It took years to recover. I got a floating-rate loan, which substantially lowered the monthly mortgage payment. With time and a little luck, interest rates dropped considerably. Now we have very good tenants, and the area is rapidly developing.

It was a terrible experience, but I learned a lot from it. Most notably, I learned the importance of bringing in consultants. It doesn't pay to cut costs up front. Three years after I bought the shopping center, I bought and gutted an old manufacturing facility that borders Midtown. It took a year to remodel the building and turn it into Asia Plaza. Our restaurant, Li Wah, is the main tenant, but another six years passed before the shopping center was fully occupied and we started getting positive cash flow. Now we're planning to expand Asia Plaza by adding a food bank within the next year.

The shopping center experience helped me to have realistic expectations about real estate. It was bleak back then, but I've always remained positive.

Beverage dealer now buying buildings too

Alan Iacofano
Title: Owner
Company: World Wines Beverage & Liquor
Founded: 1983
Headquarters: Mentor
Employees: 6

I've always been conservative. I was 22 with a wife and two kids when I won the lottery for $67,000. Believe it or not, I held on to most of that money for six years.

I ended up putting the money toward buying out my father's business, Shoregate Beverage & Liquor, in Willowick. I had no intention of following in his footsteps, but he had spent 35 years building the business, and I wanted to keep it in the family. At the time, I was managing a scrap metal business, and I really enjoyed it.

Fourteen years after I took over my father's business, I bought two liquor agencies in Fairport Harbor and Chardon with money I had saved. I needed a challenge, and I got it. Both stores were pretty run down, and I worked hard to renovate and turn the businesses around.

I barely got out of high school, but I know what it takes to build a successful business: Put your customers first and hire good people. I've had four businesses, and three of them were bought when the businesses were not for sale.

But one thing that I never thought about was residual income. My biggest mistake was not buying a building until last year. The only thing I had ever owned was goodwill and inventory. I thought about all the millions I spent on rent throughout the years and realized it was time to stop paying rent and start paying myself.

When I bought my liquor agencies, I should have tried to either buy the buildings they were in or move them to another location. If I had done that, I would have been a property owner regardless of what I had done with the businesses.

I should have sought out more financial advice a lot sooner. I waited until I had a 22-year banking relationship before I got a $500,000 loan from my bank and another $500,000 from the Small Business Administration. Six months ago, I bought an 18,000-square-foot strip shopping center and used half the space to build World Wines Beverage & Liquor.

Our store is four times larger than our former Mentor location, and we offer one of the largest wine selections on the East Side. The new space has enabled us to attract an entirely different customer base, from the casual drinker to the connoisseur. We sell bottles that range in price from $3.99 to $399.

I still maintain that the keys to this business are having the right people behind the counter, a nice selection of products and always listening to the customer. But as a business owner who is aging, I'm now thinking more about what it will take to semi-retire. I won't ever retire. I'm hoping that this building will be paid off in 15 years, my children will take over and I'll live off rental income.

Even though I'm basically a conservative guy, I am a risk taker outside my business, whether it's gambling in Vegas or on the stock market. But with six kids to raise, I've always been worried about not succeeding in business. I always wanted to self-finance because I was afraid of not being able to pay off debts.

That wasn't the only reason I didn't take out a loan sooner. First, I had to become more confident in what I was doing. I had to get to the point where it no longer felt like a big risk to me. The other problem was that I was so busy with day-to-day operations—book work, physical labor and customer service—that I lost track of that long-term plan. In my case, I never set a long-term goal for my business. I set a lot of small goals that I achieved, but I never had a long-term business plan.

I'll never forget being so proud several years ago when we finally grossed $1 million in a year from beer and wine sales. What I wasn't looking at was where that money was going. I had three locations, three rental payments, three managers and several employees to pay. Now our goal is set at over $1 million at one location in our first year of business.

Years ago one of my employees told me, "we work harder not smarter." Now I'm trying to work smarter—not harder.

No cash flow sure way to sink starter business

Sean Sullivan
Title: Partner
Company: Euro USA
Founded: 1986 (as Navillus)
Headquarters: Cleveland
Employees: 75

I had a degree in psychology with a minor in marine sciences. I considered getting a master's in psychology, but I was bored. I ended up starting a business selling fish from the back of a refrigerated truck.

It was actually a natural transition. Back then, all of my friends were marine biologists. I had a friend in the commercial fishing industry in Wilmington, N.C. I met the owner of one of the largest packing houses in North Carolina where fishermen sell their catches. For a year I'd make two trips a week to North Carolina, driving my truck about 48 hours a week. I'd haul fresh fish back to the Cleveland market and sell it to grocery stores and restaurants.

It was a cash on delivery business, and after a year I'd saved enough to open my first wholesale/retail business in Rocky River. But opening a business was all I had enough money for; I wasn't prepared to sustain it. I called the company "Navillus"— Sullivan backwards—and I thought I was ready for business. All I was thinking about was putting one-third down on leasehold improvements and equipment. I never thought about how long it takes to be profitable.

My biggest mistake was not understanding cash flow before I opened a retail storefront. I needed enough money to pay for expenses for three months, ranging from rent and payroll for six people to products and miscellaneous expenses like truck leases, insurance and office supplies. I didn't have it.

I had huge cash-flow issues. I was used to driving a truck and dealing exclusively with cash. Frankly, when I opened a storefront, I was thinking like the movie "Field of Dreams." Build it and they will come. I really thought the retail part of the business would take off immediately, because I was the first independent fresh seafood retailer on the West Side.

I spent a little on advertising, but it wasn't enough.

Meanwhile, I wrongly assumed that I would get paid when I wanted, and that I would be able to get credit to finance the retail side because I had been in business for a year selling fish from my truck. That's not the case.

On the wholesale side of the business, it was difficult to get new customers to pay cash on delivery. I had been a one-man and one-truck operation for a year. I was used to pulling my truck up to the back of a restaurant, unloading fish and collecting a check immediately.

Everybody needs cash flow, so they weren't anxious to pay c.o.d. I couldn't carry them. I could only accept c.o.d. terms.

I was in a storefront for a month before I realized that I would be out of business the following month with a lot of debt if I didn't do something quick. Getting a loan from a bank was not an option.

After I signed the lease, I spent about $50,000 for freezers, compressors, refrigerated counters and improvements to the space. I didn't mind because I just knew that more money would be coming in fairly quickly. Unfortunately, customers didn't buy fish nearly as often as I thought they would. I opened the business with virtually no cash.

Nothing was going the way I had planned. I owed money to equipment vendors, and they were threatening to pick up their merchandise.

I knew I had to take in partners. Having partners was never part of the plan, but I needed money and input. Actually, I never had a well-thought-out plan. And I definitely didn't have a business plan. Back then I knew nothing about cash-flow analysis. I didn't realize I needed cash until I was out of cash.

Luckily, I found three people who not only invested money but also gave me insight on building the business.

I didn't want to sell any of the business. But I ended up having to sell 30 percent of the business to raise money for cash flow. I sold 10 percent to each investor, and they all brought something to the table besides money.

One friend was a banker who later helped the business secure small business and economic development loans. Another friend worked in day-to-day operations. He was an excellent manager and a hard worker. And the most important investor was my father, who has vast experience in running and developing a business.

I was very fortunate to find partners who contributed their time and expertise. If I hadn't been in a position to raise money, I would have gone out of business.

Twenty years ago, when it was time to take the business in a different direction in order to grow, I bought out my partners.

If I had to do it over again I would have probably delayed opening the business for six months to a year, until I could do it right. I learned the hard way that cash flow is king.

Bargain bookkeeper fell into tax trap

Nancy Charney
Title: President
Company: NS Charney & Associates
Founded: 1994
Headquarters: Rocky River
Employees: Seven

I never had aspirations of owning my own business. I just wanted to make money and help others.

But I've always enjoyed recruiting. I have a passion for helping people find good jobs. At the same time, I didn't enjoy working for a manager whose method of motivation was intimidation. One day, a good friend and young entrepreneur encouraged me to quit my job and start a business.

I thought he was nuts until he reminded me that I had worked on 100 percent commission since 1991. I realized that the relationships I had in the medical industry weren't based on the names on the marquee at either of my previous employers. They were based on the results I produced in placing people in both the sales and service side of the business.

In the last 13 years, my company has placed about 1,000 people throughout the country in support management and as application specialists, field service, sales and technical-support representatives.

Building NS Charney & Associates has been a continual learning process. One of the first challenges was not initially understanding the importance of working with appropriate business advisers. My biggest mistake was not hiring a full-time professional accounting firm when I first started my business.

I hired a bookkeeper who worked for another company full time. He had yet to pass his CPA exam, so he did accounting on the side. I hired him because I was new in business with no employees and I was trying to save money. That was my downfall.

I remember the call from the accountant like it was yesterday. It was 1996, after my first full year in business. He casually told me that I owed several thousand dollars in taxes. It was an amount equal to some people's annual salary. I panicked.

After I got on a payment plan, I spent a lot of time thinking about what went wrong. It was very simple. I hired the wrong person to watch the finances of my business. My specialty is recruiting for the medical industry, not accounting. Business owners can't be experts at everything, but when it comes to taxes, only they are responsible.

All I could think about was, if this happened, what else has he missed? I was probably overpaying taxes. I also realized that my business suffered by not working with a firm that was easily accessible.

As a small-business owner, it's important to find an accountant who can offer advice, not someone who just handles your books. At the same time, it's not important to work with a major accounting firm. Size doesn't matter. Dealing with a firm that specializes in small businesses is key.

For years, I've done annual tax planning, so I'm never surprised. I always know what I need to pay, well in advance. I found a firm that has experience in helping small businesses manage money from a tax perspective. As the business grew, they guided me in starting 401(k) and profit sharing plans.

I learned my lesson early. The money you spend on a good accounting firm is not an expense. It's a cost of doing business—a cost that saves you time, money and headaches.

Delivery business must budget for fleet

Kris Stotz and Mike Hamilton
Title: Co-owners
Company: Stotz Hamilton Interstate Transfer
Founded: 1998
Headquarters: Richfield
Employees: Two

When you're building a delivery business, customer service is everything. Dealing with vehicle issues is not an option.

My partner, Kris Stotz, and I each had a FedEx Ground route when we met. We used to park next to each other and often talked about our plans to grow and ways to keep expenses down after we both bought a second route.

For us, getting larger meant hiring more drivers, paying for new routes and buying more used step vans, trucks and cargo vans.

Sometimes it meant working double time if a driver couldn't work. We formed a company and bought a fifth route in order to serve customers in Summit, Wayne, Medina and Portage counties.

Both of us bought new trucks before we merged our businesses. Even though those first two trucks were five and six years old, replacing them was the last thing on our minds. It became top of mind when we spent about $6,000 in repairs on each truck in one year.

Our biggest mistake was not factoring the cost of new vehicles into our business plan.

In our business, costs are only part of the problem. If a truck breaks down, everyone's schedule is interrupted. You waste a lot of time with towing, renting a van and transferring boxes. And using a rented van is much harder on a driver. An ordinary van isn't equipped with shelves, and that makes everything more difficult. We have to keep a schedule in this business. We probably pick up an average of 2,500 to 3,000 packages a day on all of our routes.

Every time we had a problem, we were grateful that it wasn't an engine. But when you deal with older vehicles, expenses never go away. For instance, a paint job on one of our older trucks cost $2,400.

In any business, you want to fix costs as much as possible. By our second year in business together, we realized that it wasn't worth it to save a truck payment when the money eventually goes to repair costs.

By buying new vehicles, our costs are fixed and we get a tax break. It's also easier to attract drivers with newer vehicles. Our older vehicles didn't have power steering.

We have a formula now. If we spend $40,000 on a new vehicle, we can sell it five years later for $15,000. We use that equity to put on a new truck payment, reducing the cost to $25,000. We will always have truck payments, but it's worth it to have newer vehicles.

With 10 vans and trucks, we still have repairs. But it's part of our budget. We put so many miles on our trucks and vans that by the time they are three years old, we expect to have a problem that's not covered by warranty.

By years four and five, we expect more things to go wrong, but we do our best to keep those costs down by spending more money on maintenance. A mechanic looks at all of our trucks every month.

When you're in the delivery business, repairs and truck payments have to be part of your budget.

Failing to charge enough

Kathleen Hogue
Title: President
Company: Mediform
Founded: 1979
Headquarters: Twinsburg
Employees: Three

I learned of the idea to help elderly people with their medical from my former partner during rides to and from bridge club.

At the time, I was a teacher preparing to return to the classroom as soon as my youngest son was school age. My friend was a hospital social worker who had been bombarded by elderly patients for help with Medicare claims, and she was sure that a business could be sustained by this unmet need. Mediform opened for business in 1979, financed by a second mortgage with an interest rate of 24 percent.

Today, there are about 1,000 similar businesses throughout the country, but we were the first. We know this because we were featured in a *Wall Street Journal* article six months after we opened. The article set off a landslide of national publicity, contacts from venture capitalists and requests for franchises. Instead of being swayed by all the acknowledgements, we should have paid closer attention to the words of an early client quoted in the *Journal* article: "You charged me $50 to clear up all of these medical claims. . . . Lady, I would have paid $300."

My biggest mistake was not realizing the value of our services and coming up with a workable fee structure a lot sooner.

Because we embarked on a business no one had ever done before, the blue-chip accounting and legal firms we consulted, and paid, were not equipped to give us the help we needed. We knew we weren't making enough money to stay in business when we started out, first charging just $25 per case, and later just $50 a case, but we didn't know how to structure fees or what to charge.

Finally, we met with two financial consultants who had recently formed their own business. They told us to charge more or close our doors, especially considering the fact that we did not take a salary the first two years.

At their advice, we reluctantly announced to our clients that we were changing our fee to a $50 per hour rate. Maybe it's because we both came from nurturing careers, but we were frankly timid about charging for our services. We fully expected that half our clients would quit us. To our amazement, only one did.

For some time, we didn't understand the value of what we were doing. We weren't thinking about what we were really offering—intangibles we provide to people, like reassurance that their affairs are not out of control.

We deal with people who think they might lose their homes because of health-care costs or people who have to switch health-care plans because of major life changes such as a spouse's death or a divorce.

We help navigate the paperwork caused by illness. With any hospital stay, patients might encounter 30 different businesses. They're medical businesses and they have to be paid, from the radiologists and anesthesiologist to the surgery, ambulance and rehabilitation companies.

The business has changed considerably, but one thing remains the same: People come to us with paperwork and questions. Our elderly clients used to refer to us as the girls who do their forms. Now half of our clients are under 65. They wonder why they're paying so much when they have insurance. We orchestrate the flow of paperwork so that health plans pay as much as they should. Claims management and benefits consultation grew as a natural extension from handling forms.

There's a fine line between being a patient advocate and being in the business of managing medical claims. We've always taken a problem-solving approach to what we do. It's not so much about the numbers. We make sure our clients are not missing any benefits. In a way, it's a sad commentary that a business like mine needs to exist.

But at the same time, it is a business. No matter what business you're in, it needs to be profitable or you shouldn't be in business. We stayed at the $50 rate for a decade or so, and I was beginning to feel that I was working very hard for the amount I was earning.

For a few years we offered clients alternative membership fee arrangements. Instead of an hourly rate, they could pay $199 per year, regardless of how much time we spent on a case. The response showed us that people preferred an hourly rate.

Various consultants urged us to charge a small percentage of the money we recouped for our clients. That didn't appeal to us because larger amounts don't always require more effort. You might be able to resolve a $5 million claim in five minutes, while a $10,000 claim might take two hours.

One day, riding home, I heard a fortune teller on the radio advertising a 15-minute session for $15. I immediately thought, What I do is worth at least as much as the service she provides. The next day, Mediform clients were informed that the hourly rate was being raised to $60. This time no one quit or even complained.

My business is about my constantly evolving expertise. The learning process never ends. I co-wrote a consumer's guide to health insurance nearly 20 years ago. Last year, to serve my clients' needs, I became an expert in dealing with Medicare Part D. I call the same customer service numbers that the patients do; I just know what to ask and how to get results.

Experience taught me the value of my service. I can clear up a year's worth of paperwork for someone who has Medicare and a Medicare supplement in 30 minutes. The average person might spend hours on the phone and still not get the job done.

No matter how passionate you are about a service business, you have to remember it's still a business. If you're not confident about your expertise and your fees, you won't make it.

Photographer had the passion but not enough capital

Billy Bass
Title: Owner/Photographer
Company: Billy Bass Photography
Founded: 2003
Headquarters: Cleveland
Employees: One

What do you do when you're 60, but you still feel like you're 21? I started a second career. Make that a third career.

I started out as a disc jockey in Cleveland. Then I moved to Los Angeles and spent the next 25 years in the music industry. I was vice president of Chrysalis Records, where I developed marketing plans for superstar recording acts including Blondie, Pat Benatar and Billy Idol.

I ended my management career as Luther Vandross' manager when he won his first Grammy. Ten years ago I moved back to Cleveland to work in radio, first at Majic 105.7, then at 92.3 "The Beat." When my contract ended I took a year to decide what I wanted to do next. That's when I took a couple of Photoshop classes. Photography has been my passion for nearly three decades.

Then I became a wedding photographer. I learned to take showbiz tricks and bring them to the wedding business. Timing is everything. I do my part to make sure the bride is the star on her special day.

My biggest mistake is classic: starting a business without enough capital.

I spent $25,000 on cameras, lighting and software and I didn't have much left for marketing. I knew better. Starting a business without access to capital breaks one of the first rules in business. But I did it anyway.

I convinced myself that my photographs would be enough. My plan was to build my business by satisfying brides and grooms who would help spread the word. My premium package involves working with three professional photographers, guaranteeing unusual shots that just aren't possible with only one photographer. I contract with five photographers who work with me part time.

Word of mouth is working. But it's not enough. When a young lady decides to get married, the first thing she generally does is start looking at national and local wedding publications—magazines that I cannot afford to advertise in. For services, they start looking online and in yellow pages. Brides also go to wedding events— venues where some longtime, established photographers have spent $30,000 to $50,000 on visual displays alone.

When I started this business a few years ago, I even thought my name alone would help bring in business. That was flawed thinking, too, considering most women getting married are out of my demographic.

Access to capital is key when you start any business. I'm one of those people who has always taken pride in my credit rating. When I came back to Cleveland I joined a small bank, hoping to develop a relationship. Then that bank was purchased by a larger bank. I didn't know anyone at the larger bank. The only thing they look at is your track record in business. They want to see a profit, which takes time.

With odds against me, I focused on what I could do to attract more clients. I focused on guerrilla marketing tactics to drive people to my web site.

I market every chance I can, even at weddings. When I take photos at receptions, I hand out business cards at each table and let guests know that they can check out their photographs online the next day. Meanwhile, I set up my laptop at the bar and show a slideshow of the wedding the guests just witnessed.

I immediately put the best 25 to 30 photos of the bride and groom online. That way they can check them out while they're on their honeymoon, which makes them more eager to see the other photos when they return.

While I don't have a display at wedding events, I pass out business cards to brides while feeding them lines that make them smile. My goal is to encourage them to check out my web site. Everybody has a web site, but not many photographers keep a blog.

Blogging is huge for me. Anybody can show off their best shots in advertising materials or in an online portfolio, but visitors know it's not a fluke when they see my quality, wedding after wedding.

My latest marketing strategy is offering couples free engagement photos that can be used for save-the-date event cards and thank-you notes. The photos are also available online.

I also leveraged relationships for another part of my photography business. While young brides might not have heard about me, many other people have. Two of my largest clients are the Teamsters and the Cleveland chapter of the American Red Cross.

The Red Cross gave me a chance because for seven years I helped that organization with "The Billy Bass Run to Help." Every week, 100 to 200 people donated $5 to $10 directly to a Red Cross representative to run or walk with me for three miles at Edgewater Park. At least 50 people were regulars, and we got sponsors to donate coffee and bagels. Those runners were among the first people I let know about my photography business.

About 90 percent of my business is weddings. I enjoy bringing showbiz to every wedding. Our photographers wear ties that coordinate with the bride and groom's wedding colors, because it's a production.

I want the couple to disappear immediately after the ceremony, for two reasons: First, they just got married and they should be with each other as husband and wife before they start greeting everyone. And second, because the next time they appear is another picture-taking opportunity with guests anticipating their arrival.

If you decide to start a business without access to capital, you'd better have a plan B, which could mean guerrilla marketing.

Lack of capital and business plan led to bad decisions

Sherri Foxman
Title: President
Company: Party411.com
Founded: 1997
Headquarters: Warrensville Heights
Employees: 16

Party411.com is a local event and party planning firm. We coordinate and decorate any size and kind of event, from fund-raisers for nonprofit organizations and politicians to birthday parties and baby showers.

The internet site offers 58,000 pages about planning themed parties and events. It also provides custom products and long-distance coordination. We've planned a birthday party in Hong Kong for a 1-year-old and a bar mitzvah in the United Kingdom.

Party411.com is the leading internet site for event and party planners long after I was told by many competitors that I would be gone.

My company's main rivals for a piece of this $200 billion industry have disappeared or shifted gears. Companies that courted me to buy my company with stock before tech stocks went bust are no longer contenders. GreatEntertaining.com closed after spending millions on marketing; iParty.com has reverted to representing brick-and-mortar stores on the East Coast.

I built my community of more than 400,000 monthly visitors through guerrilla marketing, free advice, loyal employees and lots of 18-hour days. But if I had to do it all over again, I would have never started a business like this with no business plan and no capital. I was not prepared, and it has been a struggle.

I am an impulsive person. Once I decided to go from being a consultant at a local nonprofit agency to having my own business, I had an office and employees in a day. I always thought the word "overhead" referred to a type of garage door. The day I decided to incorporate, I never even considered how I would pay the rent. I just decided, "I think I'll start a business!"

Although I had a good reputation and was known in the community, I was not prepared for the struggle that came with trying to build a client list, handle the overhead, do the creative work and run daily operations.

Had I had capital and a business plan, I wouldn't have made the succession of bad decisions that came from having no monetary buffer. I was forced into a bad business partnership designed to save my business with an infusion of cash. Every decision I made—and many still today—was based on lack of capital.

Making every decision based on cash flow is not a way to start or run a business. I'v had to take many event at a discounted rate for fear of losing it. I've had no cushion during changes in the economy, such as right after 9/11, when many clients canceled events.

On top of that, collecting money is not my strong suit. When I finally decided I needed a "money" person, she collected $12,000 within her first three days.

It has taken a toll on my staff. They went weeks without a paycheck. And I've lost some good people. But many have stayed, leaving me feeling proud but incredibly obligated.

Where does that leave me? Things are much better than they've ever been. The event side of the business has grown, and we count many of Cleveland's biggest companies and nonprofits as our clients. The internet provides us with an ever-growing client base, including Sprint, Epcot, Warner Bros. and MasterCard of Canada.

Necessity has created a wealth of products for us—customized candy bar wrappers, caricature invitations, sign-in boards, centerpieces, banners and more. In May alone, we sold on the internet $14,000 worth of graduation candy bar wrappers—a product I created solely to generate a revenue stream.

They say creative people aren't business people. I don't know that I agree with that 100 percent. I know my weaknesses. But I wonder what would have happened if I had had capital and could have made sound business decisions based not on cash flow but on what I knew was right. It's as much about heart as it is about knowledge.

Don't limit yourself to one revenue track

Victoria Colligan
Title: Founder/president
Company: Ladies Who Launch
Founder/president
Founded: 2002
Headquarters: Beachwood
Employees: 5

I've talked to entrepreneurs all over the country, and I'm convinced that women tend to start businesses in different ways than men and for different reasons.

Women tend to be more passion-driven. They start businesses for lifestyle reasons in order to balance work, family and self-fulfillment. And they're natural connectors. They use friends and family to get information for new businesses and to take existing businesses to the next level.

I started Ladies Who Launch with online content aimed at helping motivated women move forward in business and projects. We send a weekly dose of inspiration to thousands of women nationwide. We basically feature a different woman every week, noting her successes, obstacles and challenges, along with tools and tips for others.

I spent a year working in investment banking after I got a law degree and an MBA. Then I went on to work for two women-

owned small business start-ups in New York. I always wanted
my own business. I explored a lot of different business ideas
throughout the years and thought each was the one.

I got the idea of starting a business aimed at entrepreneurial-
minded women after seeing so many women around me starting
businesses. I also noticed that they weren't necessarily reading the
Wall Street Journal, Forbes and Fortune, but lifestyle magazines.

I knew there was an audience for packaging business content
in a more feminine way. I started this business because women
business owners need support. Some want to be inspired.

I launched this business with about 500 e-mails I had gathered
from friends, associates and women, many of whom had attended
fun small business gatherings I used to host in New York. I didn't
expect to make any money with this business for at least a year
or two until I built up a substantial subscriber base that would be
attractive to sponsors. Actually, I planned to eventually turn the
online content into a magazine. My biggest mistake was thinking
that the traditional online advertising sponsorship was the only way
to make money in my business.

What I found was that as women throughout the country
got pumped up through the online content, they wanted to meet
with women in their areas. They would reach out to me but I had
nothing to offer them.

Then, about a year ago, I met my partner through an e-mail.
She was doing the same thing I was doing through workshops and
meetings, and she was seeking an online partner.

We merged our companies in December, and now we offer
Ladies Who Launch incubators throughout the country. It's a
licensing model, with a cost of $6,000 to run programs in various
cities. So far we're in 18 cities.

The first part of the program is a four-week workshop limited to
12 participants who meet once a week for two hours. We put women
through a series of exercises to clarify their goals or expand their
businesses using energy and resources of other women in the group.

It works like magic. It gets people into action. It's not just about clarifying a vision. We talk about movement. About 90 percent of participants are business people, but sometimes you hear things like, "I want to start a scarf company," and "I want to lose 10 pounds."

Participants can opt to join an ongoing program that includes monthly meetings, free advertising on the web site and benefits from sponsors.

When I started the business, I couldn't foresee the potential of revenue streams coming from anything but advertising. I didn't realize that Ladies Who Launch is a community and that there was potential for a business model tied to this network of women. Not only can advertisers sell them things, but these women can also sell each other things.

The irony is that as we've built the community with more offerings. It's made the business more attractive to sponsors, including Bloom By AG, online greeting cards made by American Greetings.

I've learned not to pigeonhole myself into one idea of how to make money. Now I'm open to creative ways to grow the business.

MARKETING

WHAT SETS YOU APART from your competition? Sometimes it's your product or services. Other times it's your marketing capabilities. If you really are different, even more reason to flaunt it.

Marketing is all about making the sale. No matter why you're in business, you have to sell goods or services, or there is no business.

One of the fundamental mistakes that small and large businesses make is not having a marketing plan. Some have money, so they hire the best and brightest. The products are great and services are tight, so they open up their doors and wait for people to discover them. Customers generally don't flood in.

Marketing is about creating a demand for your products and services. Whether you try guerilla marketing, direct mail, radio, television, websites, blogs or newspaper advertising, marketing makes people aware of your business. No matter what form or forms of marketing you choose, it takes time and effort—and sometimes trial and error.

These entrepreneurs share mistakes they've made with marketing, ranging from wasting money on the wrong medium to marketing before they were ready for customers. Mistakes include marketing too broadly or not fully understanding their target market and how those customers like to receive messages.

The right medium can help a business grow. The wrong medium can kill a budget quickly, with little or no return on investments. There's no need for a small neighborhood restaurant to advertise in a national publication, when customers only come from a three-mile radius. At the same time, as long as systems are in place to fulfill orders, online advertising can brand a business and help a retailer or manufacturer grow nationally or internationally.

Dream big. Whether your plan is to brand your business nationally or you just want to target a small niche locally or regionally, marketing has to be part of your plans.

When innovating, rely on instincts, not experts

Jay Yoo
Title: Founder
Company: Koyono Co.
Founded: 2003
Headquarters: Lyndhurst
Employees: Four

I've gotten a lot of advice from people with good intentions. But when you have a unique product aimed at the technology market, you have to market directly to that niche.

Traditional methods just don't work. We make a line of outerwear with strategically placed pockets for gadgets or handheld devices as well as a line with integrated iPod controls. We also sell a T-shirt line that has two hidden pockets for an iPod and a cell phone.

The first two years in business, we sold our overcoats in 40 stores all over the United States and Japan, but sales were minimal. Looking back, most of those boutiques didn't even have e-mail accounts. Yet, before we even received our first order of T-shirts in 2004, we put a drawing of what it was expected to look like on our web site and blew through our first production run of 500 shirts within 24 hours.

My biggest mistake was relying on experts rather than my intuition. When you're innovating, you have to go with your gut and try different things until you find what works.

When I started my company, people thought I was a whack job, including some in my inner circle. I heard everything from laughter to a suggestion to put all of my merchandise on consignment. If it sold, great. If not, go out of business. Now, e-wear, or the wearable technology market, is predicted to be a $7 billion industry by 2014. In 2000, it was just an idea.

I designed the first coat as a hobby when I was working for Swagelok covering new technologies in the oil and gas markets. I used to travel a lot and I always wondered why I couldn't find an overcoat with style, performance and utility. I wanted something that I could wear on any occasion, an overcoat that didn't look like my dad's. Long overcoats and jeans look awful.

I'm a very creative person who tried to be corporate. When I was told that something couldn't be done, I would go to the technology department and they would figure it out. I loved breaking the rules. In the back of my mind, I always wanted to do my own thing. I just didn't know what that would be.

I met my business partner at a technology company that I worked at six years ago. Even though I had sold some coats to friends and family, I never intended to turn it into a business until I decided to leave the company.

I did the typical entrepreneur thing, using credit cards and going through my IRA to get the business off the ground. For two years, we struggled for cash flow.

Meanwhile, I kept seeking advice. I heard things like focus on retailers. Do one thing really well. That's probably fine advice if you have $8 million to spend. We had to just survive. The truth is, very few start-ups make it.

Part of the problem was I was asking advice from traditionalists. I didn't even have a basic cookie-cutter web site until 2004, because our focus was on retail. Now we get 2,000 web visitors per day. People also find us from blogs and search engines. Our own blog gets about 1,000 unique visitors daily.

When you're innovating, you have to go with your gut. No one has answers because you're going into the unknown.

It took us eight months to design a simple T-shirt with a zippered entry and two pockets. Then, when it took off online with just an artist rendering, before we could get a photo of the product or start an e-mail and blog campaign, we wanted to capture that momentum. We thought the best way would be to hire one of the world's largest marketing and public relations firms.

They came up with a tag line, "The zipper comes down," and shared plans for what we considered an outdated buzz guerrilla marketing campaign. We expressed our concerns but they refused to listen. Basically they experimented with us. For instance, they put 30,000 stickers on dumpsters, signs and bathrooms in New York, and 75 percent were taken down within 24 hours.

Trying to reach internet-savvy people with conventional guerrilla marketing was a mistake. Our money would have been better spent on more direct advertising.

The firm did get us two sentences and a photo in Stuff magazine. But without doing anything, our product was picked up by Macworld, PC World and a bunch of technology blogs. By acting small, being approachable and having a great product, word got out.

We're going through some new challenges and introducing new products, and we're grateful for the traffic to our site. As a start-up, we didn't realize it at first, but our strength is in marketing. We asked early adopters to give us feedback and we've been fortunate to be part of a lot of blogs, which helped mainstream media to find us.

You can't always predict what's going to happen or even whether your product will be used for its intended application. But you stand a better chance at success when you target relative markets. Some diabetics have found us online and use our clothing for insulin pumps instead of technology.

It's very difficult to predict the home run. With the resources of a start-up, you've got to try a lot of things. Fail fast. Learn from it and move forward.

Search engine rescues computer firm from ad disaster

Dean Bellone
Title: President
Company: CompSource Inc.
Founded: 1991
Headquarters: Cleveland
Employees: 22

I started CompSource in 1991 when I was in college, and it was a slow start.

Today we sell our computers and more than 200,000 products all over the world. Our web site, www. compsource.net, gets nearly a million hits a day from more than 7,000 unique visitors.

But it didn't start out that way.

When I started the company, we were building and selling computers to local consumers, but had our sights on the national market from day one.

I used to read Computer Shopper magazine all the time, and it was my dream to advertise in it.

Five years after opening CompSource, we finally had enough savings to buy a full-page, black-and-white ad in Computer Shopper. I truly believed that all I had to do was spend $15,000 a month and price our products competitively and "they will come."

Looking back at what must have been the worst day of my life with my company, I recall my wife asking what was wrong. I told her I finally realized that my dream of making it national was turning into a nightmare.

We had made a six-month commitment to spend $90,000 total for an ad each month. Five months into our commitment, we were getting only about two sales a month. And on those sales we were losing money from trying to compete with competitors that were making inferior computers.

We were nearly out of money, out of time and out of our contract when the phones began to ring.

I couldn't believe that my ad, which seemed lost in the middle of an inch-thick book, had suddenly started working. So I asked customers how they heard about us, and they would say, 'From your web site.' Well, I didn't have a web site.

At the time, the internet was in its infancy. Like a lot of people, I thought it was a fad. Back then, the average cost of a home computer was about $3,000, and the internet was mostly being used by government and universities. I found out that the owner of a price search engine had taken prices of computer components from our ad and listed them free on his web site.

I quickly negotiated a deal with the site owner allowing us to show 20,000 products we carried from different manufacturers.

To give you an idea of the scope, computer superstores generally carry around 6,000 items. Then we put together a web site. It was a bad one, but we had one. It served as a springboard to a new direction.

Our business has continually grown, and I attribute it to web advertising, our massive product range and staying one step ahead of our competitors' web sites. Because of technology, I immediately know that my advertising dollars are paying off because I can see where our customers originate. For instance, I can trace when consumers click over to our site from Google or Samsung, among others.

Now I spend about $20,000 each month on internet advertising. Today CompSource has many national accounts that have switched over from Dell and Gateway because of our long warranty, reliability and vast product selection.

But if it weren't for my biggest mistake, we probably would not be a national computer company and we definitely would not have conformed to the internet as quickly as we did. My mistake made my company what it is today.

She lost business by not doing follow-up reports

Patricia Bertschler
Title: Co-owner
Company: Northcoast Conflict Solutions
Founded: 1996
Headquarters: Independence
Employees: 2 full time, 8 affiliates and several associates

My husband, Dr. John Bertschler, and I opened Northcoast Conflict Solutions in 1996, combining our psychology practice with a new service, mediation and conflict resolution.

We primarily target businesses, churches, schools, families and retirement centers. We moved into a corporate suite in Independence, placed a Yellow Pages ad and waited for the phones to ring.

When we first started the business, I continued working in the marketing department at a local hospital for a couple of years.

I hated those end-of-the-month marketing reports, meetings and constant pressure to gain clients. I swore that when I was ready to devote full time to our own practice, I'd never work on another report.

My biggest mistake was not using the experience I gained from two hospital marketing departments and applying it to my own business. I assumed I had a good handle on our referral sources and that if I just kept loosely networking, it would pay off.

Three years ago, after watching our fledgling mediation practice struggle to get off the ground, it occurred to me that I had an arsenal of knowledge that I could use to turn things around.

I first had to get over the notion that clinicians and mediators are not good business people. That was an excuse that held me back. When you own your own business, you have to balance your desire to help other people with drumming up business. The phone is not going to ring just because you have a shingle.

We had to make some changes, including moving from a small

corporate office space to one that's more conducive for a mediation atmosphere. Then I started a multifaceted marketing campaign.

We hired a local public relations firm for several months to initiate a radio campaign and set up a web site. We got active in the Mediation Association of Northeast Ohio. I sent out media releases to promote free seminars, classes and support groups several times a month. We did radio interviews, advertised on cable television and in local newspapers, wrote feature articles and worked collaboratively on projects with other conflict-resolution practices. We also spoke at local chambers, churches, schools, businesses and employee-assistance programs.

In each of the last three years, we began to see our profits double and then triple. Still, I resisted many of the reports that I was required to do when I worked in the business world. In the mediation and counseling field, we don't want things to drag out. We concentrate on helping people with short-term resolutions. But when you have a high turnover of cases, that next business piece has to be there or you're going to die in the water.

I always kept track of referral sources by categories such as clergy, attorneys and mental health professionals. But I had no handy record of who referred a client—I had to search through every client's chart.

When I searched through the files about a year ago, I found out that one group in particular represented almost 66 percent of our annual income. By quantifying how much the categories represented financially, I was able to develop a plan that helped us maintain current relationships, contact past referral sources and discontinue marketing efforts that were not successful.

We now have formal meetings weekly. We redesigned our web site to give it a warmer, more interactive look. We report on names, not just categories, and we provide the status of developing projects. And each week, John and I meet with one new or former referral source. We also help our 12 associates to develop business.

Not keeping track of contact names for ongoing follow-up would have cost us our business as mediation becomes more mainstream.

Sales-marketing department gives balance

Steve Peplin
Title: President
Company: Talan Products Inc.
Founded: 1986
Headquarters: Cleveland
Employees: 45

When you talk about manufacturing in America, you generally don't use "high growth" in the same sentence. It's a tough industry that is suffering from overcapacity, has low margins and is hypercompetitive. But we grew steadily and very quickly for many years, and we're still having fun.

I started this company 19 years ago with two other guys. We each put in $2,100, and we clawed our way up the glass wall.

We are metal-forming specialists that make parts typically unseen in products—unless you're a manufacturer. We're in the metal stamping, tube-forming and aluminum-extrusion business. We make components for the fastener, appliance, building hardware and automotive industries.

In the 1990s we got used to receiving awards for growth. We won Inc. 500 awards in 1993 and 1999 for being among the nation's fastest-growing privately held companies.

We won the Manny award from Inside Business and CAMP for manufacturing excellence in 2000. We were named to the Weatherhead 100 list of fastest-growing private companies in Northeast Ohio from 1993 to 1997. That's kind of unique, because by the fifth year, you're not comparing such small sales numbers.

But that was the 1990s. Our sales stayed flat at around $10 million to $12 million for many years. My biggest mistake was not building a sales and marketing arm sooner. We were unbalanced. We concentrated on innovative tooling and processes of manufacturing, but I was the only one selling our manufacturing services.

After our high sales growth period settled down, we still grew at a rate of about 40 percent a year for a few years. And we made nice profits. We didn't even have a brochure for a long, long time. When you're growing fast, who needs one? We had built the business by networking and through our reputation. Our efforts were spent becoming a better manufacturer by working with an organizational development consultant.

We tried to just let growth happen. We never participated in trade shows or had reps doing work for us. Then, a few years ago, we finally decided to start marketing, and we fumbled. We hired someone, and it didn't work out. Nothing was sold for a year. After we were burned by the experience, we got cold feet.

I was a little naive, though. It takes a few years to make it work. You have to have a formal process that includes a way to create leads, such as brochures and a web site. It took a while to get qualified leads. Then, once we did, we still didn't have anyone in sales to chase them down. We ignored the sales process until we plateaued.

The good news is that in a four-year period when our sales were flat, we increased our productivity. Thanks to improved processes, 32 employees can do the same volume of business that 50 to 75 employees used to do.

Being more productive enabled me to spend more time landing a big job. After years of networking, we just closed a few deals that make us a $20 million company. Now I have breathing room to work with sales. Before, I was too busy doing what I call presidential crap. About six months ago, we hired a known entity in our industry to be in charge of sales and marketing.

We're successful in an industry that's been hurt greatly by offshore purchasing. The industry is consolidating, too. Forecasters are saying that half the metal stampers will be out of business in just a few years. The ones that remain will be twice as big.

We've been fortunate. We still have the first, second, third and fourth accounts that we landed. Now that we're generating leads, getting quotes and going after new business, I'm more excited than ever about our prospects.

It's great to be high-growth again. Now, when I go to bed, I can't wait to get back to work.

Radio hosts find earlier start time better serves listeners

Douglas Magill and Paul DeLuca
Title: Co-hosts
Company: Cleveland Business Radio
Founded: 2004
Headquarters: Cleveland
Employees: 3

I worked in corporate America for a couple decades and spent the last several years as an entrepreneur. I've spent most of my life focusing on corporate America. But when you have cancer diagnosed, you look at things differently.

Frankly, you realize how precious life is, and you think more seriously about how you want to spend your time. I spent days thinking about how I could best share 30 years of knowledge about business and organizations. Last year I helped launch the "Cleveland Business Radio" show because I have always believed in the power of commerce and economics to transform communities.

I met my co-host, Paul DeLuca, through a business networking group. Both of us are technology consultants and former high-level executives at Fortune 500 companies. We figured radio was the best outlet to reach the community.

We're a good team because we have similar skills in terms of teaching and coaching. We don't always agree, though. One of us is sophisticated, and the other is not.

One is brilliant, and the other is brainless. That's what we do on the air—good-natured bantering to explain complex things in easily understood ways. We inform people about the good things happening in Cleveland with entrepreneurs, business-development organizations, nonprofits and educators. One thing we agree on is that Cleveland is a great place to live, and we really want to help it grow.

Still, with all our good intentions and all our experience as business managers and consultants, we were messing up with this venture. Our biggest mistake was scheduling a business show at 9 a.m. instead of during the morning rush hour. We were trying to accommodate our guests rather than focusing on the business purpose of the show. We were being nice hosts as opposed to being good business people.

Business listeners can't tune in at 9 a.m. because most of them have already started their business day. We launched the show in September, and we knew that it would take some time to build an audience and attract advertisers. But we kept hearing from associates, friends and former guests that although they liked the show, they weren't able to listen to it often because of the time slot. That finally became obvious even to us because traffic was light when we were driving to the radio station.

Then when the ratings came out in December, they were lower than we anticipated. Potential advertisers liked the show's concept and the audience that we were attracting. But they refused to make an investment because the show's time slot was too late to reach enough business people.

We were putting out a great product, but customers weren't buying it. So we did what any good business owners do: We measured, analyzed and worked on changing our structure.

We were fortunate. The program director at WERE AM/1300 believed in the show and gave us the 8 a.m. Thursday slot that was held by a nationally syndicated show. It made a huge difference. We immediately gained 1,600 listeners, nearly doubling our audience. The move also helped us to secure our first long-term sponsor.

Looking back, we just got caught up in the excitement of planning this venture both online and on-air. We love talking about development issues and featuring businesses like Fairport Yachts, a growing company that builds and ships world-class yachts all over the world from Northeast Ohio. But we had to relearn some basic business lessons about marketing.

It doesn't matter how great your product is. If you don't understand the market you're trying to serve, you're not going to succeed.

In food world, make sure marketing's on your menu

David Epifano
Titile: Owner
Company: Alfonso's Restaurant and Alfonso's Tuscan Grill
Founded: 1983
Headquarters: Middleburg Heights
Employees: 70

No matter what your interests are, good food brings people together. I don't care if you're dining with a co-worker or a relative, you may not be able to agree upon the subject you're discussing, but you can definitely agree upon good food and good service.

It's one of the many things I love about the industry. I was a manager for about half of my 30-year career in the food service industry before I decided to go into business for myself. At the time, I was district manager of new accounts and marketing for Sysco Food Services, the world's largest food distributor. My job required me to go in and out of just about every restaurant in Northeast Ohio. That's when it hit me: There is a great American dream, and I'd like to tap into it.

My wife and I bought Alfonso's Restaurant in Middleburg Heights 11 years ago. It was a small pizza shop, and we worked hard to expand the menu and build upon the quality and reputation before turning it into a 130-seat restaurant with in-house catering for 100 people. In 2000, four years later, we opened Alfonso's Tuscan Grill in Cleveland, just seven miles away.

We've tried all forms of marketing, with minimal success, throughout the years. We wanted to leverage the businesses by advertising both restaurants at the same time.

We thought we were getting a better deal by doing it that way. It took me a long time to realize that the only good deal in marketing is a deal that brings customers through your doors—no matter what the cost.

My biggest mistake was taking a widespread marketing approach instead of targeting a specific territory. I've spent thousands throughout the years on ads in local newspapers and on radio shows. But the fact is, as a small business owner, I never had a lot of money to allocate to marketing.

Marketing is why the chains are successful and the little guy isn't. The repetition of your name in radio, television and newspapers conditions people to go to an establishment. The food is almost secondary to marketing because it doesn't matter how great your food and service are without customers.

The little guy usually has a better chance of selling you on food and service, because they try harder. But small operators can't afford to do a lot of marketing.

I've been frustrated with my marketing efforts for years. We even advertised in USA Today once in the early years. It was just a small blurb, and it was a one-time deal. It sounded like a good deal at the time. Hey, I saw the ad.

I've also paid money to add a quick tag line to radio spots, saying this information was sponsored by Alfonso's. That does nothing to bring in customers unless you can bear the cost of buying ads frequently. The chances of someone deciding to come to our restaurant because our name was mentioned on air as part of a sponsorship are extremely minimal.

Finally, about two years ago, I made a strategic decision to market within a 3-mile radius of my restaurants. It's paid off. Business is up about 15 percent. Now we market through direct mail, a small local paper and through a major paper that allows us to target our immediate area only.

We cut a deal with one paper by exchanging gift certificates for advertising. It was so effective that we decided to do a similar bartering deal with a radio station.

Not only is it more cost effective for us, but the marketing is also effective because the ads run much more frequently than we ever could afford to run in a cash-only deal. Every time someone brings in a gift certificate with certain numbers on it, we know which advertising medium it came from, so it's trackable.

I firmly believe that the best form of marketing will always be word of mouth. But you need other forms of advertising to drive new people to your business who can spread the word for you. For the small independent operator, marketing is the lifeblood for continued success. Small-business owners have to be extremely smart and find ways to not waste dollars allocated for marketing.

I have a passion for taking care of people. But before you can serve customers, you've got to get them into your business. My motto: Early to bed, early to rise, pray like hell and advertise.

Networking without a plan won't help you sell

Fred Johnson
Title: Principal
Company: Affluent Technology
Founded: 2004
Headquarters: Cleveland
Employees: 2

Figuring out how to penetrate a new market is just as important as having skills.

I've been in the computer industry for a long time, but running systems and creating an internet presence are two different worlds. My company, Ross-Tek Information Systems, is an outsource technology firm for small to midsize companies that don't have their own IT staffs.

For the fourth year in a row, Microsoft has awarded me the MVP designation for being among its top 33 small business server experts. Installing systems, consulting, helping businesses with IT strategy and disaster recovery have been good business for the last 10 years. It can also be frustrating, and I was ready for a change.

A couple of years ago I started a boutique technology firm to target blacks in sports and entertainment, helping them with their technology needs. My biggest mistake was not offering the right services initially to capitalize on relationships I had developed with trusted advisers of sports figures and entertainers.

Traditionally, all business is built on relationships. When you factor in the idea of getting close to athletes and actors, I knew I wouldn't have a chance of even making contact without some help.

When I first decided to target that market, I also knew that this niche market would never find me by opening up the Yellow Pages.

Sports figures and entertainers have gatekeepers and I would never have an opportunity to meet them without someone in their inner circle making an introduction.

I turned to a couple of longtime friends and clients to make introductions to financial advisers and sports agents who already worked with the people I wanted to do business with. Through various networking efforts, some of those contacts eventually led to friendships as well as invitations to meet others at places like the Grammy Awards brunch.

The problem was, I couldn't figure out how to make those prospects pay off. Once I got the relationships, I didn't know how to leverage them. The fact is, people don't generally recognize technology unless it's not working. It's not top of mind.

Whenever I networked in those circles, I would tell them what I did at Ross-Tek. Their response would be along the lines of, that's nice, but can you create web sites or an internet presence? My response was always no. That's not what Ross-Tek does.

I knew I had to make a change because I wasn't generating any sales.

One reason is that people didn't understand it or didn't know whether they needed our services. Those same people did know they wanted an internet presence of some kind, whether it was a web site, an Intranet not open to the public or a shopping cart for one of their business ventures.

We needed to narrow our focus. Instead of taking a shotgun approach saying we provide IT solutions and so forth, I decided I had to be more specific in our offerings.

The next time a sports figure asked me if I could create an internet presence for one of their business affiliations, I said yes. Then I started a second company, Affluent Technology, with my partner, Charles Anthe.

Now we offer site design, system management and we create an internet presence for our customers. For instance, right now the company is the lead designer for a web site being created for a new book by actor Courtney Vance and Angela Bassett, recently announced on "The Oprah Winfrey Show".

Affluent Technology is a boutique firm that does things that Ross-Tek would never do, like creating and managing someone's MySpace pages. The company is growing and I'm having more fun. We've added clients like actress Tichina Arnold, who stars in "Everybody Hates Chris," as well as the Philadelphia 76ers' Andre Iguodala.

I was on track by targeting attorneys and financial advisers because they have a rich network and there's a significant opportunity for future referrals.

By changing our offerings, there's also a greater opportunity that clients will spread the word if they're pleased with our services. Credentials and relationships get you in the door, but you have to be able to deliver.

When people are proud of their web sites, they talk about it.

Marketing has to be aggressive

Michael Kline
Title: President
Company: eCollect of Ohio Inc.
Founded: 2000
Headquarters: Bedford Heights
Employees: 2

I never dreamed it would be so difficult to give away a good service.

I'm in the business of recovering money for companies and organizations when bad checks are written. I get a fee from the check writer, but there is no cost to my customers.

Today, 350 organizations have signed up for the service. Some days the mail brings in as many as 60 checks. More typically, at least 10 to 25 checks come in the mail.

The business has come a long way. But the first two years, I really couldn't call it a business. I couldn't get companies to sign up. They always wanted to know the catch.

My biggest mistake was thinking I didn't have to do anything after I got a little publicity.

I was so wrong. I work just as hard to build this business as I do in my role as a certified public accountant.

After 20 years of working for large CPA firms, I started my own accounting practice in 1991, working with small businesses and individuals. Now eCollect accounts for about 25 percent of my revenues.

I first heard about the business of collecting on insufficient funds six years ago when I got an advertisement describing a new banking law that allows companies such as eCollect to go into the bad check writer's account and pull out money as soon as it was available. As a CPA, I was intrigued. In my field, you always have to hustle to sell your services. You're always trying to prove why you're better than your competitors. A lot of times it comes down to a fee.

After I did research on the company and the change in law, I thought that since the service was free, all I needed to do was get the information out there. I thought that would be enough.

That was my first problem. The next was trying to get a sales force together who could get the word out. I spent money on different ads, but after interested applicants learned it was strictly a commission job, nobody was interested.

After six months, I realized that if I were going to give this business a shot, I would be the only one marketing it. I did everything from putting an ad in the Yellow Pages to direct mail pieces to participating in various chamber of commerce events and trade shows.

At trade shows and events, I got my sales pitch down to covering everything in a minute or two, letting prospects know that debiting money electronically could cut down the turn-around time from a week to overnight—or as soon as money is available. Electronic debiting means money is available overnight and avoids the need to resubmit a paper check.

Whoever I was talking to would say they understood. Then they would ask what it was going to cost. It was difficult. The fee comes from the customer and the fee is set by customers and is equal to what banks can charge in whatever state the customer is. In Ohio, it's $30. In some other states, the fee is as low as $20.

Throughout the years, I started creating more and more advertising collateral that spelled out the process of how the service works and addressed concerns I always heard. No matter what type of marketing I tried, word-of-mouth continued to work best.

About a year and a half ago, I started advertising online, since this is an internet business. I try to maintain a regular schedule of advertising on a few hundred web sites each month.

The internet expanded my business outside Ohio and opened my eyes to clients that I would have never even thought of—such as school districts.

Parents bounce checks all the time for lunch money, after-school programs, field trips, athletics and even fund-raising. After the third school district signed on, I realized that I should create some marketing materials that target school districts. Now we service four dozen school districts throughout Ohio, and I've learned to target our marketing efforts at different industries.

The business is growing, but it's a lot of work. Marketing this business is no different from marketing any other product or service. People evaluate it the same way as if they were paying for the service.

Owner learned importance of knowing what's involved in everyone's job

Donna Zapis
Title: President
Company: Harbor Court
Founded: 1987
Headquarters: Rocky River
Employees: 60

We started The Harbor Court long before assisted living was a coined term. Twenty years ago we had to put the definition on the back of a business card.

My father, Xenophon, is a child of an immigrant who worked his way up to owning several businesses, including radio stations and an apartment for older residents. The Greek culture honors and respects the elderly, so I wasn't surprised that he developed a passion for caring for older people.

I was in law school when he asked me to help turn his vision of The Harbor Court into a reality. At the time, it was an empty building across the street from our church. He envisioned a 122-unit apartment building where residents had privacy in a community and could enjoy social activities and get necessary help.

Some days, assistance means providing transportation to a

doctor's appointment. Other days, it's as simple as opening a bottle.

A concept is a dream, though, until you build it up. We started out with five residents and thought it would be easy to attract more. Two years later we had added about 20 residents. With just four employees doing everything, I hired someone to handle marketing and admittance. Three years later we were up to 100 residents.

Needless to say, I relied heavily on our marketing director. My biggest mistake was not appreciating that marketing is not just about one person.

When you run a small business like this, you embrace employees like family. A few years after our marketing director was hired, she was diagnosed with breast cancer. Our colleague was just 42 when she quickly died from the disease. It didn't feel like a short time then, because we watched this young, vibrant woman suffer and we were there with her for support.

For a long time we were almost in shock. Could this be happening? Is this really happening? It took a long time to absorb from an emotional standpoint and longer from a business standpoint. We had no idea how she marketed this business.

We didn't understand her tracking system, her notes or her note cards. That was her job, and she was very good at it. As a young small-business owner, I didn't understand the importance of involving myself in everybody's job. I don't mean micromanaging. I mean being aware of what's involved.

That awful experience taught me the importance of cross-training. It also made me realize that as an owner, I am the one who is ultimately responsible, but everyone plays a role in making a business a success.

Even though we hired someone else to do marketing, that experience made me change the way I ran the business. At staff meetings, I started emphasizing the importance of everyone understanding our product and being comfortable with what we have to offer.

Our marketing director is in charge of public relations, brochures, fliers and networking with groups including the chamber of commerce and nursing groups. But I tell my staff that there is no better referral than word of mouth. They can play a role by being cognizant of opportunities to market in our daily activities, like picking up medication or making sure someone at a doctor's office knows to contact us when one of our residents is ready.

Now we have a marketing team that meets weekly. Sometimes we bring in others. For instance, the head of nursing might offer a different perspective that we never would have thought about. One time we considered a marketing campaign that involved going down memory lane. One staff member pointed out that it might make some people sad. That member offered a much better idea.

Ten years ago we converted a former Sheraton Hotel into a senior community in Rocky River.

Rockport Retirement Community has smaller rooms and a kitchenette instead of a full kitchen, but it offers independent living at more-affordable rates. We began the team approach there, realizing that the best way to run a business is by cross-training.

I make sure that all nurse assistants are comfortable giving older people a bath. I want our driver also to be able to lead an activity if the activity coordinator is absent. Residents should still be able to play "Let's Make a Deal" or have a birthday party.

When I started out, I assumed bad things couldn't happen. Back then, my biggest fear was that another company might try to steal our marketing director, not that she could get sick and die. The fact is, life gives you surprises. Employees can leave or move.

At one point we were paralyzed because of an employee loss. Now our goal is to make sure changes are seamless to residents and prospective residents.

Ad money spent in the wrong media

Bud Ungar
Title: Founder
Company: Mar-Lou Shoes
Founded: 1958
Headquarters: Richmond Heights
Employees: 19

I bought a shoe business in downtown Cleveland with money I borrowed from a loan shark. Each week, for 100 weeks, I made payments that included 10 percent interest. I got rid of the old inventory, specialized in unusual sizes and started advertising. I didn't have any money, but I had a great incentive to attract customers.

That was 49 years ago. Since then the business has done nothing but grow. I've always advertised Mar-Lou Shoes in all sorts of print publications, from local newspapers to national magazines. It has been key to our growth.

At one point we had several locations. Now our one location at Hilltop Plaza in Richmond Heights does as much business as all of the others put together.

We spent 40 years downtown, 29 years in Richmond Mall, 18 years at Severance Town Center. We stayed less than two years in Canton and at Randall Park Mall, but that's a different story.

We didn't lose our customers when we finally decided to have just one location. That's because we specialize in hard-to-find sizes.

Our business has been through a lot of changes throughout the years, but the one thing that has remained constant is our commitment to advertising. We've always advertised with traditional media, except once.

And that was my biggest mistake—spending money on advertising in two supermarket tabloids in the early 1970s.

I can look in my journal and tell you anything you want to know about the history of this company. You have to have records. I can even tell you what the weather was like going back to 1958.

Our first day of business we sold $170 worth of shoes. The next day we sold $65. We started a catalog on March 1, 1964.

When we opened for business, there were seven department stores downtown. It was a different time. Long before computers and the internet, people loved catalogs. Our catalogs didn't even use photographs. An artist drew each shoe. Great drawings. Some shoes were made for us, so we would have to get samples for the artist. We used to promote the free catalogs in all sorts of national magazines including Redbook, Seventeen, Glamour and Ebony.

They were very small ads. Just big enough to promote a free catalog with contact information. Advertising worked well for us. But one day I was approached by a now defunct Cleveland advertising agency that used to be in the Terminal Tower. He sold me a bill of goods when he told me that we could be getting more customers if we started advertising in the tabloids.

I hired him because I figured he was the expert in advertising. I know advertising is important, but it's not my world. I know shoes. I've been working in the shoe business since I was 14. By the time I was 22 I was managing a shoe store. At 25, I opened this business. I didn't have any money then, but I was optimistic because I knew there was a market for hard-to-find sizes. After the Korean War, I worked for a while in the corporate office of the former Wohl Shoe Co. and we could never fulfill requests for unusual sizes. I knew that would be my niche one day.

Immediately after the ads ran in the tabloids, the mailman brought a small box filled with requests for free catalogs. I had high hopes. I got really excited the next day when he brought three more. The third day he brought bags of requests.

I thought, boy, we hit the honey hole here. We're going to do great. We printed more catalogs, probably about 25,000. We did a special print run. This was long before computers, so it involved a lot of labor and time.

We sent out all of the catalogs and then we waited. And we waited. And we waited. We spent a lot of time and money for nothing. The only thing I got out of that deal was a valuable lesson.

It's not about quantity when it comes to advertising. It's about the quality of customers that you're trying to attract.

The people who saw the ads in the tabloids just wanted a free catalog. People who respond to ads in traditional publications are good, quality leads.

I have customers whom I've had since we started the business. Every day I get new customers from word of mouth and advertising. Once they get here, it's up to us to give them great service and show them our quality products. That's what turns them into loyal, repeat customers. But it all starts with advertising.

Don't bring in customers until you can keep them

Deborah Lontor-Bonham
Title: Owner
Company: Dorlon Golf Club
Founded: 1973
Headquarters: Columbia Station
Employees: 45

I inherited a golf course in Columbia Station. I'm an only child, so I knew that would happen one day. But nothing was planned when my dad died suddenly.

My first impulse was to sell the golf course. Running a public golf course was my father's dream, not mine. I didn't even golf.

At the time I was the administrator of a 100-bed long-term-care facility, a business I had started 15 years earlier. Each year it was becoming more difficult to manage in such a fast-changing industry, but it was a very successful business and I loved it.

A year after my father passed away, I was still taking a hands-off approach to running the golf course—until I found a buyer. But what happened when I finally got an offer for $2.5 million? I turned it down and sold my own business instead.

I had a steep learning curve, but that didn't stop me from

heavily marketing Dorlon Golf Club.

My biggest mistake was marketing the business before it was renovated and ready to compete with other courses in the area.

In my former business, marketing was essential due to a less-than-desirable location. Dorlon is also off the beaten path. I thought that marketing was a no-brainer, that the same thing would happen here. My father loved taking care of the course, but he was very frugal and he didn't spend much on advertising. There wasn't even a sign on Ohio 82, and we're a mile and a half south of that main road. Some people in the business didn't even know about us.

I renovated the clubhouse immediately and bought new signs for the road near our entry and other places. Then I spent money on advertising in several outlets—newspapers, radio, cable television and the entertainment book. It was expensive, but it worked. People came out in droves.

I used phrases like "best-kept secret" and "one of the most challenging courses." Business tripled within a few years. Then business started to decrease dramatically.

The problem was customers were disappointed when they got here. I didn't get it, for a while. I chose to look at the positives only, like our great facility, excellent customer service, a full driving range, a chipping green and a putting green. After learning more about this business, I realized I had to do a lot more, starting with updating our antiquated equipment and undertaking major capital improvements.

I spent more than a million dollars on irrigation and drainage for every fairway. We also began an overseeding program for the entire course. Even growing grass can be a challenge in some areas, season after season. Again, it wasn't enough.

The other lesson was a lot harder to figure out. It took me a few years to understand that the course was too long for regular play. Nobody wanted to tell me that. They just made excuses or went elsewhere. Everybody wants to score well. What was happening was some people would come out so they could use every club in their bag—once a year.

A long course is not attractive for league play. I had a lot more leagues in the first couple of years and we catered to them. But it wasn't enough. I had to shorten the course 600 yards to make it a more competitive length.

We took out half of the sand traps and renovated the 11 remaining traps. It wasn't easy making these decisions because my dad designed the course and I didn't want to take away all of the character. But we continued making improvements. For instance, there's a clear definition between the fairway and the rough.

My five-year plan turned into a 10-year plan, with a lot of trial and error. It has been a challenge even deciding the best time to undertake projects such as lake expansions or putting in drain tiles on the fairways so they remain dry and playable. Winter months are obviously the best time, but in recent years the ground was often not firm enough to do the necessary work. These projects had to be completed throughout the golfing season.

We never even had cart paths, and that's an expensive, ongoing project. We listen to customers and continue to make improvements. We even added lots of birdhouses, which helped to alleviate the deerflies.

I haven't done any advertising in the past two years. But I'm very close to showing off with a big anniversary celebration next spring.

There is no room for immediate gratification in this business. In the past year we finally started enjoying a big increase in play, with both individuals and outings. We're competitive now, and I'm encouraged every day by positive feedback from golfers.

The next time we advertise, we'll be ready to keep our customers.

Tech guy needed to see different angle

Jim Kerr
Title: President
Company: CRU Solutions
Founded: 1982
Headquarters: Middleburg Heights
Employees: 8

I started learning about these new products called microcomputers when they first came out. At 17, I was writing software. When I was in college I started CRU Solutions.

It was a different company back then, just focusing on software. Now we design technology solutions, supply the hardware, service it and manage clients' networks all the way out to the internet. But it's still the same company. Except for one corporate internship, I've never worked for anyone.

I'm a technology guy, so luckily I was able to build this company by serving customers well and banking on referrals. I never actually looked for clients. They found me. But when I was ready to grow the company five or six years ago, I started advertising. In a year's time, I spent about $20,000 on radio, direct mail and five billboards. We even knocked on doors. The result was just absolutely embarrassing.

My biggest mistake was not differentiating sales from marketing. I'm a math guy, so I know you've got to start somewhere when you approach an issue. The problem with that approach, I later found, was that I focused on trying to sell products as opposed to offering solutions.

I was selling without having created a market to sell into. One billboard, for instance, promoted buying the Pentium 4 processor when it first came out in 2001. A direct-mail piece marketed an e-mail server. We were trying to sell to businesses—businesses that had never heard of us or understood why they would be interested in the product. It took about a year and a half for me to realize that

I was wasting my time and money with my approach.

I hired a business development officer who I met at Bible study, and I credit him for helping me to better understand strategic marketing. He spent a year working at the company, just trying to understand our business. About 90 percent of our clients are small to medium-size enterprises that have 15 to 50 employees.

He made a few changes in that first year. After that, he began creating packages that were attractive to both our former customers and our new customers.

Instead of saying we have laptops, desktops and servers to sell, which was my approach, he identified solutions that both information workers and mobile workers were interested in.

For instance, some of our clients had our hardware, but we were not doing remote management for them. We created a set of benefits that made clients want to pay a small monthly fee in order not to have to worry about things like slow servers and space dwindling on a hard disk.

The way services were packaged was critical, though, and it called for a balance. We had to make a fair and reasonable profit. Meanwhile, clients had to get more value than what they were paying for in order to make it a win-win situation.

After his second year here, in 2003, our sales increased 300 percent. That's a significant increase in any economic environment, but this increase happened during the dot-com bust, at a time when technology stocks were crashing and the whole technology industry was tanking. Since that time, growth has been more modest, with 10 percent to 20 percent annual increases.

Part of our growth has come from helping clients understand that they need a lot more than just a product to accomplish their business objectives. Just knowing that they can turn to one company to handle all their technology issues has made a big difference.

If you want to grow your business, often one of the best ways is to look at your business model from a different perspective.

Golf course manager steps outside the (tee) box

Jimmy Hanlin
Title: Director of golf operations
Company: Little Mountain Country Club
Founded: 1999
Headquarters: Concord Township
Employees: 75

I got a business degree in professional golf management, then played a lot of golf as an assistant pro in Pinehurst, N.C. After my game improved, I toured as a pro for a couple of years.

When I figured out I wasn't good enough to play for a living, I went back to doing what I love—creating a great experience for other golfers.

I moved to Northeast Ohio to work as an assistant pro at Quail Hollow. Then I was recruited to sell memberships to a new course, Little Mountain Country Club, a year before it opened. I was excited about the opportunity until I arrived at my new office, a trailer surrounded by dirt.

It was supposed to be a private club with 80 homes on acre lots. The entire project was based on selling the development. Everything changed when one of the owners suffered a stroke and the other went through a divorce. The development didn't sell as quickly as expected and finances fell apart.

Meanwhile, I continued trying to market the course as a semi-private club, with plans to make it private after about a year. Four years later, we had new owners, still operating as a semi-private club.

My biggest mistake was trying to operate Little Mountain like a traditional golf club instead of thinking out of the box, emulating what has been successful in other industries.

New owners put a lot of money into this venture, turning a temporary modular facility into a clubhouse that resembles a chalet, complete with a patio and a pro shop. Actually, they took the entire project to the next level, with new landscaping and a new driving range. Lots started selling again, but the golf industry in general was still struggling.

After 9/11, businesses started cutting back on entertainment. A few years later, employers were still not spending on extracurricular activities, including golf memberships. Meanwhile, golf courses, including ours, were still operating the same as they had in the past.

A couple of years ago I became a part owner, along with our golf course superintendent. But we were just surviving. We started making changes when one of the two other owners, who is not a golfer, suggested we look outside the industry for marketing and operating ideas. That scared me. I've been golfing since I was 6, so I know it's a traditional industry. But then we thought, why not?

We looked at the way ticket packages are sold for professional sports and then changed the way we sell memberships.

Before, members who paid monthly membership dues could golf at peak times, play in tournaments and special events and bring guests for an extra charge.

Now we offer packages of 25, 50 or 100 rounds of golf that the buyer can use or give to others. The vast majority of our members transferred to the more flexible membership options. Businesses that would not even look at us before started buying these packages.

Some marketing changes were in motion earlier. For instance, we realized a few years ago that one of the best ways to communicate with our customers is through e-mail. Whenever people called to make a tee time, or when we participated at regional golf shows, we started asking for e-mail addresses. We got more addresses by promoting contests on the web site. Now we have more than 10,000 e-mail addresses.

We advertised on radio and TV for about four years, which was about the same time I was host of a sports talk radio show Saturday mornings on WKNR. What started out as a guest spot turned into four years of giving golf tips, following the PGA Tour and doing live remotes from various Ohio golf courses.

Within the past few years we've realized that having a face tied to the name Little Mountain has helped create relationships with people. It makes new customers feel as if they know somebody when they walk in the door.

Two years ago I started co-hosting "Tee It Up Ohio" on SportsTime Ohio. The show airs on Tuesday evenings and promotes great golf courses throughout Ohio.

I often am asked how I can promote other courses on TV and radio. My answer to that is I just promote golf. I try to get more people to play and love the game. If I operate my facility right, then I'll get my share of customers. We were fortunate enough last year for Golf Digest to agree with how we do things. They named us one of only 17 five-star courses in the country in their Best Places to Play issue.

I'm no longer reluctant to try marketing techniques that don't fit the traditional mold. Now I at least give everything a second look. Proof of that is the 2008 Girls of Little Mountain Calendar that features some of our bartender and beverage cart employees. When they came up with the idea three years ago, I hesitated because it's not a traditional marketing tool.

In the spring we bought a golf course development just east of Columbus in Reynoldsburg, and we hope to try there a lot of things that have worked for us here.

We started out with a build-it-and-they-will-come mentality. Then we spent some money on upgrades. But it still wasn't enough. We had to go get the customers and work on retaining them.

TECHNOLOGY

TECHNOLOGY CAN MAKE OR BREAK your business. It can put you way ahead of your competition or drain your finances and time.

Either way, it's something you have to consider to be in the game. Whether you invest in simple personal handheld devices and computers, or spend big money on state of the art media, you need technology to help communicate with customers and vendors. When things go right, it helps you shine. Technology allows instantaneous contact with employees and customers—which creates value.

Unfortunately, some entrepreneurs have learned the hard way that investing in tools not right for their businesses or failing to invest in security and back-up systems, nearly made them crave for the days of pen and paper.

Technology is a tool, designed to help businesses run smoother. Sometimes tools break so you'd better have another plan.

Even in the best case scenarios, companies that use technology well, never forget the importance of human contact. Smart business people know that high touch is as crucial as high tech. Remember, no technology ever signed a contract.

Don't be afraid to embrace technology. But don't take it lightly.

That click isn't music: Back up your files now

Sandra Wolk Graubard
Title: Art Director
Company: Spiral Studios
Founded: 1998
Headquarters: Orange
Employees: One

Click. Click. Click. Click. Click.

I heard the noise, but computers often make noises with the fan or motor. This was a noise that I had never heard before, but I ignored it. I'm a software expert, not a hardware specialist.

Maybe my mind was on wrapping up graphic design projects so I could go on a much-anticipated weekend trip. I usually do some work on weekends. I returned Monday to a computer with missing files. Data for about 40 clients was gone.

I panicked. It didn't take long for me to learn that the sound I heard a few days earlier is commonly known by hard drive experts as the "click of death." Companies that try to resurrect data from dead hard drives even have counselors on hand to help customers cope with their loss.

My biggest mistake was not investing time and money in a good backup system until I faced a disaster. I lost tens of thousands of dollars in revenue and spent many hours re-creating my custom design work.

It happened three years ago, but it feels like only yesterday because it took a good two years before it all shook out. You never know when you will get a call for more work that involves a design you created earlier.

At the time, it was stressful and embarrassing. I told clients what had happened only when necessary. Some were understanding. Some were intolerant. I recovered some things from vendors and others. For instance, a printer who had worked on a job might have copies of older files.

My design business is primarily referral-based. It has grown consistently because of excellent customer service, quick turn-around and because I am always following up on leads and planting seeds.

I'm a generalist, so my customers include retailers, kitchen remodelers, law firms, colleges and universities, lots of nonprofit organizations and smaller marketing firms. I do everything—print ads, signage, special-event marketing material, catalogs, corporate identity material and newsletters. I have to keep up with a lot of things. No client is interested in excuses.

Luckily, when my system crashed, the five projects that I was working on that week were saved. And even though I had gotten lax in backing up material, I had backed up in the past. Probably a good year's worth of designs and information were not backed up properly.

I was OK with the newsletters I produce because every issue is new and fresh. But I lost the main templates and other items that were in my archives. Instead of just dragging material to my working files, I was spending my valuable, non-billable time re-creating art.

When I lost everything, I tried to recover the information by sending the hard drive to a California-based computer restoration company. The $10,000 fee was steep for a small company like mine, but I was more than willing to pay it. Unfortunately, they could not help me.

My systems are complex with a lot of upgrades, so I have always had a computer guy in my life. Until the mishap, it never dawned on me that I should have sought his advice about backups. I hired him to customize a backup program that runs every night.

Now I go overboard so that I am never in the same position again. I back up on an external hard drive. I back up with CDs. And my current working jobs get transferred to a jump drive every night. Sometimes a surge can blow your hard drive so I even bought a large industrial battery back up.

I also check my backups. I open programs and check hardware files and CDs to make sure the copy is there. I even make printouts every night so that I feel safe.

Before I started my company, my background was in marketing and communications and sales. My degree is in industrial design visual communications, not technology. After losing data, I learned a lot about computers. The bottom line is computers are machines that are not built to last. Just like you have to constantly upgrade software, it's up to you to protect your data and information.

Wireless proved wrong choice for travel firm

Grady Burrows
Title: Owner
Company: Burrows Travel Group
Business: Corporate and leisure travel agency
Founded: 2002
Headquarters: Cleveland
Employees: 2

I opened Burrows Travel Group last year after working in the management consulting and information-technology management fields. When I started my own business I wanted an attractive and welcoming environment with bright colors and the latest computing technology—which to me meant a wireless network.

I moved into a live-work loft space in the Midtown Corridor in Cleveland. All of the technology that we have in our office is state-of-the-art, and the decision to go down a wireless path seemed perfect.

I made investments in hardware and consulting, and the network was up and running. But as more business applications were added, performance began to degrade. Our business is very data intensive, with several systems, including our client database, traditional reservations platform and a low-cost web-fare searching tool that searches multiple travel web sites at one time.

With demands from multiple machines, reliable up-time became a challenge in getting everything to work in harmony. Other wireless networks in the building compounded the problem by causing interference.

My network would often pick up on my neighbor's signals and get confused.

Even though I have wireless technology at home that works great, I learned the hard way that it's not meant to be in my current office environment.

We compete head to head with large global travel service providers and the internet, so our ability to get information to clients and cultivate personal relationships is vital in giving us an edge.

As a new business, we leverage personalized customer service as our key differentiator. It's a competitive advantage in the world of nameless, faceless web sites and mega-agent travel providers.

But in order to be effective, we have to have an IT infrastructure that's reliable.

When we first had problems, we called the manufacturers of the wireless hardware. Then we called in an IT technician. Then we called another technician. We did a lot of tweaking and talking to hardware manufacturing experts and software help-desk representatives. We were operational but never 100 percent.

Finally, we decided to box up all of the wireless hardware. We saw that wireless was not going to work for our needs and a traditional wired solution would be best for our complex environment. Now we have wires lining the walls—camouflaged elegantly. Nothing is wireless now. Everything is networked with traditional cables.

But we're able to efficiently send and receive data, access our client database in real time and leverage our web-fare tool with our traditional booking system.

No matter how sexy or state of the art I thought it to be, I am better served in this particular environment by traditional wires, cabling and networking.

Limousine service temporarily hobbled when outside vendor slipped up

Stephen Qua
Title: President
Company: Company Car
Founded: 1994
Headquarters: Cleveland
Employees: 26

I started hearing travelers' complaints about taxi service when I was in law school driving a cab at night to support my family. I started asking customers, "If a transportation service existed where they could buy on-time performance and limousine quality at a rate close to a taxi, would they take advantage of it?" I asked for a business card from everyone who answered yes.

I left school and started the business with a partner nearly two years after we started making inquiries. Company Car was founded in a Chagrin Falls bedroom. Our success has been found in focusing on the business traveler. Most of our business comes from airport transfers and corporate events, with regional door-to-door ground travel to Pittsburgh, Columbus and Detroit accounting for about 30 percent of business. Last year we were named "Operator of the Year" by Limousine and Chauffeured Transportation magazine.

Our company has matured. We celebrate our 10th year anniversary this month, but our biggest mistake happened just recently. We failed to inspect what an outside vendor was doing for us, and our lack of oversight had a profound impact on cash flow.

Our network-based accounting system failed, and we found that our backups were not working properly. Our backup tapes were blank. When our program crashed, we weren't able to access any financial data, which meant we could not send out invoices or statements.

Even worse, we were unable to close out any existing transportation jobs, rendering us unable to bill credit cards. The feeling could only be equated with the sense of immediate panic when you first realize that you've lost your wallet or purse.

It took nine days to fix the problem. We're a big company. Had we not recovered the data, we would have had to hire someone to manually input every financial transaction for the year. That's hundreds of thousands of accounting entries. All that corrupted data was crucial for tax returns, accountants, as well as our banking relationship.

Several years ago, when we first started the company and didn't know a lot about technology, we had a big scare. Our old dispatch and reservation system crashed, and we didn't even know where we were supposed to be heading in the morning. Luckily, we were able to fix the problem before it was time for our first pickup.

That experience taught us that we needed to upgrade to a network-based dispatch and reservation system with tape backups. It also taught us that because our business relies heavily on technology, we needed to start relying on others who have expertise in the field.

We assumed that we minimized our risk of data problems once we turned over the technology part of our business to a qualified company. We chose a good company that we had been with for several years. They just dropped the ball, and we got caught.

Had we been supervising properly, we would have found out a lot sooner that the network company knew our backups were not working properly. After our system failed, we learned that it is capable of sending us an e-mail every night to alert us when the backup procedure is successful. We now take advantage of this. In the words of one of our chauffeurs, you are responsible to inspect what you expect. We sleep better now.

Software unsuited to business proves costly

Anup Gupta
Title: President
Company: AG PrintPromo Solutions
Founded: 1996
Headquarters: Cuyahoga Falls
Employees: 4

I'm a big believer in small business. It's in my blood. My family has a textile company in India, and I grew up working in the business and learning to make a living by selling items to retailers.

I came to this country to get a master's degree in sales and marketing. I didn't know what field I would get into afterward, but I knew I wanted to be in a business-to-business environment.

I started a printing and promotions-product company, but we don't just offer products. We offer solutions. There are a lot of companies that try to sell you "stuff" without attempting to find out if it's the right product for your needs. When it comes to service, knowledge and targeted solutions, very few companies can compete with us. Our clients are nationwide, and our business has experienced double-digit growth every year for the last nine, primarily due to referrals.

We attribute our success to the way we take care of our clients. Anytime a potential customer inquires about a product, we spend a lot of time asking them questions.

Only after we learn about their company, their target market, their budget and the type of event that they're hosting do we offer suggestions.

When you treat people the way you would want to be treated in business, it generally decreases the possibility of getting into trouble.

That's why I don't make many mistakes. But I made a big mistake last year by spending $10,000 on software that is not suited for our business.

I take full responsibility. It's a good product that had a lot of positive reviews. It was recommended by some of my peers. Business was growing, and this software appeared to be better than our 6-year-old software. But it's been a huge pain. It takes double the time to process orders, and it's not very easy to use.

The software has a lot of neat online order-management and inventory features, but only about 20 percent of our business comes from online. The software is geared toward printing, and printing accounts for only half our business. We didn't realize that until after we were using it.

Another problem is that the print on purchase orders is too small. That's a disaster waiting to happen. Luckily a couple vendors have called us when they weren't clear about a number. We've been fortunate because an eight sometimes looks like a six. If an order of 600 shirts looks like 800 shirts on the fax, who would pay for the extra 200 shirts?

We spent a lot of time learning how to use this software. But after 10 months, I decided to go back to our old software. That means that all the work we've done in the last 10 months has to be entered into our old system.

We should have asked for a trial period. Instead, I just went for it because it was so highly recommended. It doesn't matter how many bells and whistles a product has if your company isn't able to use the features.

I wish the software company that I bought it from had treated me the way that I treat my customers. I wish they asked me some questions. If they had, I would have realized that this was not the best product for me.

On a positive note, I have gained a tremendous amount of knowledge about software. A lot of companies have trial periods. Some offer demos. Others offer to send a CD by mail so you can try it before you buy it.

I learned the importance of talking to other companies in similar businesses before making a big purchase. The software we got is great for a printing company, just not for one that offers promotional marketing as well.

Our old software now has more features to help our business run more smoothly. We can't risk using a product that takes attention from our ultimate goal of being one step ahead of our competition.

Manufacturer discovered online project needed in-house experts, not hired hands

Jack Schron Jr.
Title: President
Company: Tooling U
Founded: 2000
Headquarters: Cleveland
Employees: 18

My two sons are fourth generation family members working in manufacturing. It's a great feeling. But the world is changing.

My father started Jergens Inc. with his father, making clamping parts for all sorts of manufacturing processes that require drilling, welding and stamping.

For years, I've wondered who is going to train the next generation to use the tools that corporations around the world need for their products. More people were retiring at a time when companies were cutting back on apprenticeship programs and the interest level at high schools and community college levels was minimal.

When my son Chad joined Jergens as an engineer in 1999, he took it upon himself to upgrade our web site. After he added instructions on how to use our products, we decided that there was a market to sell online training for manufacturing parts made by other companies.

We started Tooling U, an online training company, and we figured the best way to get the content was from training materials already developed by other companies. We assumed that the best people to put the information together were engineers. We assumed wrong. Our biggest mistake was turning to technical and sales people to develop content for our web site.

The idea was that we could charge companies to host the materials on our web site after their engineers and salespeople had put the information in a comprehensive format. There were many problems with that logic—mainly time, commitment and readability.

Nobody is going to be as committed to your project as you are. It was unrealistic for us to think that engineers and salespeople could spend time developing materials for our site while doing their jobs. We found out, way too late, that it takes about 100 hours to develop every hour of content for our online training program.

The second major problem that we faced was that technical people weren't able to convey their thoughts in an educational format. It's not what they're trained to do. It was like calling in professional ballplayers off the field and asking them to put out a newspaper, or asking professional writers to hit the field. Either way, you won't get your desired result for quality that you can sell.

The material that we did acquire was inconsistent, because it was coming from so many different companies and people. When you give up control, you sacrifice part of the quality process. At one point, we even hired a writer who specialized in manufacturing publications. That didn't work. There's still a big difference in developing curriculum, especially when you're working part time. A year after we started our project, Tooling U had no classes.

We started second-guessing our efforts. Was there really a need? Will the product sell? How do you price it?

That's when we realized that although we were going into uncharted territory in the manufacturing world, online content was available in other fields. We did some research on other online training ventures and made some changes. Frankly, I also started listening more to people involved in the project—people who had been recommending changes.

We hired Greg Herlevi, a full-time professional writer, to interview engineers, trainers and salespeople. He turned the information into a readable, consistent and sellable format. Right away it worked, and our first writer became head of content development, proving that we could repeat the process.

In the last four years, we went from three employees to 18, with a third being full-time writers. Today we have a wide variety of more than 200 classes online. Our customers range from Chrysler and Caterpillar to about 80 high schools and community colleges. Our classes are technically correct and educationally sound. Just as important, they are engaging.

Parts and other images are shown with graphics. Video and audio are available in English and Spanish. Definitions pop up when words are highlighted. You can save notes on the same screen while you're learning, and the time, date and notes will reappear next time you log on.

Not only am I recharged and optimistic about the future of manufacturing. I've relearned a valuable lesson in business. When you're involved in an area that's not your specialty, the best thing that you can do is put the right people in charge and get out of the way.

Face time essential for success

Louis McClung
Title: Owner
Company: Lusso Cosmetics
Founded: 1998
Headquarters: Lakewood
Employees: 2

I got into makeup because when you're the photographer, you're responsible for the finished product, no matter what.

When I first started doing commercial photography, a lot of times there wasn't a budget for a makeup artist. When I was doing head shots, I was always wondering how I could make customers look better.

That's why I taught myself how to apply makeup. To me it's like painting. But when people started giving me feedback, I fell in love with the art. I was taking photos long before digital photography became popular, and it used to be a huge process. Makeup is spontaneous. But when it's done right, it changes people emotionally.

That's why one of my newest services is giving clients a before and after photo to take home with them, after I've selected makeup just for them. My business has continually evolved in the last eight years, but designing makeup to fit clients' lifestyles is the only constant thing I've ever done.

Listening to clients and teaching them to highlight their best features is the way I've built my business. People spread the word.

But a few years after I started the business I forgot that. I didn't have money for marketing and I just knew that the internet was the answer.

My biggest mistake was believing that online sales would account for at least a third of my revenues.

I thought that people would flock to my web site just because it was attractive and easy to navigate and my prices were competitive with department store cosmetics. I learned the hard way that people are not going to buy makeup online unless it's a major national brand. Sales were rough, and that's putting it mildly.

The reality is that when you look at makeup colors online, they're distorted. Technology is not the best way to buy makeup unless you've already seen what you're buying. It's not like buying a DVD or a product that people might buy sight unseen because they're price-motivated.

At the time, though, I got caught up. Small businesses were just starting to build web sites and e-commerce was just starting to kick off. In 2000, every time you watched the news or turned on commercials, everybody was talking about dot-coms.

I didn't have a lot of money to put into a web site, but I invested about $2,000, and that was a ton at the time. Forget the money: I spent way too much time working on the site. I thought it was my future, so I probably spent about five months working on it. Some nights I would be working on it until 3:30 a.m.

Not only was I working on the technology with a friend, I was doing all of the product and fashion photography for the site. I spent many, many hours in Photoshop. It was a really big process.

Just because we perceive things to be one way doesn't mean they're gong to be that way. Part of being a successful business person is having vision and daydreaming. That's what it's all about. What I've learned as a businessman is that you have to go for it, but you also have to let go of the outcome.

I was so focused on building my web site that I wasn't thinking about what drives my business—the personal touch. Even though I was personally picking out makeup for people every day in my studio, it just didn't dawn on me that the key to building my business was one-on-one consultations. It's what I do, and that's what people wanted.

About a year after the site was up I realized that I needed a web site, but not for sales. I turned my strategy around and made it work for me. I started using the site primarily as a marketing and educational tool.

My clients can leave the studio and go online at their convenience to see tips and techniques reinforced. It also has tools to drive business to my studio, including a link to Mapquest.

Even now, five years after I launched the site, only about 10 percent of revenues come from the internet. But it helped me to keep customers who have moved from the area and now order their products online. The site also has sales tools. You can hit a button to recommend a product to a friend.

The internet has played a role in building our database of 2,400 clients. Some people sign up for our monthly newsletter and new product announcements. The internet has also helped build our wholesale program that targets salons and spas.

When I first started the business with 15 clients, I was banking on technology, media exposure and my passion for what I do to build my client base. All of that is important in retail. But word-of-mouth referrals are what sustain my business—not technology.

Web business delayed setting up capability for credit cards

Dr. Jacob Mathew
Title: President
Company: International Cyber Business Services Inc.
Founded: 1995
Headquarters: Hudson
Employees: 4

I started a web development company in 1995, when the web was still in its infancy.

International Cyber Business Services Inc. offers web site development, maintenance, promotion and hosting. In the beginning, I decided to develop a web site that could be used as an example to show prospective clients—similar to a builder putting up a model home to show potential clients.

After several bad starts, we finally settled on developing www.holisticonline.com, a web site that provides information about integrative medicine.

It was never meant to generate revenue. It was just a reference source that got a lot of media attention. Before long, visitors from all over the globe were on the site and some wanted more than information. They wanted products.

But when I linked to another site of mine where a few homeopathic medicines and health products were available, I didn't set it up to accept credit cards. That was my biggest mistake.

It wasn't until two years ago, when I changed the focus of ICBS and devoted my efforts to a different e-commerce site, www.specialgifts.com, that the business took off. That web site offers unique gift and health products.

When I first started selling items online seven years ago, shoppers were worried about internet security. And for a small business owner, the cost of setting up and maintaining a web site with credit card capability was substantial. I decided to try the cash-on-delivery route, because at the time we were an unknown company dealing with an unproven technology. I thought that for the amount of business we did back then, fees would have eaten up all our revenues.

But, of course, I was being shortsighted. By not having a convenient way for customers to make payments, we were restricting our growth. By refusing to take credit cards, we lost valuable opportunities to develop our business early.

Looking back, the overriding issue was running an information technology business and pursuing outside projects that involved a lot of capital and took time to develop. Though the company had built up a loyal client base, I had limited financial resources and time.

By not accepting credit cards, I had a lot of problems. With the c.o.d. method, we lost a lot of money from people who simply didn't pay. And for small amounts, wire transfer was too expensive. We required payment up front for overseas shipments, but we had to wait for the check to arrive and clear. Sometimes that process could take three weeks.

As the years went by, the web was changing fast, and people were demanding convenient ways to pay. Security for handling credit cards was in place. People lost their initial resistance to using them online.

Unfortunately, I was too busy developing our marquee web site, www.holisticonline.com, to keep up. My efforts have paid off, though. It's one of the top sites on the internet for integrative medicine, getting visitors from more than 170 countries. The web log registers more than eight million hits a month.

Two years ago, I finally decided to develop my dream web site, www.specialgifts.com. The site incorporates all that we had learned, including convenient payment methods and a strong back end that assures effective and efficient e-commerce. In order to tackle the rising concern about identity theft, credit card payments go directly to a financial institution so customers don't have to divulge sensitive personal data to us.

About half the products we sell are custom gift products, many of them handcrafted by artisans in remote parts of the world. We offer bracelets, necklaces, earrings and rings that are custom-made with genuine gemstones. Some of the precious gems include genuine Ceylon sapphires, Burmese rubies, Colombian emeralds, African amethysts and tanzanites and Brazilian citrines. We also sell vitamins and homeopathic and herbal health products.

Within a short time, our web site has captured a sizable, loyal customer base. We ship all over the world. Sometime around Thanksgiving, www.specialgifts.com will be featured in "Living in Style's Annual Gift Guide," a TV program that has more than 70 million viewers nationwide.

Offering a combination of outstanding products, pampering customer service and a great web experience proved to be a winning formula. But accepting credit cards is one of the biggest factors for our success. Today, at least 95 percent of our orders are paid for by credit card.

Eagerness for latest technology led to expensive error

John Hornyak
Title: President
Company: X2 Media
Founded: 1999
Headquarters: Twinsburg
Employees: Three

Think. Create. Inspire.

It's not just a tagline. It's the foundation of our business. We help companies tell stories using video, graphics, photography and animation.

In order to sell a client's services or help educate their employees, we put the emphasis on the message. But when you see the impact that video and visuals can make on a presentation, it's easy to get caught up with technology. When visual tools are used appropriately, it helps an audience become emotionally involved.

I always wanted my clients to have the latest, greatest technology. My biggest mistake was being too anxious to be the first kid on the block with a new toy.

Six years ago, I spent $65,000 on a DVD authoring system. Just three months later that same company introduced a knock-off system for $995. Part of the system I purchased included a $5,000 DVD burner. Now you can get DVD burners included on laptops for less than $2,000.

Throughout the years, the cost of the technology always decreases. But six years ago, we thought we were going to be able to provide customers with much higher quality video and sound. The system offered interactivity that allowed users to select where they wanted to go in the production immediately.

I was excited to be among the first companies in the area to offer video and sound to the market in a DVD format, instead of a CD that had limited capacity and quality. At the time, all of the market indicators suggested that DVD was the wave of the future. And it is. The problem was, I jumped the gun.

I was sold a bill of goods at a presentation. The video production systems dealer assured me that I would be the first in the Cleveland area with the system I purchased and they told me they would provide all sorts of marketing support. Instead, we got no marketing support and the company released the cheaper system three months later.

It was like buying PowerPoint or Photoshop after we spent thousands on a similar product. It wasn't the entire turnkey system with hardware and software. But I didn't necessarily need to buy all of the hardware. My letters to the company's president were in vain. We were told that we have the system, so use it to make money. For us to get a return on our investment we would have had to charge a lot more than the cost of an off-the-shelf system. What I bought was an expensive learning lesson.

I've been in the presentation business for 24 years, long before

I started this company. I remember well the labor-intensive 35mm slideshow presentations that we used to put together long before slides went digital.

Tools have changed, but customers have not. They generally wait until the last minute to get help and then they want great results in a short time. It's the same premise of going to a dentist: People tend to wait until it hurts. That's why I always wanted the best technology to help deliver great results—so that creativity doesn't suffer due to time constraints.

Now I talk to a lot of people before I make major purchases. I want to know who has one already and how they like it.

We also try a lot of things before we buy it. Some of the best people to talk to about new technology are college students. They are privy to the latest software and hardware and they give unbiased opinions.

Now people are constantly trying to sell me on high-definition video. Will I get it? Eventually. Will I be the first on the block to get it? No. Before I make purchases now, I let the market catch up with the technology and I listen more to customers' requests. At that point, prices have dropped because of supply and demand.

We do a lot of web design and produce videos for web sites. We also help produce PowerPoint presentations for annual meetings and big events.

With all of our services, I remind customers to put themselves in place of an audience. They want to know what's in it for them. Our job is to help them get that message quickly, in a way that will inspire them to remember it.

One of the analogies I use with clients and prospective clients is that I can buy the exact same set of golf clubs that Tiger Woods has, but it's not going to make me the same caliber of golfer as he is.

Technology is a tool. In my business it's an important tool, but it's not the complete package.

CLIENTS/CUSTOMERS

CUSTOMERS ARE THE LIFEBLOOD of your business. Sometimes they're right. Sometimes they're wrong. Either way, they still deserve respect.

Entrepreneurs in this chapter share experiences that include trying too hard to make customers happy. Sometimes businesses need to improve products and services, but oftentimes it's best to find customers who appreciate your offerings.

Your work is your signature, so strive to give customers what they paid for and then some. But set guidelines. Going overboard to please customers can make you unhappy. One hairstylist spent years, altering her hours to meet customers schedules. Customers were happy, but she suffered from not having a social life, sleep deprivation, and gaining weight from all of the fast-food she ate on the run.

Some small business owners have found that being confrontational isn't good for business—especially when customers can be so loud and wrong. The best approach is to make sure your paperwork is organized and in order. The fact is, many customers will try to take advantage of you. Memories can be selective and perceptions vary, but there's nothing like a document signed by a customer. Spell out in writing what products and services you provide and your payment terms.

For the most part, people do business with people they like. Some entrepreneurs learn the hard way that subtleties have major influence on the way customers percieve them, ranging from attire to manners. Look and act the part for the role you're playing.

It doesn't matter whether you're operating from a home-based business or spacious well-lit retail space, customers want a good experience. They want to buy a good product and they want to respect you and the services you provide.

Listen to your customers. Good and bad experiences can enhance your business and make you more effective. But don't be afraid to fire your customers. Have courage to refuse clients who don't fit the direction of your business or who constantly elevate your blood pressure when serving them.

Public relations professional forgot her firm needed PR, too

Lora M. Thompson
Title: President
Company: LMT Productions
Founded: 1990
Headquarters: South Euclid
Employees: 3

I started LMT Productions more than a decade ago after leaving my job as public relations and marketing director of Gateway Economic Development Corp., a temporary position that had been created to help publicize Jacobs Field and Gund Arena.

I always knew I wanted to be an entrepreneur, ever since I was 10, selling Christmas cards to neighbors and heading street bake sales. So when my job was coming to an end, I knew it was time to make the leap and start my own public relations and marketing firm.

I am a consultant, advising businesses and organizations about media relations, advertising and community relations.

My clients are in various industries, including entertainment, education, government and construction.

Clients have received local, regional and national coverage, including "Entertainment Tonight" and the Wall Street Journal. But even with 20 years of experience in the industry, I am still learning lessons all the time. Early on, I learned a crucial lesson after wrongly assuming that a client understood the true value of services my company provided.

When I first started the business, potential clients requested quotes for media relations services including writing and placing news releases in media outlets.

I'd often give quotes that raised eyebrows from potential clients who weren't used to hiring public relations professionals.

I failed to explain the potential dollar value of getting an article placed in the media versus what it would cost to place paid advertisements. For example, a client might pay $1,000 to get a news release in the media—potentially generating several local and national articles. Purchasing this same space as advertisements might cost $50,000.

I found that I had to teach clients not just about the value of the service but also about realistic expectations.

For example, a client who has received a local award may get national attention in a trade publication but should not expect to be included in a national general publication.

I learned that securing new clients in the service business isn't just a sales process, it's also an educational process.

Not only does it give your company credibility, it can help close a deal.

Center focuses on quality, not quantity, in leasing to start-ups

Stacey Banks Houston
Title: President
Company: Executive Concepts
Founded: 1994
Headquarters: Shaker Heights
Employees: 3

We own and operate a business center that generally houses 20 to 30 tenants at any given time. Business owners and organizations rent space from us, and we provide our clients with support such as secretarial services and a conference room.

We also offer virtual offices for entrepreneurs who aren't ready for space but need someone to answer phones and have use of a workstation and a conference room. They want a professional image without overhead.

At this point, most of our clients come from referrals. But when we started the business, we used to advertise in newspapers, through direct mail and a telephone directory.

Initially we concentrated on quantity instead of quality—our biggest mistake. We wanted 100 percent occupancy, but we never reached that because we had clients whose business would last only three to six months. They could not fulfill leases, and we would find ourselves sending them to collections and dealing with legal issues.

My dad started the business a decade ago, and asked me to move back to Cleveland to help him build it. But when clients didn't work out, I spent a lot of time dealing with issues instead of trying to take our business to the next level. Looking back, we wasted a lot of time.

I used to show a space to a prospective client and tell him what it took to move in, such as signing a one-year lease, credit approval, first month's rent and a deposit. I made the mistake of not spending time talking to entrepreneurs about their business and business support needs.

It was a learning process for me as well. I was 26 when I joined the company, and I was learning about business myself. Four or five years later, after I became wiser and more mature, I began to appreciate other people's business and the importance of sustainability.

I've rarely rejected a business, only a few when the companies didn't fit in with the others in our building. Other times, I've found that by spending more time talking to business owners about their needs, I have been able to persuade some to start small and work their way up slowly.

They don't always listen, though. One company initially rented 600 square feet of space. A week later it wanted more space and doubled to 1,200 square feet. The owner purchased a lot of furniture and hired a lot of employees. And they were in business for all of six months.

I've been able to talk some start-up businesses into starting out with a virtual office, which includes phone service, a business address, a workstation and use of meeting or conference rooms. Eventually they moved into an office space.

I refer my clients to each other because I want to see them all succeed. Watching businesses come and go has made me much more passionate about entrepreneurship and sustainability.

Furniture business delayed opening to general public

Harriet Kitay
Title: President
Company: Interior Design Center
Founded: 1981
Headquarters: Warrensville Heights
Employees: 6

My husband, Allen, and I have been in the wholesale furniture business since 1960, and we've spent the vast majority of our careers selling merchandise to the design trade.

Our customers used to be furniture stores and commercial and residential designers exclusively. We started with a very small 300-square-foot showroom selling occasional furniture, art, lamps and accessories—mostly from catalogs. Throughout the years, we've grown considerably.

We now operate from about 35,000 square feet in Warrensville Heights. Our main showroom, Designers Showroom, offers transitional furniture and accessories. Interior Design Outlet Centre offers contemporary furniture. And our newest store, Modern Dwellings, is a contemporary closeout center.

Today, nearly 90 percent of our business comes from the general public. We opened our doors to the public six years ago, and since that time, business increased about 75 percent. Our biggest mistake was not opening our doors to the public sooner. We should have gone retail as early as 1990.

In 1979, we opened the small showroom and kept adding square footage throughout the years. Ten years after opening our showroom, we took the big step of opening a showroom in "The Ohio Design Centre."

Throughout the years, friends would want to buy things from us, but we could not sell to them. We didn't have the ability to charge for taxes, because everything was sold for resale.

In the meantime, I grew frustrated with the way business was changing. A lot of designers would use us as a showroom, and then they'd often get something similar from somewhere else.

I firmly believe that you should hire interior designers and pay them well for their expertise, whether they charge $50 or $250 an hour. But I had a problem with consumers paying way too much for furniture.

The straw that broke the camel's back was when a friend was charged $3,800 for a couch that was purchased from us by a designer for $2,200. What was upsetting was that the designer told the client that she was charging him 10 percent above her cost. I said, "That's it. We need to make sure that the public has access."

Around the same time, I read an article written by a well-known designer in California who said designers should be paid for their expertise and not try to make a killing on the furniture. That was the final push that we needed to open our store to the public.

It's a different day now, no doubt. Still, I wish we would have done it much sooner. The internet has created a more educated consumer. People go online to look at furniture and learn about decorating. They research pricing, decorating tips, fabrics and colors—before they go into a showroom.

We used to get a lot of women who came in and brought their husbands later. Now it's often the other way around. People watch all sorts of cable home-decorating shows, and we see as many men as women in our showroom.

We're finding that people are taking their time, buying one piece at a time. They're looking for quality, unique pieces. They want to be different.

There is no doubt about the value a designer brings to a project. We still have a small number of designers who bring their clients in. Those are designers who charge for their time and ability, allowing the client to pay wholesale prices for merchandise.

Opening our doors to the public has increased our business considerably. It's more fun, too. We love the fact that each person who walks into our store is greeted and made to feel at home. We've made many friends as a result. And we're traveling more than ever to find interesting things from more places to please the consumer.

Initially losing intended focus left business lacking direction

John Sonnhalter
Title: Owner
Company: Sonnhalter, Inc.
Founded: 1976
Headquarters: Berea
Employees: 13

For nearly 30 years we've helped market a diverse array of products and services for our clients, from established brands to new products. Our clientele includes industrial, institutional and commercial companies. But the one thing that they all have in common is that they offer products to other businesses—not consumers.

We specialize in business-to-business marketing, and I am proud to say that nearly 70 percent of our clients have been with us for more than a decade. That's extremely unusual in the world of marketing—at least with consumer marketing, where companies tend to "churn and burn" advertising agencies in search of fresh, creative ideas.

When I started the company with a partner, we identified the industrial marketplace as our target market.

We had a business plan, and we knew that while it was not glamorous, it was a big and underserved market.

The companies that we planned to go after advertise primarily in trade publications.

But in the beginning, we didn't have a track record—or any clients, for that matter—so we took any client we could get. We represented a florist, a weight-loss clinic and even funeral homes, since I had spent 10 years in the funeral business before I decided to start using my marketing degree.

My biggest mistake was not focusing on the business-to-business market sooner. Even though we initially had to take on other types of clients to generate income, I didn't get back to my original plan until my partner and I split a few years after we started the business.

It quickly became apparent that marketing to consumers and business-to-business clients takes a lot of work. Marketing to consumers means buying radio time and ads on TV, in newspapers and on billboards. But marketing to other businesses means reaching out primarily to trade publications and doing promotions through their distribution network.

When you're marketing to consumers and business-to-business clients, you almost need two staffs. It takes a different set of talents and expertise to market to both groups. So we got out of the consumer market and devoted all our energy to our business-to-business clients, which is where we wanted to be all along.

Today we're big in the general contracting, plumbing and electrical marketplaces. We may need to learn the features and benefits of a company's product, but the prospective client doesn't have to educate us about the industry or how they go to market, because we speak their language.

We can immediately talk about their threats and opportunities and put a plan together to help them grow. By specializing, we can hit the ground running and help the client to sell more. We truly become marketing partners.

When you're going in 16 directions, you're not doing anybody a favor. That's why the saying "Jack of all trades, a master of none" was created. The lesson I learned early on is that you have to focus to do something really well.

Throughout the years, I have had plenty of business opportunities that I turned away because they were not our chosen market. It's hard, but you have to know when to say no. Think about it. Do you want to work hard or do you want to work smart?

Reaching too fast, too soon not good for business

Edmond Bell
Title: President
Company: Laser Expedited
Founded: 1995
Headquarters: Solon
Employees: 35

I operate a full-service transportation company that specializes in expedited shipments. Our company offers exclusive-use trucking services, but the biggest part of our business is emergency shipments, whether it's parts needed for production or general freight.

I've been in the transportation industry for 25 years. I started out as a corporate traffic manager and later became distribution manager before going into business for myself. I owned a freight auditing company and a courier service before I started this business.

We're based in Solon, and we deliver throughout the United States, Canada and Mexico. We have offices in Atlanta and St. Louis and plan to open offices in Houston and Chicago this spring. My biggest mistake was wasting a couple of years going after big accounts at a time when we weren't prepared to handle their volume of business.

When I started the business, I should have been going after smaller companies, which would have been easier to service. I should have appealed to those companies by saying, "I'm a new company, and I want your business."

Today we have nearly 60 trucks, so we're in a position to service much larger accounts. But when I started the company, we had only two trucks, and I wouldn't have been prepared if a large company had asked for 10 trucks at one time.

I wasted a lot of energy, time and money trying to compete with much larger players in this industry. My sales staff and I did mass mailings and made lots of personal sales calls. We should have also done more advertising in the beginning as well.

At the time, I thought bigger accounts meant more dollars, which is not always true. Major players in the industry have thousands of trucks, so they were able to offer lower prices.

I made the mistake that a lot of small business owners make, thinking that a big account will put you on the map. Actually a big account can hurt your business if you're not prepared.

Now we have more than 75 accounts in multiple states, and we've earned a reputation as a reliable expeditor. We're constantly updating our fleet with new equipment, and we just purchased several new Air-Ride straight trucks.

Looking back, my strategy should have been focusing on building a track record with small and midsize businesses in the beginning.

I've learned that in this business, by having offices in multiple states, you're in a much better position to service large corporations that have plants in several states. After nearly a decade in business, we're now able to service both small and large corporations nationwide.

Reliance on big firms sapped business when bubble burst

Lori DeVore
Title: President and CEO
Company: DeVore Technologies Inc.
Founded: 1991
Headquarters: Bedford
Employees: 49

When I started DeVore Technologies, I was the salesperson, receptionist, accountant and trainer.

I was working full time for a training and recruitment firm when I fell into starting my own business. I used to spend my free time making sure people got extra training needed to get a better job in technology. And then I found my niche.

For five years, I worked three other jobs while I was building the company. My part-time jobs paid my first two employees' salaries that first year. My second year in business, 10 people were working out of my home. Bedrooms were offices. We had no air conditioning. Our "company" car didn't go into reverse.

But we grew fast because we always worked hard to please customers with our customized computer software training. From the very beginning we worked for giant corporations including General Electric Co., Eaton Corp., hospitals and banks. In the late 1990s, we had 150 full-time and contract employees. Then the bubble burst. At my lowest point, I did all I could to keep 18 employees.

My biggest mistake was relying too much on major corporations and not diversifying my services sooner. Our business has always been very sporadic, with lots of peaks and valleys, depending on projects. But I wasn't prepared for such a significant drop in business at one time.

I should have been. Even with Y2K, I could see economic pressures coming, but I didn't do anything about it. When you work with major companies, it's easy to get comfortable. We used to support General Electric's entire global North American help desk.

After the 9/11 tragedy, my industry was the first to be looked at and frowned upon. When times are bad, training is one of the first things to go. Technology is a close second. Businesses were not investing in people anymore. They were investing in keeping their companies in business. People were not an asset. Companies had to downsize to stay competitive.

Within six months, I was forced to lay off about 40 employees and dozens of contractors. I had no choice. I had to reinvent myself and find a business that clients would be interested in doing business with again. I had to add services that brought in residual income. I decided to build my own infrastructure to host and develop Web sites and offer application development and information-technology services. It was like starting over.

No one really knew me or what we were doing at DeVore

Technologies. We had always targeted major corporations, and we had grown primarily through word of mouth. I didn't know anything about targeting small businesses. I had always invested my time learning about infrastructure for the big guys. I had to learn how to open my business and service to everyone and share technologies with all businesses no matter what size.

I also had to learn to market my business. I had never spent any time in the community networking or giving back to charities. Today, I'm involved in the community, and I*m on four different boards. By giving back, I've benefited greatly. My being visible has allowed people to see that my company has grown and my leadership skills have improved 110 percent.

We diversified our services to the point that we now work with everybody from entrepreneurs who are building businesses out of their homes to all sorts of small to midsize businesses. We offer complete computer software training and software for payroll systems and medical records. A range of products and services allows us to have recurring income. Now custom-developed products are our No. 1 revenue generator.

Five years ago, training accounted for 80 percent of our revenue; now, it's about 40 percent. We've totally restructured our business. And we're going to continue adding services. In April, we launched Spanish Translation Services, a spin-off with two full-time employees and 11 contractors who focus on transcribing legal and medical records and translating Web sites for clients.

I'm going to keep reinventing the company. If you want to keep top employees, they have to feel that the company has energy and that they have a vested interest.

I used to just work all of the time with no strategy. I learned the hard way the importance of being visible and having multiple revenue streams and a strategic marketing plan. My company is healthier than ever before, and bigger things are on the horizon.

You might be an expert, but give clients information in bite-size pieces

Sunday Homitz
Title: Owner
Company: Body Technic Systems, Inc.
Founded: 1997
Headquarters: Woodmere
Employees: 2

I operate a physical therapy, fitness and wellness center with 15 independent contractors. My clients include dancers, athletes and people who need motivation for an exercise program. About 70 percent of my business comes from people who are hurting from accidents, poor posture, chronic back pain and not paying attention to proper form when exercising.

I started pilates at the Cleveland Clinic in 1989. I learned a lot from my supervisor, and I had a packed schedule at the clinic. But at one point I was so busy with the paperwork that comes with physical therapy that I had gotten away from doing what I love most—movement.

I also wanted to develop new programs, so I started my own business. I'm just as passionate about training as I am about getting people to get themselves well, fit and active. The problem was I needed to listen more. My biggest mistake was overloading clients with information.

I have years of training and a lot of information that I want to share with my clients. But they've got to be receptive and be able to digest it.

Starting this type of business is a huge undertaking, and recordkeeping and insurance paperwork comes with the territory. I was so busy building the business with physical therapy, fitness training, dancing and teaching classes that I didn't realize that I needed to pay more attention to the way I was training people.

I've had clients say, "Whoa. You've given me two weeks of information in one session." Some clients said things like, "I need to really review this and get this down before I go to the next phase." But most clients aren't that direct. They either worried about hurting my feelings or they didn't want to appear as if they couldn't grasp the information. But their actions spoke louder than their words.

For instance, I might have said, "OK, show me what you know," and they couldn't demonstrate the exercises or material that I taught them in the previous session. I was so intent on getting the latest information out to them that I didn't realize I needed to make some adjustments to my teaching approach.

Like any good business owner, I want happy clients. So I started encouraging clients to fill out surveys. The biggest criticism I had was information overload.

I learned to listen more and ask more questions.

By changing the way I interacted with clients, I noticed an immediate change in my business. Clients were more attentive. They would be more consistent with their program. And most importantly, they were proud of themselves because they actually completed the program.

I've never used handouts. But I write things on a clipboard, and sometimes clients do, too. They still have homework and reading assignments, but not nearly the same level that I used to give out.

I also started using a timer to keep things aligned, balancing what I want to cover with what clients want to cover. My main goal is to get people to take full responsibility for their care, fitness and wellness.

The greatest lesson I've learned in business is to keep it simple if you want consistency. Overwhelming clients with information makes them uncomfortable. In my business, people have to be receptive and consistent to achieve success.

Key was learning how customers viewed firm

Russ Hill
Title: Owner
Company: Ultimate Lead Systems
Founded: 1983
Headquarters: Berea
Employees: 12

The idea for starting my company came when I was selling ads for an industrial magazine. Customers kept saying things like, "I get all these leads from advertising, but I don't have a good way to follow-up and track results."

So I started working on a plan to wed new computer technology and software to better handle and manage sales leads.

I reviewed my plan with the vice president of sales at Pipeline Development Co., who said he would give me business if I could make the technology happen. Pipeline became our first customer and is now using our fourth generation of technology.

Our company offers customizable Web-based tools to manage sales leads. It also offers support services such as handling toll-free-number inquiries for our clients and sending product literature to people who ask for it.

Our clients are local, regional and national players. Most of the relationships are 10 years old or more.

My biggest mistake was having a major misread on how our customers were viewing us. They saw us as too small and without the depth of resources, because I was always the primary contact. We had failed to keep them up-to-date on how our company had grown.

Although we have expanded our staff by 25 percent in the last year alone, most clients regarded us as a "one-man band." That perception affected my ability to win more business.

But the larger issue is the way I viewed my own company and how we were presenting ourselves. We thought we were in the customer relationship management arena with dozens of competitors, including much bigger companies like Siebel and Microsoft, which offer applications that record day-to-day sales call activities, provide sales forecasting and track expense reports and other sales activities.

We saw them as a threat. Actually, seeing ourselves competing directly against these powerful players was silly because we're such a small company. We learned that our customers viewed us as a niche supplier of customized sales lead management programs and marketing analytic tools.

It all came to light within the last year, when I decided to have an independent research firm survey my key clients. The results were surprising.

I learned that customers valued our relationship, but they didn't realize our company had grown to keep up with them in terms of services and capabilities. I also learned that they never put us in the same category with companies that we believed to be our competitors, because our systems offer flexibility and serve a different purpose.

Learning that our customers did not consider us to be a provider of customer relationship management programs was eye-opening. If we had proceeded with the marketing strategy that we thought was appropriate before doing research, we would have wasted money.

I used to mention customer relationship management a lot when talking to customers and prospective customers. What I should have been talking about was how our products can complement CRM plans. Some companies need big, complex programs, but some just need simple, effective, customized sales management programs.

Now we better understand how we need to sell our services. I've made a big effort to publicize our entire team, including adding staff photos to our holiday cards and resurrecting our bimonthly newsletter. We're revamping our web site, changing at least 70 percent of the content.

Making sure you really understand how your customers view

your strengths and why they're buying your products and services is critical to success.

Oral contracts made projects more difficult and expensive

Nicole Lumpkin
Title: President
Company: TL Webdesign.net
Founded: 1998
Headquarters: Montville Township
Employees: 4

My husband and I were both working in information technology at major corporations when we started a home-based Web design company. At the time, business was slow because our target market—small businesses and nonprofit organizations—was just starting to understand the benefits of marketing with a web site.

Our company specializes in flash animation, 3-D animation and database-driven web sites.

The biggest mistake we made was doing work without written contracts—we had oral ones. Because of that, we didn't always have a clear understanding about what a client wanted for the amount of money they wanted to pay.

A big problem with oral contracts is interpretation. For instance, you might say that you'll use flash on a web site, but in your mind, flash means the door of a car opening. But in the customer's mind—because they've seen sites designed with much larger budgets—they're not only envisioning a car door opening, but also a music video playing on a navigation system inside the car.

Unfortunately, in the early years of our company, that lack of understanding led to situations in which we were putting in many hours of work that we weren't getting paid for. Because we were new, we were particularly concerned about our reputation, so we would bite the bullet and in some cases totally revamp a web site to satisfy a client. We chose to look at it as a marketing expense because the more work we had to show, the more opportunities we'd have for future business.

We realized that we should have been using written contracts when we designed a 10-page web site for a large local association. After the site was completed, the client wanted to continually make changes, such as adding sponsors and biographies. The problem was that they didn't want to pay for the extra work and time. And they didn't have to because we didn't have a contract.

We ended up adding 20 pages, and we didn't get paid any more money. It was a learning experience for us because we lost a lot of time that should been devoted to paying clients.

We've learned a lot through the years. Now our initial consultation with a prospective client includes a questionnaire that helps us to not only pinpoint their expectations for designing a web site, but also their needs for continuing maintenance, such as changing photos if they're selling products online.

As small business owners ourselves, we're empathetic to the needs and challenges that other small businesses and organizations face. But we had to change our ways in order to remain in business ourselves.

A written contract is crucial so there's no misunderstanding and everyone is pleased with a project. You can always make an addendum to a contract—for a fee.

Don't wait for a crisis to assess business

Liz and Lou Radivoyevitch
Title: Co-owners
Company: Rad Graphics
Founded: 1999
Headquarters: Cleveland Heights
Employees: 2

I remember wanting to start my own graphic design firm and feeling limited because the majority of my portfolio was wallcovering-related. That was the industry I had worked in for years, and a large wallcovering company was my first client.

Next, I landed a professional sports team. Since I didn't have anything but wallcoverings to show them, I created mock-ups of player pages to prove that I could design in the sports arena.

Relationships and hard work helped my husband, Lou, and me to build the business. Before we knew it, we were also servicing a large telecommunications client, and we had two employees.

But we lost sight of the importance of marketing our business to prospects. Our biggest mistake was relying on a few clients for the majority of our revenue stream—not taking into account the "what ifs."

We realized that losing one large client would affect our bottom line, but we never considered the impact of losing all three. A couple years ago, through no fault of our own, we lost all three in nine months.

We lost the professional sports team when it had a change in ownership. We lost the telecommunications company when the company downsized and drastically cut its marketing budget. And we lost the wallcovering company to bankruptcy.

We were devastated. There's nothing pleasant when the cash-flow stops but operating costs continue. We were very fortunate to survive. Both employees found other opportunities, and our landlord was very accommodating.

We went back to the basics and looked at our business strategically. We reduced overhead, scaled back and focused on marketing. We also expanded our creative services to include business marketing collateral, annual reports, print ads and direct mail. Before we lost those three clients, we focused primarily on developing catalogs, digital manipulation and print management.

We went through a difficult time. But the experience also underscored the importance of building relationships with clients who know they can trust us to make them look good. A few decision-makers who left their jobs with our original clients turned to us when they moved to other companies.

It took about 20 midsize clients to make up for our losses. Although it takes more time to develop each account, it's critical for our growth and business success.

The biggest lesson we've learned is that it's important to assess your business when things are going well. You have to have a formula that says if you're doing X amount of business, you want a certain amount coming from X number of clients. I'm not saying a client should account for 10 percent or 25 percent of your revenue stream—the formula has to work for you. The important thing is that you're thinking about it, and you're prepared to make changes.

When you want to start a business, landing a big account gives you a sense of security. We learned the hard way that you have to always think about what it takes to build your business.

Now, profit is the key word. We're able to take care of clients while keeping our operating costs to a minimum.

When I look back, I see that our business was like a sand castle, and nobody told me that the tide would come in. Now I know better. We're building a bungalow right now. But it's made with brick.

Young restaurant manager learns to dress for the role

Ghassan Maalouf
Title: Co-owner
Company: Nate's Deli & Restaurant
Founded: 1986
Headquarters: Cleveland
Employees: 10

When I was a student at Bowling Green State University, I used to picture myself in different fields. But in the back of my mind, I guess I always knew that I'd come back to Cleveland to take over the family restaurant.

One day I got the call. My dad told me it was time to decide.

If you want the restaurant, it's yours, he said. If not, we're going to sell it. At 22, the only major decision I had to make until that point was which bar I was going to go to the next night.

I was living the life of a college student. But trust me, I was no stranger to hard work. It's in my parents' blood. They started Nate's Deli when I was 9 years old. Before that they worked just as hard for other people. At one point, my mother juggled raising three kids with cooking at three different restaurants while my father worked as a cabinet maker. My mother was a cook at our restaurant when it was owned by someone else. After my parents bought it, they changed the menu to Middle Eastern cuisine.

Getting the opportunity to run this restaurant wasn't a hard decision. Business is good. Nate's is especially popular with the downtown crowd. I'm always amazed at how often our regulars come here. They never seem to get tired of shish tawooks, fattoosh and hummus.

I've been running the business now for five years, but I made my biggest mistake soon after I arrived. I wasn't dressing in a manner that commanded respect. It's not as if I was wearing T-shirts to work, but I definitely didn't dress the way my father does. He wears slacks and a nice shirt at all times, unless he's doing yard work or going to bed. I was wearing polo shirts or sweaters and jeans.

Even though some of our employees have seen me around since I was a kid and others since I was teenager, they always respected me as the new business owner. That wasn't the case with some vendors and customers.

There was nothing worse than seeing the look on someone's face after they asked who was in charge and the waitress pointed to me. The person might have had a question or complaint about delivery or catering and they'd look at me like, "You've got to be kidding. I've got to deal with this kid?"

I knew people didn't view me as someone who could be in a position of authority. I knew I needed to make a change to show people that I was serious about taking over the business.

After I started wearing dress shirts and ties, I immediately noticed a difference in the way that I was treated by vendors and customers. Whether I was making a deal with a vendor next door at the West Side Market or buying a refrigerator, people immediately changed the way they dealt with me.

I know that a person's attire is only a first step in formulating an overall impression. Some people command respect just by sheer presence. Other people have to work much harder to make the same impression.

I also know that if you don't have the ability to connect to make a lasting impression through intellect or good people skills, what you're wearing doesn't matter. But when you're young, you have to stay close to the parameters of business.

Right or wrong, people size up others with their first impression. I want to help sway that impression in a positive way, before they make it on their own.

We have a small mom-and-pop business. That means I'm the busboy, the co-owner and the manager. It doesn't matter what you call me because I do it all. But for me, regardless of what role I'm playing, a shirt and tie is my uniform.

Firm was in awe of Seagram, but just had to walk away

Mark Schwartz
Title: President/Creative Director
Company: Nesnadny + Schwartz
Founded: 1981
Headquarters: Cleveland
Employees: 19

We've always been in a unique position in the Cleveland market, getting a lot of awards and national attention for our work in visual communications. But when the Seagram Co. called us, we were in awe. It's a company that I had always admired, and not for their liquor. I run a graphic design firm, and I've always been intrigued by the company's art collection, the architecture at its headquarters in New York and its commitment to contemporary photography. We had never moved in those circles. To be considered to design the Seagram annual report was a great honor.

We had been in business for 13 years when they first contacted us in 1993, but we were still a small design firm with 10 employees. We quickly learned we were up against three of the biggest and best design firms in the world, including the company that previously had the multimillion-dollar contract.

All of a sudden, we were thrown into an arena that was dazzling.Luxury goods involve a different culture. We had not sought out the work, but we certainly responded and pursued the account aggressively.After three months of meetings, memos, drafts, writing, designing, plane trips and presentations, we landed the job.

Our biggest mistake turned out to be working for people who had a total lack of respect for our company, our staff and what we do. We learned the hard way that the grass is not always greener when you land a dream account.

Pursuing and winning the work was intense but exhilarating. It involved showing Seagram unique and compelling visuals and proving we could service the account, even though we had produced nearly 100 annual reports up to that point.

It also involved assuring the client that Nesnadny + Schwartz could meet the criteria for the design excellence by committing resources from our Cleveland, Toronto and New York offices. It even involved dealing with troubling behavior by our competitors, which were not awarded this engagement.

It was a different league, for sure.

But all that trouble paled in comparison to what we were headed for.Edgar Bronfman Jr., Seagram's president, was a prince to work with.But we only met with him six times. However, the people we had to work with in communications were monsters.

They asked for version after version. They felt they owned us because it was a $4 million account.

We would have meeting after meeting in luxurious places. At first it was interesting. When you*re putting together an annual report, you have to learn as much as possible about a company's business. But after awhile, enough was enough. How much information do you need to do your job?

We would get summoned at the last minute to ridiculous meetings where nothing would get accomplished. It was just a drone of useless information. You couldn't help but think, this is not rocket science. You guys sell liquor.

I started questioning why it was necessary to hold meetings in luxury suites in New York's finest hotels, especially when it was just 10 blocks from the Seagram building. One time we had to sit through a two-day conference on one of their brands, Tropicana Orange Juice. In the end, it*s still just orange juice.

You don't mind going to meetings when they make sense and help you to achieve your objectives. Unfortunately, the vast majority of meetings we went to for this client were a total waste of time.

The level of waste in terms of money and time was incomprehensible to us. It was a different world. It wasn't all bad, for sure, including the perks. Holiday gifts from Seagram took the form of cases and cases of several brands of liquor that they sent to all three of our locations, including $300 bottles of Cognac.

We really thought we wanted to work with this client. But it reminds me of the question, What does the dog do when he finally catches the car?

Part of every project includes managing the client and the process. But we never had control of this client, and it*s not that we didn't try. It was like talking to a blank wall.

Before we got this job, we had worked with all sorts of clients, both large corporations and institutional clients. Never had I had an experience that caused me restless and sometimes sleepless nights. It was tough on the staff. My partner and I had lots of arguments, and we started neglecting other accounts.

It wasn't an easy decision. But after two months, we decided to fire the Seagram Co. On top of everything, we had only invoiced them $200,000 when we made that decision. We walked away from nearly $4 million, with the realization that life was too short. For matters of survival, we needed to end this relationship.

If you do fire a client, make sure you do it publicly. It's very healthy. We sent all of our staff a copy of the resignation letter. It was an affirmation to them that they mattered more to us.

The Seagram Co. annual report was not right for us. If we were a huge firm, we could have sent account executives to those pointless meetings.

But we're small by choice. I've always felt that the best way to do creative work is by listening to the decision-makers firsthand and not have the information filtered through anyone.

We never want to be that big. We just want to be great.

I'm proud of who we are and the direction that Nesnadny + Schwartz is heading. We've been in business for 25 years. Our first client is just two doors away, University Circle Inc. Progressive Insurance has been a client for 24 years, the George Gund Foundation for 19 years, Eaton Corp. for 13 years. We've done major projects for British Petroleum, Cleveland Clinic, Columbia University, Hearst Corp., International Spy Museum, Johnson & Johnson, Planned Parenthood Federation, Rock and Roll Hall of Fame and Museum, and Vassar College.

At the end of the day, happiness and respect don*t have a price

Contractors' efforts to keep clients happy came at a cost

Doug Hill
Title: Vice President
Company: BCI Custom Cabinetry
Founded: 1988
Headquarters: Brook Park
Employees: 18

We started out working as general contractors. Then we built some custom cabinets for one dentist, and things changed. For the past 13 years we've focused specifically on designing offices for dentists.

I'm an electrician by trade and my partner, Bill Savel, is an ironworker by trade. A few years after we started D.R. Hill Builders Inc., we bought a cabinet company. We do everything from building one cabinet to designing and building a million-dollar dentist's office.

Our company, BCI Custom Cabinetry, has grown primarily from referrals in the dental community, but also from marketing to this niche. For us, building is the easy part. It's a business that requires a lot of meetings with clients and municipalities.

Sometimes we even help clients find property. We need to schedule meetings before a project begins, during construction and after construction.

Throughout the years, if we were in the midst of a job and a client insisted that we had promised another light or cabinet as part of the deal, we would just throw it in at our cost. Keeping clients happy was our main goal, so we didn't think much about it. But then it started getting costly and frustrating.

Our biggest mistake was not documenting, until recent years, all the details of what a job included.

We waited a long time to start requiring signed finished

schedules, letters of intent and other documents that ensured we were on the same page with our clients at all times. Proper documentation eliminates misunderstandings.

One dentist, for instance, waited until all the cabinets were installed before he said we put in the wrong color. You have to understand, they're choosing from about 900 different laminates on samples the size of a cell phone. A full wall doesn't look the same. In this case, all of our paperwork showed the selected color. When the job was done, the client said he had changed his mind at some point before the job began.

We've always had finished schedules, detailing colors of all sorts of items, like cabinets, carpet, walls and trim. But it wasn't until a couple of years ago that we started having clients sign off on them—including any changes or additions.

Another problem that we've faced throughout the years was one that Realtors have to deal with. From time to time, we would spend a lot of upfront time with a prospective client, only to have them go with a different business. Since we started focusing on dentists' offices, we've worked at 180 practices. We're busy. And it didn't happen enough for us to address the occasional problem.

It wasn't until a few years ago that we started having clients sign a letter of intent before we would invest significant time. Unfortunately, we waited until we got burned pretty badly. We spent about a year with someone we thought was our client. We had many meetings together working on design. We also went to various sites and attended planning and Building Department meetings.

The day before we were prepared to send crews out, we got a call saying they changed their minds. They found a company that could do the job $30,000 cheaper.

We've learned the hard way the importance of not overlooking any details. We're involved in a lengthy litigation now on a job not involving dental construction that could have been avoided with proper documentation. Unfortunately, the city we were working in lost an important piece of paper and we never got a copy.

Even though I run a business, I'm a construction worker at

heart and I never dreamed that one day I would be using a voice recorder at a job site or in a meeting. But that's exactly what we started doing recently to document changes and additions.

We take pride in our work. That's why we spend a lot of time upfront with clients. We don't want to be involved with extras unless it's at a client's request. When we quote a price for remodeling or brand-new construction, that's what the job will cost.

Sometimes memories can be selective, so it's critical that your paperwork be tight. It took us a while to get it together.

When your business is smooth, it allows you to focus on building your company.

Customers dictated time and services—Owner suffered illness trying too hard to please

Gloria Warren Watts
Title: Owner/Stylist
Company: Latest Gossip
Founded: 1993
Headquarters: Maple Heights
Employees: 3

If you don't mind waiting, I don't mind doing your hair. That was my motto—for about 10 years.

When I decided to start my own business after working at other salons for 13 years, I wanted to do my own thing. The problem was I was too flexible. Working eight to 12 hours was common. There were even times when I left work at 1 a.m. or 2 a.m., accommodating customers' work shifts.

I couldn't say no. If someone had the money and they were willing to wait, I would do their hair without an appointment. I could be walking out the door after a long day, but if a late-arriving customer asked me to do her hair, I would do it. I might complain and give her a hard time, but customers knew that a few "pleases" later, they would be in my chair.

My biggest mistake was allowing my business to run me. It took me a long time to start running my salon like a business. Unfortunately, the business took a toll on my health and happiness before I did something about it.

I used to have eight employees in a spacious salon. People were comfortable there. Some customers didn't just come to get their hair done. They came for the atmosphere and the gossip. But even that was wrong. It was a turn-off to those customers who just wanted to get their hair done at a scheduled time and leave as soon as possible.

I would work hard to please customers, even doing styles that I didn't enjoy, such as quickweaves—applying hairpieces over natural hair that has been covered in gel—or dying hair with bright colors. And even though I worked hard to accommodate other people's varied requests, some of those same people didn't respect my time.

For instance, I might drag myself in at 6 a.m. because a customer pleaded with me to help her get ready for a big event. Then I'd be waiting around for a long time because she overslept. When the customer did arrive, she would have the nerve to want her hair done as soon and as quickly as possible, with no regard for messing up other scheduled appointments.

Part of the reason I let things get out of control is that I didn't have to rush home to a husband or children. But not having a family was a poor excuse for sacrificing my health and well-being. I spent so much time at my salon that the vast majority of the food I ate was fast food. I gained a tremendous amount of weight. I had other poor habits, too. When I wasn't working, chances are I would be shopping, spending money as fast as I made it.

I was in business with my sister, Kathy, but she never allowed the business to take over her life. She was flexible at times. But for the most part, she had a schedule that she didn't deviate from. She had a life outside the business.

I started pulling back when I got sick with an illness that attacks your immune system. My joints were hurting, so I cut back the hours I spent at the salon. But after I got better, I went back to my old habits. It wasn't until I got married five years ago that I started making changes.

The first thing I did was take a break from the business. I closed Hair Emotions for about a year. When I was ready to start working again, I decided to downsize. I had a new attitude, a new location in Maple Heights and a new name for the business, Latest Gossip.

I converted a dentist's office into a hair salon. I was attracted to the smaller space because it has walls and doors so that three stylists can work in separate rooms. If I was serious about making changes, I knew I had to start with the atmosphere. The new name is not about promoting gossip. It's supposed to refer to talking about great styles.

The two stylists who work with me, Charity and Yvette, have the same philosophy. We all have our specialties and we work well with each other. I no longer do styles that I don't enjoy. I pass that business on to my colleagues, and vice versa. My clients are professional women who respect time and good service. About 90 percent of my business now is weaves—sewing supplemental hair into natural hair. It especially makes me happy to help women who suffer from hair loss caused by various reasons, including alopecia and chemotherapy.

With any business, you have to be flexible at times. But customers know that the only way I will accept walk-ins now is if I don't have any other customers at the time. The funny thing is, part of the reason I used to be flexible is that I thought I was offering good customer service. When I made changes, I learned that there wasn't much loyalty with some long-time customers. If I couldn't do their hair when they wanted, they would just go to another stylist.

Most important, I go to the gym every day. Nothing keeps me from the gym. My husband, Michael, was a big influence on me. But my new focus on good health was a greater factor.

Never again will I allow customers to control me and my business. I have a new attitude about life, and I'm happier.

Digital cameras force photo studio to change focus

Mort Tucker
Title: Owner/President
Company: Mort Tucker Photography
Founded: 1971
Headquarters: Cleveland
Employees: 5

I'm a third-generation photographer. My father always said photographers were like doctors and lawyers: You had to have one.

I still believe that's true, even in this digital age, but for different reasons. I run a commercial corporate photography studio. Our quality has never been better, but the services that we provide our clients have changed dramatically. Today, we concentrate more on the organization of the creative process than on the mechanical aspects of photography.

We've always focused on the corporate market, illustrating catalogs, advertisements and much more. Architects and the development community have been among our core group of clients for three decades.

But now, with the proliferation of digital cameras and technology, the business has changed. For instance, construction companies used to need professional photographers to take photos of a building's progress every two weeks.

Today a professional isn't needed for that job. That's just one of several examples that led to a drop in sales. Revenues have been cut in half in the last five years.

My biggest mistake was not recognizing sooner the effect that digital photography had on our clients.

Technology changed the way clients viewed the value of professional photography services. When digital photography first hit the market about 12 years ago, it wasn't easily accessible or affordable, so our business continued to grow for several years. But after more people started using digital cameras, we were still trying to run a business the same way we always had, going after all sorts of clients.

Digital photography eliminated a lot of billable services that used to be very profitable for photographers and processing labs. We used to charge a daily rate on top of fees for film and processing. We also used to charge a premium for proofs. It was a profit center because people valued a product that they could see and touch. There are no excess revenues after a job is shot. Today, we hand over a disc.

Digital cameras demystified the basic process, but did not do justice to the artistic side. We had to change the way we billed services to encompass all of the work that we need to do at the shoot and afterward.

New buyers of photography services didn't understand that taking the photo was just part of the equation.

One way of stopping the revenue loss was focusing on a narrow base of clients who appreciate our services. We can't make someone buy a service that they don't deem necessary.

For instance, a prospective out-of-state client called recently and asked if we could take 80 pictures of four buildings. I tried to explain that that's not how we work, but he insisted—so I had to decline the business. When you have been doing this as long as we have, you can go to a building and know that you need one or two exterior shots and four or five interior shots that show what's unique about a property.

We didn't anticipate the tremendous consumer appeal or the knowledge gap that digital photography created. A novice can take 80 shots and still not get the photos they need. If that's good enough for them, though, they can't use our service. It's not a good fit.

We do phenomenal things with digital photography, like enhancing color or changing a color if needed. We can remove signs, put new signage in, add bushes, fix concrete, take out bushes and replace grass. We can even add clouds to a sky, or a sunset. Technology has made our touch-ups more precise and realistic.

Technology has also allowed us to get better photographs because I can put lights wherever I really need them. We used to spend hours trying to figure out where to place lights and hide cords. Today, I can easily remove a cord from a photo using the computer.

No doubt, digital photography has changed our industry— mostly for the better. It's forced us to pare down our clientele and do more target marketing. We've also added more revenue streams like trade-show banner stands and online archiving services.

We're best known for our collection of Cleveland photographs. We've been capturing the changing skyline for over 35 years.

I got hooked on photography as a kid. I got to see every aspect of the city, from hanging out with politicians and local and national celebrities to going to factories and salt mines. It doesn't matter what the scene is, or what a camera offers, it's the photographer that makes the difference.

That's why I'll never get used to people who say, "My camera takes good pictures." Cameras don't take pictures. People do.

EMPLOYEES

JUST THE THOUGHT OF BRINGING IN EMPLOYEES or partners is enough to make some entrepreneurs figure out ways to curtail their growth or subcontract services. Their business is their baby and they want to avoid excess drama that can come with employees.

Employees and partnerships can feel like a blessing or a curse.

The bottom line is, if you're overextended, turning down assignments, missing deadlines, or spending way too much time on clerical tasks, you need to hire someone. If you want lots of customers, you need help.

Employees help manage pressures, deadlines and clients expectations. But they're also the public face for your company, so it takes work to make the right hires. The next step is to monitor whether or not you're still on the same page. Happy employees translate to happy customers.

Forming a partnership can also be great. It can bring in different talents, a capital infusion and a greater potential for success. But choose partners wisely.

It's not easy running a business with people who have different goals, priorities and values. Problems with partners can eat away at profits and friendships. Buying out a partner can go from bad to ugly. When tempers flare, the working environment can feel past unstable. That's when you have to work hard assuring clients and employees.

These entrepreneurs share mistakes they've made with bringing in people who were not good matches for their companies.

Mistakes in hiring often happen when people get emotionally involved. People hire people they like. But people change and duties change. In some cases, details about jobs, goals and policies are left out during the hiring process. One entrepreneur said her biggest mistake was not having an employee handbook sooner that would have outlined the definition of business casual and her no-smoking rule.

Sometimes employees and partners fall out over small things, like communication. Other times its hard for entrepreneurs to trust and delegate. Sometimes it's the opposite problem, not having a back-up plan when valued employees leave.

It takes work to find good people and create fair structures and incentives. But it can be done. These entrepreneurs prove it.

Timing, lack of knowledge foiled unwieldy three-way partnership

Anthony Debevc
Title: President and winemaker
Company: DeBonné Vineyards
Founded: 1971
Headquarters: Madison
Employees: 15

We have a very typical family-owned and operated winery and vineyard operation that has diversified extensively throughout the years in both the retail and wholesale markets.

My grandfather, Anton Debevc, started the business as a family farm in 1916. In the early 1940s, my father expanded the business at the same location in Madison from a general farm to a more commercial grape and livestock enterprise. He used to sell grapes to companies such as Kraft, Welch's and Smucker. I came on the scene after graduating from Ohio State with a degree in horticulture.

Today, DeBonné is the largest estate winery in Ohio, growing 95 percent of the grapes used for our wines.

We sell grapes and juices to wineries and consumers. We also sell wholesale bulk wine to wineries and bottles of our branded products to distributors throughout Ohio. We offer custom-labeled wines for restaurants and sell wine and food at our winery.

I made my biggest mistake about 20 years ago, when I tried going into a business that I had very little experience in and over which I had very little control because I was involved in a three-way partnership.

We operated a retail lawn and garden center in Madison, called "Madison Pet and Garden", which offered everything from animal foods to Oshkosh shirts to lawn and garden supplies.

I was given the opportunity by one of the partners, who was the lead coordinator of the proposed venture and was seeking investors.

He was a great salesman, and he was in charge of day-to-day operations. The other partner's background was in insurance. I had an agricultural and business background and considerable retail experience with wine.

There were several problems. The company was losing money before we bought and expanded it. It took a lot of time, money and effort to build the business up.

We had a lot of expenses from the start. We did extensive renovations on the building and expanded the product lines.

Together, we invested a total of $100,000, but we also leveraged way too much capital debt. We had an 18 percent bank loan and a 14 percent land contract loan with the previous owners.

Besides that, it was not the best time to get involved in that type of business.

Interest rates were extremely high, and it wasn't the best of economic times for retail businesses in the '80s.

The landscape was changing. We had new competition from big-box retailers, like Kmart. Even large grocery stores were starting to offer some of the same products at lower prices than we could.

Reaching decisions in a three-way partnership was troublesome.

I believe strongly in private businesses that are run under a dictator-type philosophy rather than a democracy.

In other words, someone in the company should always make the final decision. With our former partnership, it wasn't always the best decision that we reached. It was one that everyone could agree upon.

The pet and feed business created a financial drain. But more importantly, it was a huge time drain on our winery. We operated the winery, but we didn't continue to reinvest in the family enterprise to the extent necessary to capture the wine industry's growth at that time. We missed an opportunity to build upon rapid growth in the '80s by devoting our funds, energy and time to the new retail business.

The wine business was at a peak in the 1980s. Wine sales were more aggressive at our business than ever. At that point, about 90 percent of our business was in retail, and we had not begun expanding in the wholesale market.

I got out of the feed and lawn tractor business three years later, after losing about $40,000. The business ended up lasting about eight years.

If you are going to diversify, you really need to know the industry that you are getting involved in. You also have to be able to devote the time and energy necessary to make it successful, without it affecting your core business.

Psychological tests filter out bad hires, loads of frustration

Daniel Schuman
Title: Owner
Company: Fidelity Home Loans
Founded: 1998
Headquarters: Woodmere
Employees: 5

I started my own residential mortgage company after being a mortgage loan officer and branch manager for about five years.

We don't advertise. Most of our business comes from repeat customers and their referrals. We also get business from financial planners, CPAs, real estate agents and attorneys.

We want to be here long-term, and we want employees who have the same philosophy. Our customers are treated like family, and we view our positions as careers, not just jobs.

My biggest mistake in building the business was hiring people without making sure we were a good match for each other. When you hire someone who is not a good fit for a position, it's a disservice to that person and to your company.

When I started the company, my father-in-law, who has owned an insurance agency for more than 30 years, suggested that I give psychological tests to all serious applicants. He explained that his company had had a great deal of success using the tests to find the best candidates. I thought the cost of the test could be better spent elsewhere. After about a year and many hours of frustration, I decided to revisit the topic. My father-in-law suggested that we test all applicants, even good friends or family members.

He told me that many applicants look good on a résumé and perform well in an interview. However, he said, testing applicants helps employers learn about their personality traits as well as their strengths and weaknesses. Test questions are multiple choice. There are no right or wrong answers. But when the testing company compiles the answers, it can tell if an applicant is empathetic, sociable, assertive, or has a sense of urgency or thoroughness.

Many companies do such testing. I decided to use the one that my father-in-law uses. Although it is more expensive than other companies, it is among the most thorough.

Different positions require different traits. Being empathetic is key in this business. In some positions, being highly organized is most important. We have a 96-point processing checklist for every loan to make sure that nothing slips through the cracks. Attention to detail and deadlines are important.

The key to success for any company is to have great employees, and testing has helped us tremendously. Besides getting immediate feedback about an applicant's suitability, the tests forced me to think about the responsibilities involved in each position and the attributes someone needs to do the job. As a result, we created employee manuals for every position, describing the responsibilities and skills necessary.

Finally, test results have proved to be a useful tool in managing employees after they are hired. Knowing how people work and what motivates them is very helpful in creating everything from compensation packages to designing workspaces.

In this job market we can get 150 applicants for one position. Sometimes there are two or three applicants whom I really like, and testing helps me to make my decision. In the long run, doing my homework up front has saved me time and money.

Entrepreneur's early partner's had different agendas, skills

Alexandria Johnson Boone
Title: President and CEO
Company: GAP Communications Group
Founded: 1994
Headquarters: Cleveland
Employees: 3

I love people and I love to talk. Those two traits seemed to go together in the communications business, so I became a public relations professional.

I own an advertising, marketing, public relations and special events coordination firm. We specialize in developing and implementing programs targeting minorities and women, such as the annual Women of Color Foundation's executive development retreat.

With the support of National City Bank's office of corporate diversity, we are taking this programming to nine cities in the next few years. My business is diverse. Clients range from the Cleveland Clinic and Mega Church to the Frasernet Powernetworking conference in Atlanta. We also work with Eric Snow of the Cleveland Cavaliers.

I've been in the communications business for 27 years, most of that time as an entrepreneur. While I enjoy what I do very much, every business has its ups and downs. The lowest period for me was when my first business, GAP Productions, closed after a 12-year partnership with two other entrepreneurs.

Unfortunately, it took me nearly 10 years before I realized that the partnership was not working and I needed to move on.

Like any other relationship, you hold on as long as you can. My biggest mistake was starting a business with partners who had different agendas and skill sets.

When we started the business I thought we had complementary skills. But their skill sets were not at the levels that I originally perceived. One of the partners had a lot of experience in printing. The other had experience in graphic design. Both skills are critical in a marketing firm. But they were only valuable if we had clients. I had to do business development, proposal writing, oral presentations and the actual public relations work.

Their skills kicked in once we got the clients and they were given specific assignments. When we didn't have a client or project that needed printing or graphic design work, all of the work fell on me. I was burning myself out.

Even though you like your partners as people, you can*t help but develop bad feelings when money is being split three ways. I was bringing in about 60 percent of the revenues. Back then, our clients were small businesses like us and some smaller nonprofit organizations.I was looking at developing business relationships with corporations and larger nonprofits, but my partners were focused on smaller projects.

I'm a strategic thinker and I was trying to develop strategies for growth and development. Too often, my partners didn't agree.

They wanted to pursue areas of business that were not consistent with our original mission.

It didn't help that I was a woman with two male partners. Back in 1984, there weren't a lot of women CEOs. Taking direction from a woman was not the norm.

My frustration level became unmanageable and I started to develop my current business simultaneously. While I felt bad about ending the partnership, I channeled my emotions toward building a new business without partners.

That experience made me reluctant about having partners in the future. Don't get me wrong. I know that partnerships can work. I know of successful business partnerships that have lasted 20 years or more. But it takes time and commitment. While you have to work at the work, you have to work at the partnership as well.

I learned a lot from my first business. If I ever were to take on a partnership in the future, I would do things a lot differently. I would not have more than one partner. I would have a written agreement that describes roles and responsibilities. I would make sure both parties had equal capital investments. And I would make sure we had an out clause in our written agreement.

I would also make sure the partner had complementary skills. I'm a strong communications professional, so I would be looking for a strong business management professional as a partner. That*s an area that*s never interested me, but it*s important to a business*s growth, development and sustainability in this economic environment.

A business partnership is like a marriage, you get out of it what you put in.

The right people were in place, but he didn't let them do their jobs

Augusto Mastronardi
Title: Founder and President
Company: N.A.M. Properties, Inc.
Founded: 2000
Headquarters: Highland Heights
Employees: 1

When I was a kid working for my father mowing lawns and tending to flower beds on my hands and knees, I often dreamed about buying and owning real estate. I set a goal, and when I turned 21, I bought my first rental property in Mayfield Heights with $9,000 in savings.

Within the next two years I accumulated six rental properties. One day when I was getting the sixth property fixed up, a building inspector persuaded me to sell the property I had just purchased. A week later I made $20,000 from the sale, and I was hooked.

I bought and sold property for the next four years. But I had always wanted to build a home in my old neighborhood. Ten years ago, I bought a vacant lot and built my first home. Two years later I tore down that first piece of rental property in Mayfield Heights and built a second home.

In 2000, I got out of the rental and rehab business and into new construction full time. Since then I have built four homes each year. But I could not figure out how to grow faster until I realized I was my own worst enemy.

My biggest mistake was getting involved with every aspect of building a home instead of putting more faith in the 37 subcontractors I work with on each home.

It takes time to build relationships with the right people who specialize in various fields—all necessary to build a home. But even when I finally got all of the right people in place, I was still treating each home as if it were my baby.

At the end of last year, I thought about how I wanted to build 10, 20 and eventually 30 homes in a year. I did a lot of self-analysis, trying to figure out how I could grow faster. I thought, I know how to build a home. I know I have a good product. But how do I build more?

I was forced to admit that I was micromanaging. I recalled several times when contractors made comments like, "Gus, how long have we been doing this?" Or even, "Why don't you go do something else?"

I realized that instead of micromanaging every aspect of framing, for example, I should have just told the framers my overall objective and left the details to them.

Even when it was time to sell a home, I would meet with the prospective buyer as soon as the real estate agent met with them. Now I wait to meet with prospective buyers to reassure them about any concerns when the agent is nearer to closing the deal.

In thinking about my strengths and weaknesses, I came to the realization that my true specialty is acquiring and developing land and construction management.

I am good at accessing land, determining what types of properties to build and figuring out whether I can get a good return.

It's easier now. By assessing subcontractors' talents and strengths, I'm able to build more. They in turn get more work and make more money. The homeowner benefits because he's getting a consistent product in a timely fashion.

It takes time to build good relationships. But after you've got the right people in place, you have to trust them to do their jobs so that you can spend your time focusing on moving to the next level.

Providing employees ownership had created complacency

Bill Salm Jr.
Title: President
Company: ImagePro Ltd.
Founded: 1999
Headquarters: Broadview Heights
Employees: 20

I sold copy machines for 14 years before I started my own business. I'd always wanted my own business, but I also knew that entering a 50-year-old market with no name recognition would be a tough sell. There were already 10 to 15 very capable and solvent companies that did what I wanted to do.

I used my own savings to start my independent dealer of office imaging technology, a fancy word for digital copier printing products. We also got financing from one of the first manufacturers we represented. We've had three consecutive years of revenue growth and profits, and we're on pace to double sales in 2004.

It has not been easy, though.

Initially I attracted a couple of talented employees by offering them a sweat-equity position in the business based upon performance and tenure served.

I told them I needed their knowledge and reputations to help start the company, and while I couldn't pay them the six-figure salary they were accustomed to, I would give them shares in the business for taking a risk to join a fledgling company.

And that was my biggest mistake—providing ownership of a company to people who had no financial stake in the business.

Since they didn't have a financial investment in the company, their sense of urgency was not the same as mine.

They were making a decent living, but I was bringing in about 75 percent of revenues. I think what transpired is we created complacency by providing people with opportunities that they didn't earn.

After a couple of years we were able to get a bank loan because we had sales and profits. But the company was not growing at the pace our business plan demanded. We weren't meeting anticipated goals, and I realized that this sweat-equity incentive was not working.

I was creating most of the business and giving it away. We had to make a change. Forfeiture of company stock did not challenge the two sweat-equity shareholders to deliver results. They did not have the same passion for the company's success as I had, and they were let go.

We changed our ownership philosophy in 2001 to one in which talented personnel could purchase an equity position in the company. I needed investors, but this time I knew I had to find true equity shareholders.

When I started the company, our accounting firm established a baseline value for the limited shares that we made available. By 2002 we had revenues, profits and projections, so I was able to go after three high-profile industry peers by offering them an opportunity to buy shares. I asked them how much they could afford, and they bought in at different levels.

These guys liquidated their 401(k)s and employee stock ownership plans and refinanced their homes to invest in the business. With a combined 42 percent stake in the company, these vested equity shareholders had the motivation and entrepreneurial spirit to build the business.

In just two years, the company's sales have grown 300 percent, and we went from four to 20 employees. In 2005 we expect to double our revenue. These equity shareholders are now accountable for the company's success, and they are rewarded for their efforts annually in appreciable stock value.

Leave emotion out when hiring staff

Alan Strauss
Title: Chairman/CEO
Company: Sales Concepts
Founded: 1987
Headquarters: Westlake
Employees: 6

I've been in business for myself for 27 years, and between my former insurance agency and this sales management training firm, I've probably made about 40 bad hires in different positions. Some hires might have lasted a week, others as long as a year or more.

We're in the business of helping salespeople sell more. We work with individuals and companies that are frustrated with the results they're getting out of their sales teams. I've worked with hundreds of businesses and thousands of salespeople, and it's easy for me to see what's wrong in the hiring process of other companies because I'm not emotionally involved.

I have my own sales team to sell our service to other companies.

My biggest mistake was getting emotionally involved in hiring people for my sales team who—once they got on board—just flat didn't perform. Throughout the years, I was emotionally involved in those bad hires, either because of the need to fill a vacancy or because I was excited about the candidate. We hire people we like.

In some cases, the person I hired wasn't comfortable in the market I wanted them to be in. Some weren't comfortable with my management style. I didn't have a process for managing others, and not everybody is self-managed.

Some didn't have the drive. I've seen people spend a week researching a potential client in order to get the confidence to pick up the phone to call them.

In some cases, the only sale they ever made was the day they got me to give them the job. Twice I hired people who had the same drive as I do. But they were too much like me. Both were self-disciplined and both ended up becoming my competitors.

In some cases I lost all objectivity when I hired because I liked the candidate or I thought they'd be great for our business. That is, until I realized that I put these plow horses onto my race horse team. And some of them weren't even plow horses. They were mules.

The difficulty in firing people is exponential with the amount of time they've been on board. Years ago, when I made a bad hire, I used to make it so uncomfortable that they'd quit or I'd finally have to let them go.

Whenever I made the wrong hire it was costly for me and unfair to them. If a guy is costing me $5,000 a month with a salary and expenses, it hurts my pocket.

Maybe if I had had the right structure, the right management process or time to work with them, some of them might have worked out. But since I didn't, they were costing me money and they weren't performing.

They might have excelled in another situation. Too often, people don't realize that a top IBM salesperson might fail miserably at a startup business. It takes a hunter to sell an unknown product for Putz Inc., as opposed to someone who is good at selling an extremely well-known brand.

I didn't see a pattern for several years. One thing we did to fix this problem was implement a new pre-employment testing system. Initially the tests we used were expensive, and we didn't want to spend the money until we already liked the candidate. By that time we were emotionally involved. So even if the results said don't hire him, we didn't believe the tests. And we hired him anyway.

We finally have a system in place where we test all our candidates up front. Now we have a farm team of prescreened, prequalified candidates who will sell successfully for us. So whenever we need to add a salesperson, we don't have to worry about getting a return on our investment.

Keeping business, employees on same page

Fran Fisher
Title: President /CEO
Company: Body Sculpting Inc.
Founded: 1985
Headquarters: Hudson
Employees: 6

It's funny how some people start businesses. I had no plans of making Body Sculpting Inc. a business, much less a career. I just wanted to get in shape, and then I decided to share a weight-training program that worked for me.

It all started when I couldn't do all of the moves in a Jazzercise class even though I had taken professional dance lessons for 10 years. They were hopping around and jumping to the music. I got a good sweat, but I didn't see my body changing. So I went back to doing what I knew worked—training with weights at home.

I altered my body and felt healthier, and I created a weightlifting program. I approached a wellness center to see if they would offer it to women.

They were skeptical, until the class sold out. That was 20 years ago.

Today we offer strength training and exercise classes at recreation centers, schools and corporations in about 200 locations throughout Northeast Ohio. The business got bigger and bigger by happenstance. Nearly 70 percent of our 300 instructors are former clients. But until five years ago, I ran the business from home along with four employees.

My biggest mistake was not getting an employee handbook in place sooner.

Before we moved to an office setting and hired more employees, I didn't have employment issues. We were like buddies, so they didn't mind not wearing perfume since the smell gives me a migraine headache. It was a problem for new employees, though.

Then other problems started arising. For instance, when the business was run from home, people just took about 15 minutes to eat lunch and then they returned to work. At our current office location, people started taking lengthy breaks for lunch, abusing the paid lunch privilege. It's no big deal to be paid for a short lunch break, but I had a problem with paying people who were gone 60 to 80 minutes.

I didn't have guidelines in place, so it was a problem when I told employees that they couldn't use their cell phones at work after I noticed company phones ringing too long because they were on personal calls.

Lots of employment issues started creeping up when I moved to the new office space, from disagreements with the definition of "business casual" attire to disagreeing with employees eating at their desk or tracking mud or slush into the office. I felt as if I was being held hostage at my own company.

But it all came to a head when I let an employee go after she refused to adhere to my wishes. She threatened to sue me for discrimination after I told her that she could not smoke on the company grounds, even though employees working at other offices in the same building were allowed to smoke in front of the building. It was my unwritten rule. I don't want to smell it, and it's not part of the healthy lifestyle that body sculpting is all about. None of my longtime employees smokes, so it was never a problem before.

When I called an employment attorney, he quickly let me know that I had a problem. He said that if that employee tried to take us to court, she would probably win. I was nervous. I felt scared. I didn't sleep.

After he explained things to me, it was clear that I was doing a lot of things wrong. We had to change our entire company culture. We even had to stop telling jokes that could be offensive to some people and eliminate talk about things like dating in the workplace.

Most important, my attorney told me that I needed an employee handbook. Employers are so susceptible to being sued for issues like wrongful termination, discrimination and harassment.

Having an employee handbook in place alleviates these worries because it clearly states rules and policies that small-business owners need to convey to their employees.

Changing a company's culture is not easy. One employee refused to sign the handbook because she thought it was too strict. I really didn't want her to leave, so I asked the attorney if I could let her slide by not signing it. I learned that by making an exception, I would in turn be discriminating against all of the other employees who signed it. It was tough.

Our company is much more professional because of our written policies. The best part of an employee handbook is that it conveys to employees what I don't want to have to say to them. Small-business owners don't often have a human-resource director or employee-benefits manager who can say things on behalf of the company.

For instance, our dress code is business casual. But my idea of business casual, I found, is quite different from a former 18-year-old employee who used to wear huge bell bottoms. One time, her pants caused her to fall down a few stairs while on the job. My idea of casual attire is not looking at distractions to business. I don't want to see bare midriffs and tattoos that can be evident with low-rise jeans.

An employee handbook protects the company because your policies are clearly stated in a fair manner.

A lack of organization led to poor customer service

Dinesh Bafna
Title: President
Company: Mont Granite Inc.
Founded: 1992
Headquarters: Solon
Employees: 50

I feel great about our company. It's come full circle.

Sales have more than tripled in the last five years, and we've opened showrooms and warehouses for our natural stone products in Pittsburgh, Detroit, Columbus and Solon.

My challenge now is looking for markets to expand to, and I'm excited about the possibilities. Fifteen years ago when I started this company, my challenge was staying afloat. Actually, my first hurdle was making my first sale—which didn't happen for two years.

I put about 40,000 miles on my car visiting fabricators, architects, builders and design professionals, and I didn't make one sale until I was finally ready to throw in the towel. That's when fate stepped in. One of those prospective customers finally called me and gave me a shot.

After that, the business started growing slowly. By the mid-1990s, I had built the company to 10 employees. The market had changed dramatically, with commercial designs and residential customers seeking our products for large developments all the way down to small kitchen projects. The problem was our company was still small, trying to keep up with demand. Our customer service suffered. My biggest mistake was taking too long to define duties and responsibilities for all employees, including myself.

When my company was real small, I depended on a few people to do a lot of things. In the early years, the truck driver was also a salesman. He would make a delivery and then he might say, "Hey, we've got this new product. Are you interested?"

We were hardly formal around here. The warehouse guys also drove trucks.

The person who sold materials might also be the same person who packaged them. We always did whatever it took.

Then when the company really started growing for the first time, it was easy to let key people do all sorts of things. We quickly got to the point where there were too many decision-makers and not enough doers.

Too many people thought they were responsible for tasks and not enough people were willing to complete them. Paperwork was getting messed up and orders started falling through the cracks. Customers were not receiving materials or they received the wrong materials.

Before we recognized that better organization was crucial to our growth, it could sometimes be chaotic. Even customer service was an issue. The person who generally greeted visitors might leave the area to take care of something else. Meanwhile, someone who should not be working with visitors would be left to fill in.

By 1998, it was clear that I had a real problem. Employees were unhappy, and customers were unhappy. It didn't matter that employees had titles when we had never identified clear responsibilities. We had no system for accountability.

Finally I sat down and wrote out job descriptions for everybody: the inside salesperson and the outside salesperson, the receptionist, the truck driver—everybody. It was a consuming task, but I made sure every detail was clear, down to who was going to fill out the UPS receipt for shipments. They knew exactly who was going to prepare the load for the next day and who was going to submit the paperwork for that job.

Game plans were set up with goals in mind. Everyone knew what his or her job entailed. Admittedly, there was a period of growing pains. Accountability was enforced. Excuses were unacceptable for poor customer service.

Once all of our departments became more structured, we found that we had more time to focus on our duties. That's what ultimately allowed me to take the next step and expand our operations.

In the mid- to late 1990s we were growing because the industry was growing. If we hadn't set guidelines and parameters, we would not have been able to keep up with the demands of our industry. We sell our products primarily to fabricators, people who actually cut, polish and customize stones for all sorts of applications. We also invite the public to visit our showroom and warehouse to select materials for their projects.

I started this business right out of school when I got my MBA. I had identified a supplier in India, but I didn't know who my customer was back when I was trying to be a broker. For two years, all I had was a bag of samples to show. My brother finally persuaded me to buy my first container of 70 slabs, but 60 arrived broken. It was fate that my first customer wanted those 10 good slabs. Today we have more than 400 varieties of stone shipped from all over the world.

Growth forced me to plan and develop a structured approach in our organization. Once the system was in place, the business ran more smoothly. By 2001, I started giving more of my responsibilities to others, allowing me to focus on expanding to other markets. With a system, policies and procedures, I realized the company was ready to expand. I knew exactly what it would take to replicate what we do here with high-end showrooms and state-of-the art warehousing facilities.

We've continued to look at every level of the business to make sure we're running it as efficiently as possible. Today we carry more than 10,000 natural stone slabs in our inventory. But four years ago we had one location and about 3,000 slabs that we kept track of manually. We spent hundreds of hours working with a software developer who created a program just for us. The program not only helps us keep track of our inventory, it also gives contractors immediate feedback about products their customers are interested in.

I attribute all of our growth to developing a structured approach to business operations.

Repairman had to fix training, expectations of others

Fred Bucci
Title: President
Company: Fred's Heating & Cooling Inc.
Founded: 1982
Headquarters: Euclid
Employees: 10

It's no secret: Nobody is going to be as motivated to work as hard in your business as you are. If you own a company, you should expect to care more than anyone else.

I've been in business for 24 years and I'm still learning to delegate and adjust my expectations of others.

The guy who works for the company wants to bring home enough money to make a good living and provide for his family. The guy who owns the company wants the job done right the first time because it's his name and reputation that are on the line.

I'm in the heating and air-conditioning business. My job is to fix it up, heat it up and cool it down. Our customers are all over Northeast Ohio.

I no longer go to people's homes, and I miss that. But the fact is, you can't build a business when you're always in the field. For about 10 years, I was the one who made the sales, went out on service calls, did the installations, took care of the books and oversaw the billing. I knew I was burning myself out, but I still kept my hands in everything. In the back of my mind, I knew no one's reputation was at stake but mine.

My biggest mistake was not trusting people's work ethic enough to delegate and ease my workload. I didn't think that employees would do it the same way I wanted things done.

I feel fortunate to have the employees I have now, but throughout the years I've been very disappointed in the work force.

It's tough being in the service business. I've dealt with employees who don't present a professional image at all times. For instance, they might come to work with no uniform. I don't understand how a technician can go to a job without the proper parts and tools.

Then there have been other issues that happen because employees don't take into account an employer's costs. There really is no excuse not to call a customer first before heading out to a home that is 40 minutes away, only to report that no one was home. It's no different from asking for ketchup at a fast-food restaurant and being handed a fistful of ketchup that's larger than the small burger you just ordered.

It took a long time for me to realize that I also had to take responsibility for some mishaps, like when a technician had no idea how to price a job correctly—even though he thought he did. When you own a business, you understand overhead costs that have to play a factor and you price the jobs accordingly.

I pay a lot of attention to details, so it was hard for me to understand how a technician could go to a no-heat job, fix the problem but forget to re-light the pilot light.

I realized I needed to do a better job at training and to alter my expectations of others. I also realized that employees needed more than my appreciation and approval. I needed to develop some incentives to motivate them to give their best.

I have a lot of energy. I work hard and fast because I come from a family with a strong work ethic. I finally had to realize that everyone is different and I could not control the way they worked. They're going to think and act differently. I had to learn to give them room to do things in the way that works best for them within parameters.

It took a long time, but I finally made some positive changes in the company. I learned to do a better job at delegating. More important, I learned to do a better job at communicating, sharing my knowledge and talking about expectations.

I started offering bonuses for selling maintenance agreements, installation jobs and for recognizing and offering other services to homeowners.

We've got a strong team now, and Fred's Heating & Cooling Inc. has grown and improved greatly over the past few years as a result. Now I'm always on the lookout for more ways to encourage and empower my team so they can take pride in helping to make this business the best it can be.

Assuming employees were happy was folly

Mike Adams
Title: President & CEO
Company: C.TRAC Information Solutions
Founded: 1972
Headquarters: Strongsville
Employees: 50

Everybody always says that customers are most important. I
don't understand how you can differentiate between who is most
important, because employees are the ones who take care of
customers. Happy employees translate into happy customers.

I bought this company seven years ago with three other
partners who were also part of the former management team.
We're in the information business. About 75 percent of our
business comes from direct-mail and database hygiene and analysis.
We do everything from bringing databases together to cleaning
up and validating addresses to helping companies save money on
mail. A growing part of the business is helping companies and
organizations figure out who their primary customers are.

We analyzed one pro sports team's customer database. They
went from calling 50,000 prospective customers to 10,000, with
the same results. There's so much power in databases if you use
them right.

We've experienced double-digit growth in the last several years.
That's one reason I value our people and all of their experiences.
They've been dealing with data and software for many years. We
actually created a policy that says we'll hire only the best and we'll
retain the best.

My biggest mistake was assuming that everyone was happy,
because employee turnover was low and people seemed satisfied.

We use a lot of tools for our customers, including surveys. Last
year, we decided to do a gut check. We hired a company to survey
our employees for the first time. The results were surprising.

We decided to do a survey because we're committed to making C.TRAC better for our customers and employees. At the same time, you're always reading about how the work force is getting tighter and tighter as baby boomers retire. We were looking to position ourselves for the future.

My advice—don't do a survey unless you're ready to take action. Before they participated in the survey, I assured employees that results would not be shuffled under the carpet. When we got the results, I put together a PowerPoint presentation. For the most part, the results were positive. For responses that weren't clear, we set up a committee to get more information from employees.

One of the biggest surprises was that employees didn't like the way their twice-a-year evaluations were handled. They were based on performance and getting things done for the company. Employees wanted more focus on setting mutual goals and help in developing their skills, which obviously still helps the company.

We compromised and formed a committee to develop a new system.

One question in the survey asked whether they were compensated fairly. Most people said they didn't know. We learned from that response that we needed formal job descriptions. We're a small company, so we don't have a human-resources department. Not everybody had a job description. We hired a company to develop job descriptions and assign salary ranges.

Now employees are more likely to set career paths here. When you have job titles like programmer 1, 2 and 3 and you know that it takes a different set of skills to become a data analyst, it's easier for employees to identify what kind of training they need. We've always offered a lot of training, but it helps to have written job descriptions with necessary skills.

Several people said they didn't get enough vacation time. We found out through an outside HR company that we were fine in that regard with salaried employees but that we were not competitive with hourly employees. We gave hourly employees another week of vacation and even added two holidays.

Input from the survey said we were not treating everyone the same. As a result, we added flex time for salaried employees, not just for hourly employees. But at the same time, the survey allowed us to clear up a misconception. Apparently there was a widespread assumption that hourly and salaried employees got different medical benefits. Actually, everyone had the same plan.

We also added a basketball hoop, yoga and Pilates as a result of the survey. We want this to be a fun place to work. You can't stop employees from considering working for other companies, but we want this company to be so attractive that they'll have to think twice before leaving.

One thing that really surprised me was that some people claimed that I was micromanaging with some high-profile clients. I'm the type of person who likes to plan and stay organized. Those traits have helped me to succeed throughout the years. If you're going to ask employees for feedback, you have to have thick skin. That was personal, and I didn't see it. The bottom line is, I backed off.

We received some tough criticisms, but we made a lot of changes as a result. We even changed our recognition program. Anybody can acknowledge associates for going above the norm in their job responsibilities. We were just throwing all nominations in a box and drawing one name each month. According to the survey, that wasn't handled fairly. Now winners are selected based on the reason for the nomination.

I want people to feel that they're heard and that we care, because they're our greatest asset. You can be assured we'll conduct another survey this year to track our progress.

Photographer didn't see need for help

Eric Mull
Title: Owner
Company: Eric Mull Photography
Founded: 1996
Headquarters: Cleveland
Employees: Two

When I was working on my degree in visual communication at Bowling Green State University, I was also shooting pictures 60 hours a week. Getting into photography was fate for me. My mother literally bumped into the university photographer during pre-registration and after a short conversation, he agreed to hire me as his assistant.

Before I knew it, I was taking pictures every day at campus events. I ended up working as newspaper photo editor, then yearbook photo editor, in internships and at side jobs. I never said no to weddings or to assignments from the county newspaper. I went through about 10,000 rolls of film when I was in college.

I ended up using my degree to become director of advertising for a construction rental company. After a few years I took another job as marketing manager at an auto finance company. I lasted six months. I left with no irons in the fire. But I wasn't having fun and I knew that I wasn't going anywhere in life fast working for someone else.

I started out with industrial clients before I finally found my niche: fashion photography and talent head shots.

It's a creative business and I love it. But it's also a lot of work. When you work for yourself—by yourself—practicing your craft is only part of the business.

My biggest mistake was taking so long to hire some help. I didn't hire anyone until 2002, after I had been in business for six years. When you're the one who has to sweep floors, pay bills, answer phones, schedule appointments and return calls, it's difficult to manage that side of the business and still live up to your creative potential. You can sell yourself all day long, but if you're exhausted creatively, your work suffers.

It took me awhile to realize it's worth it to pay someone to be here. I didn't make any more money as a result, but I felt so much better. I had to learn to look at that hire not as a profit center, but as someone who saves me from losing business. Before I hired someone, I was getting slower at turning around projects.

I take a lot of corporate head shots and photos of actors in Cleveland, Columbus, Pittsburgh and Cincinnati. I also do work for Ohio magazines. It can be hectic. I'm not complaining because I remember a time when I wished I had this issue. The truth is, that's one of the reasons it took me so long to hire someone. I spent the first four years making ends meet and building the business through word of mouth. But I was barely breaking even.

When I finally turned the corner and started making more money, my first thought was to save more, because I had been through the tough times.

Unfortunately, it took one of my best customers to tell me that I needed to hire someone. A lot of times you don't see the box you're in. That client was giving me a message. That's not good.

The big question then became whether I could afford to pay a salary. It was hard for me to justify giving money to someone who is not bringing in any revenues. And you have to pay a decent salary if you want to attract someone who is trustworthy, competent and capable.

I needed a studio manager. Returning calls alone is worth the salary. I'm in a very competitive business. If a client calls you and you don't respond in a timely fashion, you've just lost the business because they've moved on to the next photographer who can meet their needs.

I needed someone to pay bills, schedule appointments, cut photos, run errands and send e-mails to clients. Hiring someone made all the difference in the world. I felt better just knowing that someone else was on top of the business when I was traveling—or right here, for that matter.

It can be a difficult decision, though, for sole proprietors. This business is my baby and only my reputation is on the line. One lesson I learned was I needed to do a better job at training. I lost a $10,000 job one time because my manager told the prospective client that I was already booked. I was booked with a $300 job. That was my fault. At the time, I hadn't told my manager to check with me first. I could have easily adjusted my schedule and handled both jobs.

Still, all the benefits of getting help have been worth the costs. When you're at a point in your business when you start thinking about getting some help, it's probably an indication that you should make that move.

It's a leap of faith. But for me, it's worth my peace of mind.

In business, as in life, choose partners very carefully

Loree Connors
Title: Chief Financial Officer
Company: Vita-Mix Corp.
Founded: 1923
Headquarters: Olmsted Township
Employees: 200

It's natural to think about answering the obvious questions before you launch a business.

Where will the company be? Who will the customers be? How will the business be marketed?

But when you start a company with partners, you really need to think about issues that are not so obvious.

Several questions come to mind: Do you treat employees with an authoritarian or a participatory style? How should business be generated? What do you expect of each other?

I worked as a public accountant for 25 years, primarily with closely held businesses, and I loved it. I was a partner in the last two businesses.

My biggest mistake was being in business with partners who had different values.

Having different values doesn't necessarily make anybody's ways wrong. It just sets you up for disappointment and resentment. In our case, we didn't put those feelings on the table. I just kept thinking that things would get better when we got bigger.

The first time I became a partner, I went from being one of four partners to one of eight when our company merged, taking the business from about 20 to 80 employees. I had been with that company for 15 years. But after dealing with all sorts of cultural differences brought on by the merger, I stayed just two years after making partner.

When I decided to join a business with two former colleagues, we knew each other's skill sets. But it's a different world trying to manage a business as partners. After about three years of working together, I realized how different our management styles were. It's hard for employees when they work for partners who approach situations so differently. They would get conflicting messages.

For instance, one partner wanted employees to help set the direction of the company. Another preferred to delegate.

Employees were just one difference. One partner had the hunter mentality when it came to generating business, on the prowl to get more. Another partner had the farmer mentality, believing that the best way to grow was organically. In other words, if you do a great job for clients, the company would either get more of that client's business or that same client would refer others to you.

Several differences led to a lack of appreciation for each other's efforts. For instance, we never talked about the different levels of customer service before we started the business. We didn't think about whether we should always just provide a basic service for a fee or customize services for certain customers. Things like that create conflict.

Looking back, our biggest problem was that we never had a clear expectation for each other's roles.

I ended up leaving the company less than a year ago to work for my family's company—Vita-Mix Corp. It's an 82-year-old company that sells high-powered blenders all over the world. No doubt, the company has always had a superior product. It can turn peanuts into peanut butter in seconds, make soups and all sorts of healthy smoothies.

More important, it's a company that has continually tried to improve its core values. I had briefly worked here as an accountant nearly 20 years ago. It's a much bigger company now.

I had been on the company's board for the past five years, so when Vita-Mix had a big event to roll out its mission statement and corporate values a couple of years ago, I was invited. Family is our top corporate value, followed by customers, quality, integrity and teamwork. All employees have a business card that states the company's mission, business objectives and key strategies.

I remember driving home from that event thinking, Wow, wouldn't it be awesome to work for a company that had values aligned with my values?

Several months later, an opportunity was presented and I was able to join the company as chief financial officer. It was difficult for me to leave 25 years of public accounting. I loved the diversity of clients and outside interactions with so many other professionals. In the end, it came down to being at peace with myself.

When you go from working at a 20-employee firm to one with 200 workers, it means you're dealing with a lot more layers and a lot more oversight. Believe it or not, even though I work with way more managers now, there's not as much conflict. It's easier to make a decision when you know that the other executives would approach an issue the same way.

When you have issues, you've got to get them on the table. If I had to do it all over again, I would have a different conversation with my prospective partners before we decided to launch a business. I suggested that to a friend and, as a result, he and his partner ended up not going into business with a third potential partner.

I think it's important to have this conversation. Even better, I would suggest doing role-playing to find out how each partner would approach a situation. Then think about each other's responses. If you like what you hear, go for it.

Hire outside professionals to safeguard business

Richard Perry
Title: President
Company: Pinkney Perry Insurance Agency Inc.
Founded: 1961
Headquarters: Cleveland
Employees: 15

It's important to surround yourself with professionals who don't work for you directly. We got a little lax at one point. It can happen when you've been in business for more than 30 years.

Pinkney-Perry Insurance Agency was started by my father, Charles Perry, and Arnold Pinkney. When they met, it didn't take long before one tried to sell the other insurance, not realizing that they were both among the first people of color to work at Prudential Insurance. The more they talked, the more they realized they should form a partnership.

They started the business selling homeowners', auto and life insurance. Today it's a different company, specializing primarily in commercial insurance and employee benefits for companies of all sizes. Only about 10 percent of the business involves personal insurance, and that's generally for people who work with businesses that we already serve throughout the region.

When I talk to people who want to go into business for themselves, I always suggest that they include in their business plan a wall of protection—that is, hire a good lawyer, accountant and insurance representative. Over the years, I learned to add another stipulation: You need to hire disinterested third parties.

My biggest mistake was bringing all of our accounting functions in-house after contracting the services to an outside CPA firm for about a decade. Several years ago, we hired a gentleman who was both a CPA and a lawyer. It didn't take long for him to be named chief financial officer, overseeing all the company's day-to-day financial transactions.

After a couple of years, when we felt comfortable that he could handle all of our needs, we decided there was no need to keep the outside CPA firm that primarily handled our taxes and prepared year-end financial statements.

Everything was going smoothly. Reports were produced in a timely manner and we were happy with our decision—until he left our company after four years for another opportunity. Before leaving, he put together a detailed report of when and how to file various reports so that his replacement and the company could make an easy transition.

The problem was, we hired someone who did not have the same skills and expertise. He had an accounting background, but no letters behind his name.

We eventually decided we needed outside guidance and ended up rehiring our former CPA firm. The outside firm got us back on track and helped us find someone to serve as our controller.

The firm looked at resumes, made recommendations and someone from the firm sat in on interviews. That was important, because you want your controller to work well with your outside accounting firm.

If I had to do it over again, I would never have brought all of the accounting functions in-house. We were fortunate because we hired a competent and honest person. But without a disinterested party looking at your numbers, you set yourself up for fraud and other problems.

Most people don't value the need for a professional until something bad happens. That's something I hear about all the time in my industry. And it's a philosophy I lived by until we stumbled.

Small business owners can be exceptionally vulnerable because we wear all sorts of hats.

When you're in business a long time you can become overly confident. There's comfort in longevity, but you can't let your guard down. If you do, you take a chance at jeopardizing your company. For us, the matter involved accounting, but it could have involved legal matters, real estate or insurance.

Hire quality people within your company, but never turn everything over to them. Always engage outside professionals. It's how you catch mistakes. Just as important, it's how you find better, more efficient ways of addressing issues. As a small-business owner, you need to build a wall of protection.

Offering benefits lures the right people

Terry Maynard
Title: CEO
Company: Medsource Home Care
Founded: 1999
Headquarters: Euclid
Employees: 200

Sometimes you have to make changes if you want to be competitive.

When I started my company seven years ago, it was a temporary-staffing agency that targeted skilled-trades positions in the manufacturing industry. Three years later, we moved into medical staffing, helping hospitals, nursing homes and long-term care facilities find registered nurses, licensed practical nurses and state-tested nursing assistants.

Our medical staffing division took off. So that same year, we introduced a home-care program. In 2003, we became certified by Medicaid, which allowed us to serve both Medicaid and Medicare consumers. Today we serve about 200 home-care consumers in

Cuyahoga and Lake counties.

Home health care is one of the fastest-growing industries today. Getting business is not a problem, especially since we have a niche of serving inner-city residents. Our challenge has been getting and retaining qualified employees.

My biggest mistake was taking so long to offer health-care benefits to our full-time and part-time employees. It's an issue that had always been on my mind while I was building the company. But I felt it was a Catch-22 situation. I wanted to attract the best employees, but when the vast majority are part-time employees, it wasn't cost-effective for the company. It's also an industry with a high turnover rate.

It's the nature of the business. For the last five years we've gotten referrals through PASSPORT, a program that's funded through state and federal money. Under PASSPORT and the Medicaid program, money for home health aides generally is available for only three or four hours a day. So the vast majority of our employees are part-time.

Even though the company has continually grown, it's been frustrating. When you run a company that doesn't offer health benefits or a savings plan, it's hard to retain talent. Whenever I interviewed prospective employees, it was always a topic that came up. What type of insurance do you have? Do you have a 401(k)?

Too often, we weren't able to get nursing candidates that we really wanted to hire despite being able to offer a competitive salary. Finally I realized that I had to find a way to offer those benefits in order to take the company to the next level.

At the beginning of this year, I talked to a few insurance brokers and reviewed plans from several traditional health insurance companies. We ended up offering two health-care options. One is offered to our full-time employees through Medical Mutual. We chose the second option for part-time employees through Aflac. The company offers short-term disability plans and a variety of other plans including life insurance plans that employees can purchase directly through them. Employees get a reduced rate because the premium is taken out on a pre-tax basis.

With that plan, it's no cost to our company. Employees are happier, and our taxable income is reduced.

Starting this month, we'll be offering an open enrollment for our new 401(k) plan with a company match.

Now when I interview RNs and administrative staff, I can tell them that I have health insurance and a 401(k). It makes our offer stronger. In this economy where there's a shortage of nurses, that's very important.

New hires have to fit into the culture for all to succeed

Bill Onion
Title: Partner
Company: Briteskies
Founded: 2000
Headquarters: Cleveland
Employees: 14

It's a fact: Hiring is a subjective process. Some people hire people they like. Others hire people strictly because of their skills.

We run a technology-based consulting firm and we've been really lucky when it comes to hiring. Since we started the business six years ago, most of the people we hired were former long-time business colleagues of myself or my partner. Or we met them through friends or relatives, so we heard about their skills and personalities before we met them.

Our business centers on IBM hardware and software, with a particular emphasis on helping companies sell products on the Web. That means, at some point in the process, just about everybody deals with clients. Our customers range from mom and pop retail stores to large manufacturers and distribution companies throughout Northeast Ohio.

We like to hire people with a personality that fits into our culture because we share a lot among ourselves before and during the process of consulting with clients. It's what works for us. It's what makes us effective. It's what's helped us to build the company.

We went against that unspoken rule once—and that was our biggest mistake. We knew what we were getting, but we were blinded by the new employee's technology skills.

We were starting a new product line and we knew that person's skills would be beneficial for development. We didn't realize that by working with someone who had core values so different from everyone else's, it affected the mood and productivity of the company. We like to hire great people with great communication skills. This person was extremely talented, but lacked those skills.

It wasn't fair to the other employees, to the new hire or to our clients. That person ended up quitting in less than six months. The sudden departure delayed the growth of our new product, and we lost revenue. A customer project was delayed about four weeks. We had to scramble to hire a replacement.

As small business owners, my partner and I are always trying to figure out how we can improve and be more effective in running the business. The wild part of this story is that a few years before we made the bad hire, we put ourselves through a process that helped us determine who we are, what we do and, more important, how we do it.

We read Verne Harnish's book. He's the author of "Mastering the Rockefeller Habits: What You Must Do to Increase the Value of Your Fast-Growth Firm" and runs two world-renowned entrepreneurship organizations. After we saw him give a presentation, we decided to take a different view of our business, making changes based on some of his recommendations.

One of those recommendations dealt with hiring. He said that a person's core values help them to fit into an organization. When someone fits in, it allows the company as a whole to stay focused on the customer and alleviates unproductive activity. We knew how important it was to fit into our culture. But we apparently developed a case of temporary amnesia.

One of the measuring sticks we use to hire great people with great skills is thinking about our goal to cement relationships with customers. I like to think that my customers would be comfortable having any of our associates at their house, relaxing on their deck on a Friday evening.

I know this may sound strange, but we're a people business that uses technology to reach goals. So personalities and core values matter. Briteskies is a very open, energetic and positive group. The hire who didn't fit was a loner. We've hired four more people since then.

Only now we use a very structured hiring process. The company has continued to grow because of our talented people. It's growing because they all contribute in different ways. One thing they share, though, is that they all enjoy thinking outside the box and sharing their thoughts.

We decided to listen to our own advice, and it's paying off. Now, whenever we hire someone, we make sure that person's values align with our corporate core values.

Finding a more rewarding way to pay

Kathleen Dangelo
Title: Vice president and general legal counsel
Company: Ohio Valley Group
Founded: 1989
Headquarters: Chagrin Falls
Employees: 40

Doing things the same old way doesn't work when your business is growing fast.

We started our landscaping company from the second bedroom of a tiny house while I was in law school. Then we spent five years working from the basement of a larger home before we finally bought a fixer-upper zoned for commercial use. That's where the company really grew in the last 10 years. But we were bursting at the seams, with 30 trucks and people going in and out of the office and barn located on just an acre and a half.

Ohio Valley Group does tree work, and everything from designing small perennial gardens to outdoor environments, complete with a waterfall that flows into a stream ending in a reflecting pond filled with koi. We can put in brick patios or wood decks with landscape lighting—or we can just mow the lawn, if that's all the customer wants.

As the company has grown, we've hired more specialists in various areas. Last year, we bought 15 acres and moved. At the same time, we've tried to create a team atmosphere where everyone helps each other.

Our biggest mistake was having a sales commission structure that hindered our growth.

My husband, Andrew, is the president and a certified arborist. He has been in the business for nearly 20 years, ever since he got his degree in landscape design.

For about 12 years he was also the only salesperson for our company. The first time we hired someone in sales, commissions became an issue.

If a salesperson's client wanted other types of work that the salesperson didn't handle, did that mean the salesperson still got a commission? For two years, there was always a problem because the other salesperson was less than enthusiastic about helping clients that he didn't bring in.

As we grew, it became clear that our bonus structure was fundamentally unfair and caused conflict between salespeople and the production team.

All I wanted was for customers to have good service and for their experience to be seamless. I didn't want customers to have to worry about who they could talk to for service. We have four salespeople now, but even when we were smaller I could see the writing was on the wall. We had to make some changes.

I spent six months thinking about how we could not only

scrap the old bonus program for salespeople, but also how we could come up with a system that included everybody. We put a lot of thought into it because we knew the company was going to continue to grow. We had to come up with something that was not only fair but also promoted teamwork.

Everybody's efforts contribute to the company's bottom line. The old system didn't take into account all of the crew leaders, field workers and managers whose jobs come into play after the sale is made. Their efforts can make or break the company. For instance, a field worker's hard work might be the reason a project came in under budget. Everybody plays a role in satisfying the customer and building the business.

With our new profit-sharing bonus plan, everyone gets points. If the company makes its sales goals and nets a profit, a percentage goes into a big pool available for bonuses. At the end of the year, everybody in the company shares in the pool, based on the number of points earned.

Having a bonus plan makes employees responsible for the bottom line. A couple of times a year, we share financial information about the company's performance. It gives team members an indication of where we are at the time, where we want to be and how their bonuses will be affected as a result. Depending on how good the year has been, bonuses can range from about $100 to several thousand dollars.

With the new bonus plan, there's a much greater spirit of cooperation. When we talk about the bonus plan, it's a good time to remind everyone that when customers are happy, so are we.

Worth the effort to retain valuable workers

Grant Alexander
Title: President
Company: GK's Custom Polishing Inc.
Founded: 2000
Headquarters: Avon
Employees: 10

Working hard is all I know. It's how I was raised, and probably the reason I decided to turn my part-time passion into a full-fledged business as soon as I graduated from college.

I had already spent six summers detailing cars and boats, and I loved it. I thought about getting a conventional job, but that clearly wouldn't have been as fun. And I figured if I was going to work hard, it might as well be for myself. The problem was figuring out how I would survive the inclement weather in this market.

The answer was to expand the business. I learned how to maintain and restore countertops and floors made of natural stone, such as marble. I also added heated indoor storage for the prized possessions that longtime customers trusted me to detail. Now, we store everything from a 1937 Packard with original paint to all sorts of sports cars and even a wooden boat.

But when I started the business, I had just one employee – and I was broke, flat broke. For about a year, I spent just as much time juggling finances as I did working on the business. Finally, I was able to start hiring, and I have hired a lot in the last six years.

My biggest mistake was not trying harder at first to retain good hourly employees.

I was winging everything in the beginning, so I didn't take time to think about issues that were bound to occur when you advertise vague job descriptions. I've dealt with everything from girlfriends calling in sick for employees to people coming in late for shifts.

I've even been in situations where I was forced to take back an employee who didn't show up for two or three days. Now, with 10 employees and the appropriate systems in place, it's easy to recover if one person doesn't come to work. But when you have just five people, with several accounts, you're in trouble when that happens.

I didn't see it then, but looking back, I could have been clearer with job descriptions and scheduling when hiring. It would have clarified certain situations, such as when someone had to leave early to pick up a child.

The fact is, I didn't value my employees initially the way I should have. My attitude used to be that I'm giving you a job, so you should show up on time and work hard like I do. I didn't take into account that everyone doesn't have the same core values and nobody is going to work as hard as a small-business owner does.

A few years ago, I started offering incentives to employees, and it has paid off. It has been so effective that I spend a lot of my time trying to come up with more creative incentives.

We offer a Wal-Mart list. Every employee gets $10 a month for snacks that I go out and purchase.

I started preparing schedules much further in advance. Employees can generally have any day of the week off, as long as they give enough notice. I also started empowering employees, giving team leaders and assistants more responsibilities and rewards. I want to keep them for years.

I try to come up with ideas that build camaraderie, like celebrating every employee's birthday with a cake and renting a house on Kelleys Island for five days in the summer, just for employees.

Some things I did helped the company as much as the employees, like providing clean uniforms that are laundered daily and stay at our facility. Other things don't cost the business much money but make employees happy, including closing the business during Christmas week and sending different employees to various states each month to service one of our restaurant chain clients.

I learned the hard way that it pays to invest in your employees. I spend a great deal of time trying to figure out what matters to employees. Sometimes, incentives are just as important as money.

Making assumptions can hurt you

Shawn Braxton
Title: CEO
Company: Braxton Educational and Technology Consulting
Founded: 2004
Headquarters: South Euclid
Employees: Three

I was teaching adult education when I met the owner of an educational software company. He knew that I was one of those teachers who believed that technology was being used to replace teachers, so I was confused when he asked me to become a trainer for his company.

This man, who later became my mentor, explained that he asked me to become his first trainer because I was such a pessimist. I was a former English teacher who knew very little about technology. He thought I would be a good instructor because he was able to convince me that integrating technology is beneficial to a classroom.

I spent 10 years working for his company, first as a trainer and later as a salesperson. When he died, my relationship with the company did too. I decided to open my own professional development company a few years ago, working with school districts, nonprofits and businesses.

Today, about 75 percent of the business is educational services. In three years, we went from working with three independent contractors to 35, mostly veteran teachers with five years or more of experience.

My biggest mistake was assuming that people came with a certain skill set based on their vocation.

I wrongly assumed that if job candidates taught during the day and interviewed well, they would be able to integrate technology into after-school programs. I also assumed they had the ability to vary the instruction to meet a student's needs. We have a model in place that meets state standards, but we encourage all of our trainers to bring their own flavor to the programs.

Last year, we were in 10 sites in seven school districts. Unfortunately, we quickly found out that many of the trainers were not meeting the instructional style that we were accustomed to delivering.

We work with kindergarten through 12th-grade students and our company offers a variety of technology. We use handheld computer-based technologies as well as video-based technologies, including multimedia players that load educational videos and audios.

At each site there is, at most, a 5-to-1 student-teacher ratio, and every student has his or her own device. Through site visits we found out that too often our contractors were allowing the technology to do all the work. Technology is supposed to be a tool. Our contractors had become too comfortable with technology doing all the work.

It's up to the teacher to make sure the student remains challenged by using the right tools. Technology is a draw, but it can also become monotonous. It's up to the instructor to reassure students. The instructors are there to help guide the students and to answer questions.

For instance, one aspect of our program involves software that creates curriculum specific to a child's needs. We also use a whole system from the Leapfrog company that automatically shows how the student is doing. But there's no excuse for keeping students on one system when our company offers all sorts of options.

I realized that part of the problem had to do with us being a small company with a sudden, significant growth spurt. We had to do a better job with training and interviewing.

The first thing I did was create a learning-style survey for all of our students to help empower our instructors. The survey informs us of a student's learning preferences. Some learn best by visuals, by touch or by doing. Some work best alone, others work better in groups.

We had to terminate some of our contractors. Those who

remained with the company have personalities necessary to motivate students to stay engaged.

This time, before we hired instructors for our summer programs, we did a better job in learning more about their teaching styles. We also worked harder to make sure they can perform in a technology-intensive environment.

We still have one-day training, but it's much better now. We listen more and we pose issues that might come up. We might say, if a sixth-grader doesn't understand fractions, which technologies would you use to help him or her?

We used to rely on our instructors because they are veterans. Our thinking was that we provided the technologies, but it's up to them to manipulate them.

I'm immersed in technology now. I order talking pens that walk students through multiplication and division without giving them the answer. In the fall, our students will be able to load educational videos and audios to watches.

But after my experience, I'm often reminded of my former mentor and the English teacher I used to be more than a decade ago. Technology is a helpful tool, but good teachers will always be needed.

Don't fail to value a differing opinion when you pay for a consultant's expertise

Gary Baney
Company: Boundless Flight
Title: President
Founded: 2002
Headquarters: Strongsville
Employees: 34

Technology companies always have a healthy tension between sales and marketing and product management. I managed that tension for more than 20 years at various companies, but it became extreme at my own company.

Salespeople always say our product is not good enough. We're not innovating fast enough or listening to customers. Meanwhile, the production side is always dealing with talent retention, missed deadlines and estimates. They generally want to slow down and focus on doing one thing well, rather than caving in to every customer demand. It's expected.

I was a professor for 25 years, and my goal was to start my own software development company before I turned 50 by hiring the best and brightest young people. When I started Boundless Flight, I expected tension in building a fast-growing company. I've hired many people, both full-time employees and dozens of contractors. But one came into the organization and magnified tension, hurting the morale of the company's management.

A year into the relationship, conflicts heightened. I spent a lot of time trying to alleviate it by holding weekly meetings and encouraging open communications.

It wasn't working, so I brought in an outsider to help with the situation. My biggest mistake was not taking a small-business consultant's advice about firing a manager who created rifts in the company.

Boundless Flight offers custom software development in Java, Javascript, .net, HTML, XML and other platforms. I love software. It's the reason I don't believe in hiring people strictly from a resume. You're hiring personality as much as you're hiring the technical skill set.

In the last five years we've had about 150 clients. The work has ranged from spending 10 hours of consulting to get an accounting system running to developing web sites or software for Fortune 100 companies. We have 22 technicians working in Beijing right now.

When you're a fast-growing virtual company, you can't afford to spend 25 percent of your time managing personalities. Spending $7,000 on a consultant to free up my time was money I thought was well spent.

But after three months of trying to work with the employee,

the consultant recommended that I get rid of him. He said it was clear he had no intention of changing any of his disruptive behaviors. He said the employee would never get me where I want my company to go.

I weighed his advice. Then I allowed my ego to get in the way. My loyalty is very intense. I wanted to do everything possible to help the employee succeed.

This person was creating tension in the company. It wasn't fun. But it's not as if he wasn't trying. I had sympathy for him. A few months later, the employee resigned anyhow.

I learned the hard way. If you're going to hire a consultant, you have to be willing to give the consultant's opinions equal weight, or more, to your own. You're bringing in a consultant for a different perspective. If you're not going to listen, don't even bring one in.

When you're a CEO or a president of a company, your value to the organization is not just about how right you are. It's how good a listener you are and how adept you are at valuing differing opinions.

Finally hiring others led to a more balanced life, bigger business

Terry Granzier
Title: President
Company: Lakeside Produce Distribution Inc.
Founded: 2002
Headquarters: Westlake
Employees: 4

We have contracts with vegetable growers to buy 1,600 acres of produce. We market cabbage and other vegetables to salad manufacturers and help farmers with packaging, sales, food safety training and logistics.

It's great to use the word "we." It's good to have a team to service customers spread throughout the eastern half of the United

States. Selling produce is what I love, but it's not easy.

For a couple of years I did it all by myself. I was working with major customers as a sole proprietor. My phone line was professional, directing people to five different areas, but my friends used to give me a hard time because they knew all lines came to me. At night I kept my phone by my bed, in case there was a problem with a truck. I never took time off.

My biggest mistake was being afraid to hire someone. I didn't hire the first employee until I had been in business for a few years—when I was totally burned out. Even then, I hired him first as a contract employee, to free me to focus on sales.

Sales from 2002 to 2006 were $6 million. I couldn't have built this business that fast by myself. I was no different from a lot of small-business owners who are afraid to take on the challenge of being responsible for someone's livelihood.

I knew that I couldn't grow without help. But at the same time, I had a nagging thought about the possibility of failing. In this industry, a lot of companies are much bigger and they squash small competitors.

A big part of my fear had to do with a legal dispute with a former employer that caused my business to shut down for more than a year. When you go through something that devastating, being responsible for someone else was the last thing I wanted. At the same time, I was in over my head, trying to run a business with a new wife and baby. You're always on in this business.

Just managing the truck dispatch part of the business is a 24 hour deal. We contract trucks and use owner/operators to haul products from farms to salad manufacturers. Deliveries might arrive at midnight or pickups might occur at 4 a.m. The bottom line is, whenever you say a delivery is going to be made, it had better be there. Your reputation is in a trucker's hands. You can do everything right with pricing and customer service, but if your truck doesn't show on time and a production line is down as a result, that customer will be gone.

I was fortunate to find Chris Breninghouse, a former co-owner of a trucking company who is great with customers. He knows what it takes to find and work with reliable trucking companies and what it takes to baby-sit deliveries.

Finances were another reason I was afraid to hire someone initially. I was trying to build the business from scratch, so I had to live off my savings. I didn't take a paycheck because all of the money that came in was needed to help build the business. I was a sole proprietor working in a niche market with a lot of competitors. I hate to borrow money, so I had to do whatever it took to get customers and establish credit. I'd pay quickly, sometimes in cash.

Now, one employee spends a lot of time traveling to farms and manufacturers. Another takes care of administrative responsibilities, giving me more time to work on sales. I can even take time off. I'm continually seeking ways to have a more balanced life and be more efficient.

I'm much more confident about the idea of expansion. Sales are expected to grow 20 percent this year. But I still have a fear about hiring new employees and growing too fast. I believe it's a healthy fear because I'm fiscally conservative.

Just because you have employees doesn't mean that you should take the business for granted. You can get too comfortable, and then someone will pick you off.

Perfectionist learned hard way respect extends to employees too

Willie Bradford
Title: President
Company: Bradford's Beautiful Hardwood Floors
Founded: 1987
Headquarters: Woodmere
Employees: Four

Be on time. Get the job done and get out.
Our specialty is repairing and refinishing hardwood floors. But

with the word "beautiful" in my company's name, you know what's most important to me is doing the job right.

I've been in business for 20 years and one thing hasn't changed: I'm a perfectionist and I want to please customers.

Unfortunately, it took several years for me to realize that I was working toward that goal at my employees' expense. I've been accused of being rough, short-tempered and direct. Too direct.

My biggest mistake was not being respectful in the way I used to communicate with employees. In some cases, I wasn't communicating at all. I was talking down to them or even yelling. I'd scold them and let them know that they messed up.

I've said things like, "Come here and let me show you what you did, boy. Right now. Come here. I'm paying you. You're not paying me. You only have one chance with a floor."

There were signs before, but I ignored them. I used to run a commercial cleaning business in the evenings for several years.

I knew that employees preferred to deal with my wife. But that didn't bother me. I had a contract and I had to fulfill my obligations.

The floor business is different because I work side-by-side with my employees. It takes a good eye and training. The goal is to catch flaws before my people put down any stains or polyurethane. If not, you have to sand out the whole job all over again. I don't believe in cutting corners.

There are different techniques that you use on different floors and it takes time to learn them. One time, a guy wanted to cut corners by staining steps to hide the carpet lines. Instead, he should have been sanding them completely out. I told him that wasn't going to work.

Another time, an employee walked off on the job. My wife was dropping off supplies to me that day and she told me the way I was talking to workers was all wrong. She said my tone intimidated people. I knew I had to tone it down. I did, and it made a big difference.

Now I try to make a point of saying things like, "We made a mistake" before I show an employee how to do something correctly. I might even show him a shortcut in making the repair.

Before I changed, I would say, "Look at the mistake you made. Now come here and straighten this out." Then I would let him scuffle with it.

You can say the same thing with a different tone and get an entirely different response. When I talk to people with respect, I noticed that they're not defensive. What I've found is that they're eager to learn.

When I point out a flaw now, I show the worker what I see and feel. For instance, if a guy is bearing down on an edger machine, it leaves waves on top.

This is my company and my reputation is on the line. But now I try to run this business as if we are teammates. I want employees to make a good living and to be happy on the job. I've helped employees buy houses.

Incidents will happen. Once I overheard an employee telling a client that we could match a stain. That's not true. You can never match a stain perfectly to an original stain. Sometimes the sun makes a color darker or lighter.

I talked to the employee outside and reminded him that his job was not quoting estimates. Then I explained to the customer that she had to decide whether she wanted us to get close to the stain or redo the job.

Before I changed my ways, I would have told the employee to go home right then. I wouldn't have said it in front of the client, but I would have told him that.

It took me a while to learn that in order to do a good job, you have to treat workers with as much respect as clients.

Now I give a lot of positive feedback. I let them know when they do a good job. I learned that lesson over time. I even have to give my daughters some credit. At home, when I'd tell them what to do, they'd say, "Can't you ever say thank you or please?" They were right. It builds self-esteem.

Whenever an employee makes a mistake, I'm still going to point it out. The difference is, after I show it to him, I might say, "Now let's correct it together."

FAMILY

BUILDING A BUSINESS and keeping it all in the family sounds great in theory. The reality is most family businesses don't make it to the second generation.

Lack of interest among family and unhealthy communication styles is a big reason some family businesses never get to the succession planning stage. Forget strategic planning, sometimes working with a spouse is challenge enough.

Millions of family businesses have figured it out, though. Mothers, fathers, sisters, brothers, cousins, in-laws, grandparents and grandchildren are committed to succeeding. They're committed to the business that supports their family and other families.

But it's not easy. Working with people you love is hard. It means dealing with secrets, arrogance, and strong-willed opinions. It involves a sense of entitlement and making exceptions for people who would have been terminated long ago—if they weren't family.

The following entrepreneurs share experiences that range from creating a work-life balance between someone you work with and sleep with, to figuring out the fairest way to pass on a third generation business when some family members are more involved than others.

It also deals with raw emotions that come with working with someone who knows better than anyone how to make you smile or cut you down. It's not easy firing a father, child or cousin, especially when you have to face them at family gatherings.

One of the biggest mistakes I've heard from family business

owners is they get lax when it comes to dealing with family. A lack of accountability is common. Contracts aren't always as important as a family member's word. Discussions about growth, future products and results from the previous year can be difficult. It doesn't help when people with less control think outside of the box while other family members refuse. Of course that's the same reason the business can destroy family relationships.

These family members continually work hard every day to resolve conflicts. They've been there, talking about harsh or preferential treatment, dealing with money issues and coming to a consensus about the direction the business should be headed. They want to keep the business in the family and the family in business. Sometimes that means grooming people outside of the family.

Home, office didn't work together

Barbara Davis
Title: President
Company: Davis Custom Framing
Founded: 1987
Headquarters: North Royalton
Employees: One

I'm a perfectionist. When I worked in a gallery in Illinois I had control of a custom-framing project from start to finish. When I moved to Ohio, I worked at a gallery where I mostly cut mats. Often I felt that jobs were not completed with quality and the customer didn't get the value. I lasted a year there.

I started my business when I was pregnant with my second child, working full time and moving into a new home.

My biggest mistake in running a home-based business was not separating my public space from my private space sooner—both mentally and physically.

I didn't even have separate phone lines for the business. So when a call came in at 8 a.m. on a Saturday morning, not only would I take it, I'd act as if it were fine. It's the curse that most start-up entrepreneurs suffer from. We act like if we turn down business, the phone will never ring again.

Dealing with family was an entirely different issue. Unfortunately, the layout in our first house required customers to walk through both the kitchen and the family room, the two rooms that families spend the most time in.

When the layout is not right for a home-based business that requires customers to come to your home, you have to factor in extra cleaning time before a visit, especially when you have small children. You have to give talks before the bell rings, reminding them to lower their voices.

Sometimes it made customers feel awkward or uncomfortable when they walked through a kitchen where the kids were having a snack or dinner. I know it bothered my kids.

Another problem I faced with working from home was that I loved being there and it was a chore for me to leave to network. Some people find it difficult to work from home, especially if they used to work in big corporate settings. Often those types of people are energized by other people. Others, like me, are drained by a lot of interaction. It doesn't matter what type of personality or work structure you have, every business owner needs to promote their business.

When my business was five years old, I decided I had to make some changes by creating boundaries. My husband agreed. The first big step was physical. We enjoyed living in our old house, but it was far from ideal for a home-based business. We decided to build a home in the same area with my business in mind.

Now, as soon as a customer enters our home, the first door that they see to the right is my showroom. It's a small room with walls covered with hundreds of frame samples. My husband built a large table in the center of the room with storage underneath. That room is the only area a customer sees. A bathroom is next door.

My workroom occupies half of the basement. The other side is for my family. In our old house, not only did customers have to walk through two rooms upstairs in order to get to my combined workroom/showroom, they could hear and see my family if they were in our basement watching TV or playing videos.

Taking my business into consideration with our home's design has made all the difference in the world. In this business my house needs to look decent or it will leave a bad impression.

My customers range from the general public to interior designers and commercial accounts. I no longer feel as if my private life is on display. If my kitchen is a mess, oh, well. Since I don't have to clean right before a customer arrives, I can better focus just on the work.

The physical change was immediate. Making physical changes, including separate phone lines, made me realize that other problems were out of control.

It took a long time for me to realize that great customer service does not mean having your private life being controlled by every customer request. It does mean doing your job well, meeting deadlines and offering whatever extra value I can. In my business it also means going to customers' homes or offices to develop and execute a design for artwork for their walls.

I no longer take calls at 8 a.m. on weekends. I do work evenings, because that's when clients are available.

Networking has never been my strong suit, but after being in business for more than a decade, I stepped out of my comfort zone. A lot of my business is from word of mouth and I realized that if I expanded my network, my business would also grow. Now I participate in five business organizations.

When my business was a start-up, my daughter was just a baby. Now she's 19, so she has grown with my business. The other day, she said she almost forgets the showroom exists in our house. It made me feel that I had managed to keep my home-based business from intruding on our family's private lives.

Grooming next generation of managers

Christopher G. Axelrod
Title: Vice president
Company: National Concession Co.
Founded: 1978
Headquarters: Cleveland
Employees: Seven

My vanity plate reads KID 4VR. I've had the same plate for the past 30 years: Kid forever.

When I was 20, my brother, Tuck, and I revitalized National Concession Co., a business that the Axelrod family has been in since 1929. Now we serve 10 million people a year. Generally, when someone asks me what I do, I just tell them I sell hot dogs. That's an oversimplification for all of the coordination that goes into each event.

My family has handled the Cleveland National Air Show concessions since its inception, when it was called the Cleveland Air Races in the late 1920s. We'll feed 100,000 people during the three-day event. Today it's the only Cleveland show we participate in. I spend half the year on the road, because we're the largest outdoor special-event food and beverage firm in the world. We can't participate in an event unless at least 35,000 people are attending per day. We operate a tight system that guarantees an adrenaline rush. As soon as I step off a plane, I start coordinating 500 to 1,000 volunteers who work at these festivals, concerts and motor sports events.

Part of the proceeds goes to volunteers who represent charities. We designed a niche business that got so big that it consumes our personal time.

My biggest mistake was not even thinking about developing newer and younger management to take over this business until recently.

We've been running this business as if we would be eternally young and forever successful. Our operations and relationships are so tight that all we ever thought about was unlimited potential for our niche services.

It's an unusual business in that we never had to market our services. Event planners find us. We get calls from Japan, Europe and South America, but we only operate in the United States. We have five family members who work in the business and there's only so much we can humanly do.

Big is not necessarily better. It's the reason we resisted getting a web site for many years. We didn't want to field calls from organizations putting on small events.

Now that I'm 50 and my brother is older, we realize how fortunate we've been to build a business on our family name and experience. The problem is, we've become slaves to this empire.

If I get a call to handle the air show at Nellis Air Force Base in Nevada or the Marines' MCAS Miramar Air Show in San Diego, one of the largest in the world, they want to know which Axelrod is going to be there . . . no exceptions. We should have been introducing other management to these event planners so that we could make an easier transition.

It's a complex business that involves lots of part-time managers and supervisors. Some of these people have worked at other jobs for years, but they fly in to different cities to help run weekend events. When parents ask me about letting their college kids work summers, I warn them: We breed tigers. It's a tough business that teaches a balance between offering great customer service and juggling on the fly. They have to learn quickly or they'll get eaten alive.

We love this business so much that it took a long time for us to even think about grooming younger managers to work full time in this business. Frankly, we thought we were invincible. Welcome to middle age.

We started training younger managers and grooming them to get them to a point where we don't have to get on so many planes each month. We've also started thinking about restructuring our business some, going after catering large corporate events for the first time.

I believe in empowering the next generation. We have to be willing to properly train others and pass the torch.

I've realized that I'm no longer KID 4VR. Now I might need to change my license plate to AARP.

Changing concept, name proved expensive lesson

Peter Strang
Title: Executive Vice President
Company: Strang Management Corp.
Founded: 1942
Headquarters: Cleveland
Employees: 75 locally

My grandfather opened and ran a Howard Johnson's restaurant for nearly 30 years. When my father took over the business, he turned it into a steak and seafood business named after him, Don's Lighthouse.

In the early 1970s, people enjoyed dark restaurants, so we covered our arched windows for a more intimate setting. We called it casual upscale, offering features such as one of the first salad bars. It started out primarily as a steakhouse.

Then, as steak prices climbed, we branched out to seafood. We were among the first in the area to have fresh seafood flown in from Boston several times a week.

My father opened four other restaurants in the 1970s, all named after him. Some things worked; some didn't. We still have Don's Pomeroy House in Strongsville.

In 1985 our company, Strang Management Corp., bought into Applebee's. Now our operations include 27 Applebee's in Florida and Texas and 24 Panera Bread restaurants in Philadelphia. Franchisers develop most menu items and training, so we are able to focus on operations and growth.

We did great business at Don's Lighthouse for almost 20 years.

But around 1990, sales started declining with more competition in downtown Cleveland. We're just five minutes away, near Edgewater Park. We decided the restaurant needed an overhaul, so we spent $1.2 million on renovations. We gutted and revamped the entire restaurant. We figured we had to change the name to make customers aware.

Our biggest mistake was changing our concept and the name from Don's Lighthouse to Bistro 89.

We're in the same location where my grandfather opened Howard Johnson's, so it was time to make gas, electric and other infrastructure changes. We removed walls to completely open up the space, so people could see throughout the restaurant. We extended the bar and replaced carpeting with hardwood floors. We worked with an architect to make it a little more contemporary and trendy with new furniture, lighter paint and a mural.

We thought we would attract more guests with a lower-priced menu—$12-$18 for an entrée instead of $16-$30. Don's Lighthouse has always been a great place for business lunches and dinners, special occasions, or a place for dinner before heading to the theater. We believed adding comfort foods, like meatloaf with special cheeses, would attract people more often to the restaurant.

With new décor and a new menu, it was a completely new restaurant. We started brainstorming and looking at restaurants in other cities. We wanted to generate a buzz about all of our changes. From a marketing perspective, we thought that keeping the same name wouldn't generate any buzz. So we renamed the place Bistro 89, as we're located at 8905 Lake Ave.

We thought the name sounded hip. Everybody wants to try something different, so business was good for about three to six months. Then we started hearing more complaints than compliments. Some guests thought it was too loud. We had kept the low ceilings, and the new wood floors made it noisier.

I don't think people liked the menu selection, either. I think we were way ahead of our time, in some respects, with our comfort foods. There may have been some positives, but the negatives reverberated. We wanted more repeat customers, and we thought we would get more people from this neighborhood if we added more comfort foods to the menu.

We found out that the people most likely to come here are from the suburbs. If someone makes more than a 10-minute drive to a restaurant, they want it to be more special. We call it destination dining.

It was a learning experience that helped us understand our customer base. It was a costly lesson, though. After two years, sales were 20 percent below projections.

Customers complained that they liked the old menu. Our older clients didn't like the noise. They complained about feeling like they were on stage because it was too open.

It was a very challenging time. We considered three options: close the restaurant, pick a new name or make it Don's Lighthouse again.

We decided to go back to what made the restaurant successful for the first 20 years. We changed the name and the menu, again featuring steak and seafood. We also got more creative with staples like scallops.

Then we put carpet back in the dining room, added tablecloths, painted the walls darker and made other changes to make it feel more intimate. One immediate advantage was being able to market both Don's restaurants with the same direct-mail pieces, print and radio advertisements.

The funny thing is that some customers who hadn't been here for a couple of years never even knew about all the changes. Business grew over time, by taking advantage of our reputation.

We took away something that meant more to people than we thought. Then we brought it back. It cost another $150,000 to make changes including signs, uniforms and beverage napkins. Our family used Bistro 89 matches for years. I think they're finally all gone.

Business continued to grow. Now we're celebrating 35 years.

Except for that one name change, we've never been real creative with business names. All of the previous restaurants were named after my father, Don. Our management company bears the family name, Strang. We've found that keeping it simple and consistent works best.

Dad, you're fired! Letting an employee go is one thing, quite another when he's kin

Robert A. Schepens
Title: CEO
Company: Champion Personnel
Founded: 1964
Headquarters: Garfield Heights
Employees: 34

My father, Ralph A. Schepens, opened a small personnel agency in downtown Cleveland four decades ago in the spot where the 200 Public Square building stands now. Then he set out to make his mark on the industry on a national level.

He spent 30 years on the board of directors of the National Association of Personnel Services. At one point he was president, writing the code of ethics. Other times he served the personnel industry at the local and state levels while building his company up to 25 employees. No question, he was well-respected and loved.

I worked for him for 15 years, and he taught me a lot. But he was a micromanager. Unfortunately, I couldn't get along with him, so I left and went to work in corporate America. We didn't talk for five years. Then, gradually, we started communicating a little.

In 1992 my father got ill. His heart stopped on the golf course. He was in a coma for six weeks, and it took two years to recover. By then, Champion Personnel, his small but solid company, was in big trouble, on the verge of bankruptcy.

After he got sick, all of the bad stuff went away. I was right by his side throughout his recovery, but I stayed away from his company.

One day he asked me to buy him out so he could attempt to retire with dignity. I didn't have the money, so we agreed to a leveraged buyout in which he'd get money from the company if I could turn it around.

My biggest mistake was letting my father come into the office every day after I bought the company from him.

He was 72 at the time, but he still spent five hours a day at the company. The deal was, I would be president and decision maker and he would be vice president and non-decision maker. But he spent most of his day getting in my way.

Every day he made suggestions about what I should be doing or told me how he didn't agree with what I was doing. It was awkward, and I worked hard to sympathize with his plight. He founded the company and then, through no fault of his own, he was losing the company. But he second-guessed everything I was doing.

It wasn't just tough on me. It was tough on everybody. At the time we were down to six employees. These were people who didn't know me and wanted to show respect to my father. We would make minor successes and put the money back into the company.

I was torn. It's not easy trying to move a company in a different direction while having your father second-guess every decision. The first thing I did was get rid of the general manager. Next I tried to give the staff positive feedback so they would follow my lead. We were changing the types of jobs we filled, moving away from 95 percent permanent office placements to more temporary office placements.

I was spending more time dealing with my father than I was running the business. When I was away from the office, I was still thinking about the issues 24/7. It was absolutely horrible. I knew it was tough on him to go from being well-respected with a solid company and money in the bank to someone who had no money. Just before he got sick, he spent a lot of money getting the temporary division started. He was a man who had no bad habits, so he took his frustrations out on me.

We blew up at each other all the time. I tried very hard to make him feel important and respected. At the same time, I was trying to keep him from meddling with everything. It was no fun. Finally, I couldn't take it.

One day, after about four or five months, I called our attorney and confirmed that I was president of the company. I told him I intended to fire my father. My attorney told me that I could do it legally. Then he told me I had a lot of guts to try to do that, reminding me how strong-minded my father was.

My dad had already gone home after a typical Friday blow-up. I drove to his condominium. While he sat in his favorite blue chair in front of the fireplace, I explained that he was fired. I told him that he was never to set foot in the Champion office again unless I invited him.

It didn't go well. He said, "I'll give you six months to make the company a total success. And if you don't, I want it back."

"Fine," I said. "You're my father and I love you." And then I walked out.

I was scared to death. My immediate thought was, What did I just do? My next thought was that I had no one else to blame if we weren't a success.

I faced a lot of pressure, and I was relieved that my stepmother supported my decision. Her only regret was that my father would be spending a lot more time at home.

At first he would call me once a week to check on the company. Eventually he started calling every couple of days, or I would call him. At the time, sales were less than $1 million; today they have grown 1,800 percent. Now, 98 percent of our workers are temporary and 2 percent are permanent. We've won many awards, including the Weatherhead 100, over the past two years. We just won the NorthCoast 99, the Employers Resource Council's list of the 99 best companies to work for out of 60,000 in Northeast Ohio.

My dad died about a year and a half after he left Champion, so he never got to see the company we are today. But he played a huge role in getting us here.

After I fired him, I consulted with him when I felt his expertise and wisdom were needed. For instance, he helped me put together an advisory board for the company. It includes a certified public accountant, an ISO standards consultant, a former vice president of a Fortune 100 company and two former nationally recognized entrepreneurs.

When you take over any business, especially a family-owned company, make sure you're very clear with everyone about reporting and decision-making responsibilities.

Working around the older generation's arrangement

Huey Haynes
Title: President
Company: Haynes Enterprises Inc.
Founded: 1959
Headquarters: Cleveland
Employees: 5

I graduated with a computer science degree from Texas Southern University, knowing that I was coming right back to Cleveland to join my family's Sohio business at East 131st and Harvard. Some people just didn't understand why I chose pumping gas and changing tires over working for a big corporation.

But while a lot of the work was far from glamorous, I also got an opportunity to manage 15 people right out of college.

My father, Huey—along with his brothers Johnnie and Willie Haynes—started the business in 1959 at another location in Hough.

I knew exactly what I was getting into, working with three men who liked their customers and worked hard to build their reputation for service. It wasn't easy trying to measure up to their standards.

By 1983 we had three Sohio gas stations along with Haynes Firestone, which my father started in 1975 at East 134th and Miles. The service stations eventually became BP gas and minimarkets as the Sohio brand was retired.

I ran a 24-hour station for five years until 1997. When someone can't make it to work, you're there – no matter what time it is.

Working 60 hours a week was tough when my two kids were little. I wanted out.

After more than 40 years, my father was ready to retire, so I bought his 66 percent stake in the Firestone store. My two uncles owned the remainder. I had worked for both of them since I was a teenager, and I was happy about this new partnership.

My biggest mistake was buying a majority stake in my family-owned business without taking into account some important details that could have kept the business from growing.

At the time, my Uncle Willie's involvement in the business was mainly financial. He didn't spend much time here because he was still running another gas station. My Uncle Johnnie had a financial and a managerial interest. He beat me to work each day.

The relationship worked great for several years. But after a while, I started realizing that during lean times, like when it was time to buy equipment, it always fell on me. There was no financial support. That was the way the deal had been structured with my father. It was his idea to branch off, buying a Firestone store. My uncles followed suit with their support.

My dad had put up most of the money to buy it, and he continued to invest the most to keep it going. That might have worked for my dad. But it wasn't working for me.

Unfortunately, that was the deal I had bought into. A couple of years ago, when I finally got serious about expanding, I realized this deal was a problem. Long before I had any ownership in this business, I had thought about how my dad could be generating more profit by putting to better use the land he owned next to the Firestone store.

At one point he had a couple of buildings on it that were used for storage. Then he had a car wash, along with space that he rented to a kung fu instructor. I decided it was time to renovate the block and turn it into a block of businesses: an expanded space for kung fu, a beauty shop and a barbershop. Renovation is not cheap. The roof alone was going to cost $25,000.

Our business arrangement didn't specify how improvements would be paid for. We had never had any reason to take out a loan.

We used our general business account for payroll and expenses like taxes and insurance. Improvements were not part of the deal.

I assumed that my uncles would put some money toward the roof, equal to their share of ownership. I assumed wrong. They had no interest in investing or expanding. They were thinking about retirement. That's when I realized something had to be done. I started thinking that if something happened to one of my uncles, I might be in business with another family member who assumed their share.

I didn't mind having them as business partners. In fact, I enjoyed it. I had been asking them for advice on all sorts of issues for two decades. If I had a problem with an employee, a customer or a vendor, chances are they'd know how to handle it. The last thing I wanted was to inherit a partner who knew nothing about this business.

I called a family meeting with my dad and my two uncles. I started the meeting talking about where I saw the business going and my plans for renovating both the Firestone store and the adjoining buildings. I told them about my costs and my concerns about what I considered an unfair business structure. I told them I would be the one shelling out money up front, but they would reap great rewards with the current business structure.

They listened and they said changing the way the company was set up was a good idea. The meeting lasted four hours, but not because we were disagreeing. My uncles quickly offered to let me buy them out. The rest of the meeting was spent with them reminiscing and offering advice on my plans.

Now I'm the sole business owner. I know I'm fortunate that we worked things out. Some families aren't able to turn businesses over to the second generation. I'm optimistic about the future, knowing that my father and my uncles are in my corner.

Succession plan needed professional guidance

Sanford Leff Jr.
Title: Executive vice president—finance
Company: Leff Electric
Founded: 1921
Headquarters: Cleveland
Employees: 86

We've heard the statistics. Whether it's due to a changing business climate or a lack of interest from the inheritors, it's not easy transferring a family business to a third generation. We're fortunate, but it wasn't easy.

Our grandfather started Leff Electric by selling wiring devices, cable and lighting fixtures to contractors. After World War II, our dad, Sanford Leff, and Uncle Phillip Leff joined the business. Dad bought out his brother nearly 30 years ago and continued working in the business until he was in his 80s.

We were all encouraged to work for other companies in other industries. Two of my four siblings ended up working in the family business, along with a few cousins.

We all did our part to build the business, expanding sales and relationships with business partners, including banks and vendors.

Throughout the years, we became more confident that we could eventually run this business. The problem was our father never discussed it. He was happy owning, operating and controlling day-to-day operations. We were left wondering about our future. Talking to our parents about wanting an ownership interest got us nowhere.

Our biggest mistake was thinking that we could manage our succession plan without any type of assistance.

My father was happy gifting all five of his kids small and equal interests in the company. The three of us working in the business, including my sister, Deeda Shubert, wanted more of an interest in the company. Each of us had worked in the business 10 to 20 years, and we encouraged my father to look at his estate plan. We didn't think he was doing it quickly enough. He was nearly 70 in the mid-1980s, and there was no formalized succession plan.

He was president, CEO and owner, and he was very content. He had three of his children working in and growing the business. We helped to expand more into institutional, property management, commercial and industrial markets, and we shifted our focus to labor-saving and energy-conservation products. Nothing was rocking the boat. Everything was seemingly good.

By the early '90s we really wanted to improve our stake in the business. We were happy with our compensation and the roles we all played. But we wanted more of a stake.

The difficulty was approaching our dad. He was open to talking about it, but he didn't want to give up control. Both our mother and father looked at the business as their livelihood and security blanket. They were comfortable. Some people have stocks and bonds. They had a business.

My brother and sister and I would get together to talk about what needed to be done to transition the business. We had several meetings. Each of us had ideas and we discussed them all, including my sister's plan to retire before age 45 and roles for the entire management team. We really thought we considered everything.

But when we presented our ideas to our parents, the discussion ended fairly quickly. They were very cordial and congratulated us on our thought process. But there was one problem: They were just not ready to let go of their baby.

I don't think there were hard feelings, but what we thought was a great plan apparently wasn't complete. After listening to them, we realized there were some ingredients we were missing. We didn't completely fail, because at least the lines of communication were finally open. But we didn't succeed, either, because there was still no succession plan.

We recognized the importance of getting the business out of our father's estate and the importance of making sure our parents were comfortable with their own personal estate plan. During the next three years, we met with accountants and attorneys, as well as succession, estate and financial planners.

The more we dealt with different advisers and consultants, the more we realized there were factors that we didn't think about from our parents' point of view. For instance, I was going through a divorce in the '90s, and I'm sure they wondered how that might affect the business. We were thinking about things from our point of view.

Finally we developed a good plan that everyone was happy with. Bruce and I are primary owners, and our siblings have a minority interest in the company. My father continued to work here as a consultant and adviser for several years following the agreement, which was great.

But a succession plan was necessary, and not just for us—for our employees, vendors and customers, too. They needed to be assured that we plan to be in business for many years to come.

We're fortunate that as siblings we always worked well together. We've been successful looking at everyone's interest, while taking into account what's best for the company. We're optimistic about our future. We've expanded on our solid foundation and made a going concern a growing concern.

Married business partners say 'I do' to finding balance

Gwenay Reaze-Coniglio
Title: President
Company: The Coniglio Co.
Founded: 1994
Headquarters: Cleveland
Employees: 20

When you work together and live together, it's not easy finding a balance, especially when you're trying to build a construction company.

My business partner, Tom Coniglio, is also my husband. Even though our desks are side by side, we don't see much of each other.

He's in charge of operations and finances, while I spend most of my time focusing on business development and marketing.

I'm president of the Coniglio Co., which Tom started a few years before we got married. It was a different company then. We used to build houses. We've been general contractors for about 10 years.

We're opposite in so many ways, including our backgrounds. I started out in psychology and he started out as a mechanical engineer. He's a big-picture person and I'm detail-oriented. Often, our differing views have been good for the business. Other times, not so good. Good or bad, we found ourselves talking about work all the time.

Our biggest mistake was not recognizing sooner the need to create boundaries between work and home.

When you work so hard to build a company, it consumes your life. We go to different business meetings during the day, so the ideal time to talk shop tended to be at home – which takes away from family life with our two children.

Sometimes, it just made sense to discuss business matters at home. Other times, if we disagreed about an issue at work, we would tend to bring it up at home. Somehow the problems at work got blended with personal matters. I might say something like, "You threw your clothes on the floor. The mess looks just like your desk."

Doing things like not taking a salary in the beginning also impacted our home life. It took away from what we could do as a family. We were so concerned about taking care of our employees that we didn't even think about any impact on our family.

Sometimes, the roles we played at work had a direct effect on our home life. For instance, I might come home from a meeting or networking function on a high, ready to celebrate a success from the day. Meanwhile, he might have come home directly from a job site where he dealt with one issue after another.

It's tough, because he might want a shoulder to lean on after a rough day. Meanwhile, my success for the day means more talk about work. That's a good thing, of course, but the timing might be all wrong. When you don't work together, it's a different world.

The lines were constantly blurred. If we were in a meeting and he slipped and called me "honey," I would cringe.

We would talk business at dinner. We might be watching TV at night and something would come on that sparked a conversation about work. Business played a big part in our personal lives, even impacting our decision of when to have a second child. It's the reason our daughter is 14 and our son is 2.

We were so busy just trying to make the business work that we didn't realize how badly it affected our personal life. It started to take a toll on our family. A couple of years ago, Tom finally decided enough was enough. We had to work hard at creating boundaries. We decided not to discuss work at home at all, unless it was an emergency. We try not to discuss kids at work unless there is a problem.

Have we stuck to that rule? We try hard. It's gotten easier, because we're growing. The fewer hats you wear as an entrepreneur, the easier they are to keep separate.

Let's put it this way: We finally took our first family vacation in June.

A good rule of thumb is finding an appropriate time to discuss business at home, whether it's after the kids are asleep or over coffee. It's helped us to act more like husband and wife instead of just business partners. It takes work to stay committed. You truly have to be conscious of blurring the lines.

EDUCATION

WHY DO PEOPLE START BUSINESSES? Some people just want to make money using a skill set they enjoy. Some people see a way to offer a product or service that's better, in some way, than what's already offered by competitors. Some people don't want to work for a corporation, so they find a business venture to invest in, even if they don't enjoy it.

It really doesn't matter why or how somebody goes into business. What matters most is a goal to succeed. It sounds reasonable enough. But too often, entrepreneurs face challenges that could have been avoided or corrected sooner, if they just sought help.

Beginning and seasoned entrepereneurs in this chapter share mistakes they made because they didn't reach out for help. Assistance is available. Many organizations offer free services that help analyze products and services from a customer's point of view. The first step is taking a harsh look at what you bring to the table.

Seasoned entrepreneurs in this chapter found paying a consultant can be worth the investment. Consultants cut to the chase with objective, bottom-line questions, which led to greater success.

When sales slow down or top customers give you less business, some entrepreneurs find it's best to listen to and learn from customers. Sometimes small business owners find that there's no substitute for doing your own research and keeping emotion out of deals. Some entrepreneurs find that they're the ones that need to do a better job educating customers about their products and services in order to build sales and relationships.

Find a mentor in your field. Find mentors in other fields. Talk to all sorts of business owners. Some people will share more than others. Take it all in.

Just about everyone considers starting a business at some point in their lives. Consumers buy thousands of products and services, so there are plenty of opportunities.

But don't get carried away with research. Some people never start a business until they think they've figured everything out. That's why some never start. Get going. Once you're in business, remember anything worth doing, is worth improving.

Not researching before publishing made start rough

Mike Shea
Title: CEO/Founder
Company: Alternative Press
Founded: 1985
Headquarters: Cleveland
Employees: 17

I started Alternative Press as a "fanzine" out of a bedroom in my mom's house in Aurora. I was 19 and had just dropped out of Kent State because it closed down the film department. It's hard for me to believe still, but today we're the leading magazine for punk and underground music and culture.

Our monthly circulation is about 225,000, and our readers are ages 13 to 24. About 55 percent are females who hang out in malls and other youth spots and are into the punk scene. The guys tend to be skateboarders and video gamers who see themselves as outcasts.

When I started the publication, I had just been introduced to the punk scene by Jim Kosicki, a guy with an 8-inch purple mohawk whom I met while waiting in line to buy tickets to the Police's "Synchronicity" tour. He started taking me to concerts at

Cleveland punk haunts such as The Pop Shop in the basement of the old Agora and The Underground in the Flats.

I quickly realized this was an audience that was ignored. I had been editor of the high school newspaper and yearbook when I started the fanzine, an amateur version of a magazine made for fans, which eventually morphed into a magazine. But I still had very little idea of what I was doing when it came to running a business—much less growing one.

As a young entrepreneur, I walked into a number of situations in which I didn't know anything and I took the advice of the first person I talked to.

My biggest mistake was not doing my homework to learn more about my industry.

Instead of learning everything I needed to know about how printing companies price jobs, I chose to focus on the fun areas of my job and just let fate take its course.

In all honesty, I was scared, and I think all new business owners are (we just never admit it).

You don't want your staff or investors to think that you don't know everything there is to know in your line of work.

So about 50 percent of the time, you just fake it, praying to God that you don't make a huge mistake and blow $10,000 on something that should have cost $25 at Home Depot.

I just stumbled around until I found a dad. When I speak of finding a dad, I mean finding an older mentor to take me under his wing and not judge me for being young, naive and wide-eyed to the world. I needed someone to teach me the basics, not to mention secrets of the business world.

I kept switching printing companies until I learned more about the business.

Until I found a mentor, I was looked at as a stupid kid. I was charged exorbitant fees and I accepted excuses for printing mistakes. I had problems with lawyers and accountants as well, until I gained more confidence as a business owner.

My first mentor used to work at Gazette Printing in Jefferson, Ohio, where they used to do their printing.

Even though I was publishing a magazine featuring a lot of punk rock bands with pretty wild names—Alien Sex Fiend and The Exploited are among the more tame ones—he took a laid-back approach and taught me how to put out a better product.

Eventually we moved our business to Carrolton Graphics, where I met my second mentor, Jack McConnaughy. He not only became my No. 1 fan but also my No. 1 dad in the printing and publishing world. He was an ex-hippie who took me under his wing and truly taught me about the printing business. He encouraged me when times got tough, and he also negotiated for me with the financial guys and the printing company.

He has always been there for me, and I know that without his support, I would not be in business today.

In my experience, doing your homework and finding a mentor is crucial to helping a young entrepreneur survive and thrive.

Salon owner learns lesson working in, not on, her business

NeCole and Orlando Cumberlander
Title: Co-owners
Company: Noire et Blanc Salon
Founded: 1996
Headquarters: Cleveland
Emplyees: 12

I spent about 10 years working at other salons before I was encouraged by clients to start my own business. I had a busy clientele, but that's not a good reason to open your own business. I didn't realize it then, but it takes an entirely different skill set to run a business.

I don't think I've ever been more excited than when we opened Noire et Blanc across the street from the Cleveland Clinic. I spent a lot of time picking out contemporary furniture and art and finding what I considered to be the right staff. Our marketing plan basically consisted of our existing clients spreading the word.

Despite our lack of a formal marketing plan, the business grew very quickly, because we focused on a quality product and great customer service. But after a few years, not having day-to-day operational systems in place and focusing on sales instead of profits caught up with us.

My biggest mistake was working in the business, not on the business. I was a stylist. And all I really did was buy myself a job when I started the business. I didn't realize for a long time that we weren't doing well, because money was constantly coming in.

Our salon is 9 years old, but it wasn't profitable for the first six years. I didn't realize it until I got an accountant, who showed me that we weren't making a dime. From the outside looking in, you would think that the business was doing very well. Sales were high, but profits were extremely low.

We were open about five years when a friend suggested that I read the book "The E-Myth Revisited," by Michael Gerber, and it changed my life and the way I do business. The book is about why small businesses don't work and what to do about it. Basically I was doing everything the book said I shouldn't be doing. I learned that as the leader of my company I should focus on setting up good systems and letting those systems manage people.

I immediately started making changes, from the way we greeted our guests to adjusting commission rates and putting service benchmarks in place for employees.

It wasn't easy turning the company around. I was devastated when we had a walkout of employees after we changed the commission rates. We also changed our culture, starting with making employees' attire more consistent—they began wearing all black. This is a creative industry and initially they felt like their creativity was being stifled.

About six months after I read the book, I stopped being a stylist and put a management team in place. Before then, there were only two managers—including me. By empowering others, it encouraged them to take more of an ownership role and allowed me to focus on growing the vision of the company. Our profit margin went from 1 or 2 percent to about 9 percent. In our industry, the average is 7 to 10 percent.

Turning the business around allowed me to work on my vision of starting a cosmetology school. I've always been passionate about education, and as a salon owner, I understand how important it is to have access to good quality staff.

I took my knots and hits with the salon, so I understood what I was doing when my husband, Orlando, and I opened the Ohio Academy Paul Mitchell Partner School three years ago. I bought a Paul Mitchell franchise because systems were already in place for this caliber of school, and because it's a company that I believe in. In September, we plan to open a second school in Columbus, our hometown. For the last 17 years, I've been a Paul Mitchell educator, traveling extensively to participate in hair shows and taking part in national advanced education.

As president-elect of the National Salon Association, I'm fortunate to network with salon owners all over North America, and I've learned a lot from them. I know I'm not unique. I am just one of millions of salon owners around the world who have had the same problem—not realizing what it takes to run a business.

I used to be a busy hairdresser who loved the beauty industry so much that I opened up a salon. I didn't know what it took to make the business a success. Now I do.

Winging it caused big errors

Darrell Williams
Title: Chairman/CEO
Company: Ultimate Auto Care Technical Institute
Founded: 2000
Headquarters: Cleveland
Employees: 8

The school of hard knocks sounds like such a cliché, but it's real to me. I've been there.

Ten years ago, I had two unsuccessful auto detailing businesses. Both times I rented space from auto dealerships and both deals involved spending most of my time taking care of their cars. One business lasted six months, and the other lasted a year.

It didn't help that I didn't have a clear head back then. Not only was I an alcoholic, but I was also using drugs. I ended up detailing cars for years at other shops, but I never gave up my dream of becoming a successful business owner. I knew I had to turn my life around first.

I started Ultimate Auto Care Technical Institute five years ago with just $200 from an Alcoholic Anonymous sponsor. Today we've got contracts with several car dealerships, a car rental business and the city. Our auto-detail school just graduated its first class of students. We're opening a satellite school location in Akron and starting a mobile detailing service, both this fall.

We've come a long way. But I've made so many costly mistakes along the way. My biggest mistake was not doing any research before I started the business. I just opened my doors without a business plan or funding from a financial institution. I didn't incorporate until I was in business for a couple years. I didn't have an accountant, and I didn't know anything about payroll services.

I had a skill, and I wanted a business. I just didn't know things, so I winged it.

The problem was I never took the time to reach out to any associations or business services aimed at helping small business owners. I didn't have a business mentor.

And once you're in business, it's hard to get away from day-to-day operations to seek help. Besides that, I never got my high school diploma, and I didn't want other people to know that I didn't know things.

I made so many unnecessary mistakes that took my attention away from the business, and it made me want to give up.

For instance, my first year in business I had a vendor's license, but I didn't know anything about an S corporation, which separates personal taxes from business. By the time a neighboring business owner referred me to his accountant, I owed two years of back taxes. I also had to pay about $6,000 in fines to workers' comp, unemployment and Social Security, because I had been paying employees with business checks, but we weren't incorporated.

Meanwhile, one of the biggest problems I faced was finding competent employees. I had to train everybody I hired. I'm naive because I really thought I could just open up a school to teach the detailing trade. I quickly learned that everything is regulated, and opening my school involved answering 300 questions, developing a curriculum and hiring a consultant at $60 an hour. My wife, Latonia, joined the company to help get the school off the ground.

When you start a business with no money and you have no plan to get capital except from sales, it's easy to make a ton of mistakes because all your decisions are based on survival mode.

I had been in my house for just a couple of years, so I could get only a $15,000 home equity line of credit. I couldn't get financing from traditional banks, so I turned to a high-risk lender and paid 27 percent interest. I knew there had to be a better way to get the money, but I was also determined not to fail again, so I did what I had to do in order to retrofit the building and make it appropriate for a school and business. I also had to pay the consultant.

I made countless basic mistakes that could have been avoided if I had just reached out for help or even taken the time to research things. We didn't realize that every time we were denied credit, it affected our credit score.

It took me a long time to learn to say three words – "I don't know." I started hanging out with successful people, asking questions and seeking suggestions. I wish I had done it a lot sooner, and I could still do a better job at it. I just learned about the Urban League's small business development center this year, and that's just one of many organizations out there that offer assistance, training and resources.

I prefer to look toward the future. But I don't mind talking about my past to students at our detailing school, because most are recovering addicts and ex-offenders who need a second chance. I can relate to them, and I want to inspire them to start their own businesses. I also want to save them from the frustration and ill health that I endured from worry.

Last year we trained several individuals referred to us by city and state programs, and we graduated our first class in April. It's a good feeling to see people excited about getting a second chance at life. For those who want to start their own business, though, I tell them to do their homework first.

Success obscured need to keep developing the business

Rebecca Morgan
Title: President
Company: Fulcrum Consulting Works Inc.
Founded: 1990
Headquarters: Cleveland
Employees: 1

I went from making macaroni and cheese one day to making jet engine parts the next. To me, it's all the same. All manufacturing plants have control and flow issues. All of them deal with questions about adding value or adding costs without adding value.

I love the manufacturing process. Whether you're processing a chicken or building a machine, you start with raw materials, add value to it and ship the finished product to a customer. How well you do that is critical. I help companies do it better.

It's hard to believe that I've been a consultant for 16 years, especially since I didn't have a high opinion of consultants when I held various senior management positions in the corporate world. I've worked at several companies and I used to think that consultants were not worth the money. I've seen companies pay a half million dollars to get a report that was not actionable in any way.

Running a successful consulting business requires having

content expertise, consulting skills and being a good business person. I was good enough in all three areas that the first 10 years of my consulting business were a strong success—but I was bored.

My biggest mistake was accepting the apparent success of my business and not reaching out to a business development expert sooner.

It was really my boredom that got to me four years ago. I had a full calendar, a good reputation with referral business and a nice revenue stream, but I was lulled to sleep by that basic sense of success. I didn't realize how much better I could be until I hired a growth consultant to help me redefine what I was doing. I didn't know how he was going to help me, but I knew that he could.

One of the first things he did was interview about a dozen clients. I thought they would say I did a fine job, but they didn't really understand how I did it.

Instead, I found out that what they valued most was my strategic thinking, which was not why I was hired.

They told me that they wanted more of me. They saw me as a peer. This may sound bad, but I didn't let them treat me like a peer. I thought that because they paid me by the hour to do a job, that I should do it as fast as I could. Spending time talking to them about topics other than the project at hand was contrary to getting the job done as fast as I could.

I was surprised and confused initially. I had always associated myself with high-end professionals who are my competitors. I am on national and regional manufacturing association boards. And I've always worked hard to stay abreast of the latest strategies and techniques in supply chain management, information systems and consulting. Never before had I been told that I needed to change the way I ran my business.

I thought companies hired me to do a task or tweak current operations, like implementing software that helps run operations or to recommend and implement efficiency improvements. I didn't realize they wanted to hire me for my strategic input.

It took me awhile, but I finally figured out how to change my fee structure. I thought they were buying guaranteed results because they were paying me by the hour. If the company didn't do its part of the project, I thought I had to step back and do that too, with a day rate.

Now I charge a fixed project fee that we agree upon up front. That means we have to have real clarity about my role and responsibilities, and theirs. It forces clients to better understand changes they're making. Basically, I'm not a hired hand anymore. I'm a partner in improving the business.

I am doing much more interesting work now because I'm helping them to define and implement a strategy instead of working on a little project that's not really part of an overall strategy.

In making those changes and others, my gross sales have grown to record levels, except in 2004, a down year.

When a company is successful, it's easy to think that things are fine. Many companies focus inwardly. They figure that costs are under control, we're making money, therefore we're a great company.

The real question is, What is the potential for what you could be doing? That takes an external focus.

It's true. Sometimes you can't see the forest because of the trees. I was too close to my business to see some areas I needed to address to grow.

Waiting to get female-owned business status

Sandy Heath
Title: President/Owner
Company: Sandra Heath & Associates Inc.
Founded: 1995
Headquarters: Parma Heights
Employees: 3

I started working in the temporary employment business as a single mom just trying to pay the bills. Within a relatively short period I was able to work my way up to the management level in a national agency.

After several years, I started an employment agency with a partner. After my partner and I split, I decided to do things differently, on a more personal level. One of my top priorities was to treat people who worked for me the way I want to be treated.

I built my company around the premise of a temp agency, but we're so much more. I want to make sure that people who work for me earn an honest wage, have paid holidays and medical benefits. For our corporate clients, we accept all the liabilities and responsibilities for our employees. That's why we screen prospective employees thoroughly. We interview them, test their computer skills, do background checks and verify education and employment history.

Our clients may call us a temp agency, but the reality is that less than 6 percent of our business is temporary assignments.

In most cases, our people work at companies for several months, or in some cases a year or more. Right now we have 48 people in the field.

When I started the business I knew what it took to run a good employment agency.

But I did not realize how critical certification was to my company's success in obtaining larger, private- and public-sector contracts. My biggest mistake was not getting certified sooner as a female business enterprise.

A couple years after I started my business I was competing for a three-year, $300,000 contract with a larger firm. I was awarded the contract. But when I went to sign it, the company wanted a copy of my FBE certificate. I didn't have one. I didn't even know what it was.

Early in the process, the company had asked if I owned the business. I said yes. I didn't know I had to prove it. I quickly obtained the paperwork to get my company certified as an FBE with the city of Cleveland and other entities.

It was too late for that contract, but I didn't ever want to be in that position again.

Getting certified involves a ton of paperwork. You have to prove that you are who you say you are. They actually want your birth certificate.

You have to prove that you have the expertise to do what you say you do. You also have to prove that you own the company. They want to make sure you make the decisions and are not a front for anyone.

After you've completed the paperwork, an inspector comes to check out your office. He wants to see bank statements, leases, utility bills, invoices and contracts.

I have earned Female Business Enterprise certification with the National Women Business Owners Corp., city of Cleveland, Cuyahoga County, Greater Cleveland Regional Transit Authority and Cuyahoga Metropolitan Housing Authority.

Getting certified is so important for female and minority small business owners. It allows you to earn your reputation and hopefully go from a subcontractor to prime subcontractor. Having your FBE or MBE certifications does not guarantee you business.

It's not a gift. What it does do is give your company credibility. And it gives you an opportunity to compete for business you ordinarily would not have known about.

Large contractors often find FBE and MBE certified businesses through local government and other entities that certify businesses. Certified businesses may also receive e-mail notices about job opportunities. It gives you a chance to get in the game and to prove yourself.

I never thought about it before now, but I would have to say that about 40 percent of our business is a result of our FBE status. I was a business owner for five years before I knew of the value of being certified.

In June, my company was awarded a five-year Federal Supply Schedule contract by the U.S. General Services Administration to provide temporary administrative and professional services.

I used my FBE certificate to open doors for the GSA contract, but the government proposal required 10 times more paperwork and documentation.

While we've had the GSA contract for only a few months, it's already opened doors that had been closed for years. It's called a contract, but it really just gives us an opportunity to be eligible to provide services for government entities.

I have had several meetings with government contractors that are promising. Until we got the credential, we could not even get a phone call returned.

A lot of business owners don't want to deal with the scrutiny of the certification process. It's a pain. But from where I sit, it's been worth it.

Research is needed when taking over existing business

Joy Asamoto
Title: Owner
Company: Hana Asian Food
Founded: 2003
Headquarters: Lyndhurst
Employees: 1

I like a challenge. But what I thought was an opportunity felt more like a disaster. Six months after I bought an Asian grocery store, I really wanted to quit.

My partner left the business after a year, and I don't blame her. We didn't do the appropriate research and due diligence, and we paid for it. Start-up investment costs ended up being about three times what we expected.

Ten years ago, I bought a dry-cleaning pickup station and converted it into a profitable full-service plant within a year. I still run that business, but I needed a new challenge. I had been visiting the grocery store for 10 years as a customer, so when the owner was ready to sell it at a decent price, I bought it.

I had been in that store two to four times a month as a customer for all of those years, so I thought I knew what I was buying. I didn't know anything about the grocery business, but I thought I was buying goodwill and a loyal customer base.

My biggest mistake was not starting a business from scratch. I gained nothing but headaches from taking over a business without doing research to know what I was getting into.

I quickly learned that the previous owner owed a lot of suppliers and even the landlord. I couldn't get a lease and was forced to move a month after I bought the business. Three months later, I changed the company's name to Hana Asian Food.

At first, 90 percent of the items I stocked were either Korean or Japanese. That was a mistake, because I misunderstood my customer base. I had moved only about two miles from the previous location, in a much busier retail area, but the customers were different.

What I found was that more than half of my customers were non-Asian, and they expected very different things in an Asian grocery store. In other words, a bottle of kimchi was not going to sell, but a single serving would.

My store is one of several Asian food stores in the Cleveland area. The grocery business is a very low-margin business. I knew that to survive and succeed I quickly had to carve out a niche among the competition.

I was very discouraged, though. I felt as if every time I climbed over a mountain, there was another one facing me. It was especially tough since suppliers didn't want to extend me credit. They thought I was affiliated with the previous business. I decided that the only way to turn my business around was to pay close attention to my customers' desires.

I immediately noticed a strong affinity for Thai cuisine. Customers were probably asking for the food because a Thai restaurant is directly across the street. I knew nothing about Thai cuisine, so I made efforts to familiarize myself with ingredients from this culture. I studied the food, visited Thai distributors and eventually started stocking the items. Now, nearly three years after I started the business, Thai food accounts for about 25 percent of sales.

Next, I asked customers for input. I asked them if they were able to find what they were looking for. If the item was not in our store, I asked them what they wanted and made sure I got it for them.

Then I took what might seem like a logical step: I put labels on shelves describing the items in English. However, that's actually unusual in the Asian grocery store business. Adding labels or translating the names of the foods was critical for customers unable to read explanatory print in Korean and Japanese. Not only did the move reinforce the organization of the store, it created a far more informed shopping experience for new customers and regulars alike.

Finally, I responded to another frequent customer request for pre-made Asian food. I started a catering operation about six months ago, and more recently we started offering to-go boxes of sushi and Korean food. We also offer bentos, which are Japanese lunch boxes that include dumplings, Asian salad or sashimi.

It took two years, but we're finally on the right track. I really thought this would be an easy business to take over. I learned the hard way that outward appearances can be very deceiving. If you decide to take over a business, make sure you do your homework.

Real estate investing requires a lot of time, research

Graig E. Kluge
Title: Owner
Company: K Group Properties LLC
Founded: 2001
Headquarters: Cleveland Heights
Employees: 2

I became intrigued with real estate when I was a law student living in Cleveland Heights. I started thinking about all the rent I was paying. And I knew how much the people downstairs paid. It looked like an easy way to accumulate wealth.

I kept thinking about real estate, even after I became a lawyer. I was practicing criminal law and family law, but in the back of my mind I kept thinking that one day I would be able to buy real estate. When I was finally able to invest, I found out it's not easy. It's work.

I was a sole practitioner for seven of the nine years that I practiced law. I became a real estate investor full time about a year ago. After my experiences, I'm convinced that when it comes to rental property, if you want to build a business as an investor, you need to do it full time.

My wife and I were able to buy three properties in 2½ years, and we overpaid for all three. My biggest mistake was not doing a better job at researching the market before making offers on double and triple units.

When I bought those properties, I really believed I was ready. I had worked hard to save money for the investments, and I had been looking at homes and listings in Cleveland Heights for years. But the fact is, my focus was on law. That was my career. Like most homeowners, I relied on my real estate agent to help make decisions when it came to counteroffers.

In 2003 and 2004, when interest rates continued to drop, I looked into refinancing the properties. That's when I discovered that I had overpaid by about $40,000 for the three properties.

The first property I bought for $159,000, $10,000 less than the asking price. Yet I overpaid by about $5,000. More than a year later, I paid $205,000 for a triple unit that was listed at $215,000. I later learned it was worth only about $185,000 at the time of purchase. I paid less than the asking price for the third property, too, only to find out later that I still overpaid.

When you invest in real estate, there are a lot of variables to consider, like tenants and mortgage payments – and no guarantees. The fact is, you invest in real estate for profit. I was hoping for appreciation of at least 5 percent a year. The property values increased only about 2 percent.

I learned from my mistake and I decided to get serious about investing in real estate. First I got a partner and merged my former company, K Group Properties LLC, into a new entity called Phoenix Partners Property LLC. It's nice to have someone who has a vested interest in every purchase. He puts in more capital, and I do more grunt work. We both understand that if a deal isn't working, there will always be others.

I started looking at the county auditor's web site, which lists recent sales on any street in the county. Then I started checking out various listings to see what other investors were charging for rent for similar properties in the area. I also started developing connections with bankers to see what interest rates were available and to get breakdowns on property expenses. If a double brings in $1,500 a month in rent, I need to make sure that money covers my monthly mortgage, taxes, water and some profit.

I learned to keep emotions out of deals. When I first started investing in real estate, I would listen to a real estate agent's advice to raise my offer by a few thousand after a counteroffer came in. I used to worry about losing the property. I know better now.

Now, when I look at the numbers and determine what a property is worth and what I'm willing to spend, I won't go over that price – no matter how much cajoling an agent does to complete a sale.

Analyzing properties on a financial basis has made all the difference. The last five properties we purchased were all immediately appraised at a higher value than the purchase price. If we invest x amount for a property, we expect an 8 to 10 percent gain.

If you're going to buy real estate as an investment, don't get caught up with emotions. It's strictly business. Now, instead of immediately agreeing to a higher purchase price, I always ask myself if it makes sense. If it doesn't, I walk away. It's not worth taking a risk and losing.

Visiting overseas no guarantee of business

Larry Yankow
Title: President
Company: International Transport Services
Founded: 1986
Headquarters: Cleveland
Employees: 17

I've traveled overseas a lot, and I'm often embarrassed by the lack of cultural sensitivity among other visitors. It's hard to believe that I used to be the same way while trying to develop business relationships.

My business is like a travel agency for cargo. About 11 years ago, I decided it was time for International Transport Services to expand. Today, imports from Asia account for about 40 percent of sales, with about 1,200 shipments a year. But at first when I was attempting to increase business with additional freight forwarders in Asia, it was a struggle to get one or two shipments.

I continually sent business to my contacts, but they didn't send me any. I was confused until I talked to a businessman who had been doing business in Asia for many years. He told me my approach was all wrong.

My biggest mistake was expecting business to flow my way just because I made an effort to visit several business owners in one trip.

When I first tried to develop business, I basically picked some companies from a business directory and tried to start a relationship through fax machines. Then I scheduled a trip to Tokyo, Taipei and Hong Kong for a site visit to make sure they were viable businesses. I had done the same thing when I started doing business in Europe years earlier.

In Asia, my so-called partners were very friendly, and they agreed to send business to Cleveland. I spent a week going to different cities, and I thought it was a successful trip.

I went back home thinking everything was great. Days passed, and nothing came across my fax machine. Then six months passed and still nothing. I was sending business their way, but I was not getting any business from my Asian counterparts.

I thought about my trip, and I was confused. The people I met with were so friendly. We went out to eat. We went out to drink, and everyone entertained me. I even got gifts. I was walking on air because I thought we had an understanding. I really believed it would be that easy.

I turned to a friend who runs a similar business on the West Coast. He explained that they were not agreeing to do business with me, as I had thought. Just because people were saying OK, that didn't mean that they wanted to be my partners. It only meant that they were acknowledging that they heard what I was saying.

For the first time, I realized that I was acting as if I were the big American coming over and they should be happy to do business with me. I didn't take time to understand their culture, and I didn't think I needed a translator. They were agreeing with me simply because they didn't want to disagree with me.

My friend told me that you cannot go to Asia and expect to get partners on one trip. He told me that I could expect to make several trips to show I was sincere about developing relationships.

I made my second trip to Asia a year after that first trip, and I had an entirely different attitude. I made sure we were communicating and clarified agreements. I asked them to repeat what I was saying to make sure we were clear that I was seeking a reciprocal relationship. In the process, I learned that sometimes they didn't understand what I was saying. We started a dialogue, and I got some business when I returned home.

Less than a year after the second trip, I visited a third time and I worked even harder trying to educate them about what Northeast Ohio has to offer in the freight-forwarding business. I brought along maps and made other graphic literature to help them understand Cleveland's central location. I talked about how close we are to cities that they might be familiar with, like Cincinnati and Procter & Gamble, or Akron and tires, or Sandusky and Cedar Point.

They basically knew of Los Angeles and New York. But that's

no different than my initial knowledge of China. I had no clue how close Shanghai is to Ningbo, and I didn't appreciate how large their country is. While we have only a few cities with a million or more people, China has hundreds. It's continually changing, too. Just 21 years ago, Shenzhen was a fishing village. Now it has all sorts of industry with westernized hotels.

On that third trip they took me more seriously and introduced me to more colleagues, including export managers. They started opening up to me and even introduced me to some of their clients. It's sort of like a dating process. It takes time to figure out if it's a good fit.

For the last 10 years I've been going to Asia twice a year. Now that the United States and China have better relations, my visa is good for multiple entries. It used to be good for just one trip.

I've continued to work on building the import division of my company. Now we have four employees dedicated to that part of the world, including a young woman from China who speaks Mandarin and Cantonese. I no longer have to worry about losing details in translation. Working with an international group of freight forwarders has also made it easier to do business.

I'll continue to travel to build business. Whether it's to Europe or Asia, I'm conscious about doing my homework and being sensitive to other cultures in order to build relationships. In other words, I leave my American attitude at home.

Packaging proved key to making product sell

Dianna Dunlevy Seufer
Title: President
Company: D'Marie Inc.
Founded: 1999
Headquarters: Bedford Heights
Employees: 3

When you're the one who makes and sells your product, it's a balancing act trying to manage growth.

I've heard too many horror stories about mom and pop business owners who have managed to get their products sold by a major retailer only to have disastrous results. Stories range from putting all their eggs in one basket and losing the account to being hurt by mandatory term payments or not being big enough to fill a big order.

My opinion is that you get one chance with these people, so you have to be ready.

We've been cautious promoting our D'Marie Tuscan Triangles. They're a cross between a cracker and a chip, and they've been a hit with my corporate catering clients for years. Three years ago, my husband and business partner, Mark Seufer, and I finally decided to focus on selling the triangles at retail and wholesale gourmet shows. We soon had 500 wholesale accounts with wine shops, interior design shops, gourmet and gift shops scattered all over the country. Having 500 accounts means nothing if they're not reordering.

Our biggest mistake was not educating our wholesale customers on how to sell our products.

Buyers who discovered the chips at the shows loved them. But they bought such small quantities that they got lost on the shelves. Besides that, they weren't offering samples at their stores, which is key for a new and unusual product. Since they weren't selling, they weren't reordering.

In the past three years, our business growth was managing us, instead of the other way around. We were winging it. We went from leasing space in a church kitchen in Bainbridge Township to building out a 4,000-square-foot facility in Bedford Heights where we run the business. We leased a packaging machine from another company in Strongsville until we could afford to get our own this year. We brought a trailer to get our product to retail shows, only to turn it in for a larger one in order to accommodate demand.

Everything costs a lot when you're trying to bring a product to market. And we were being cautious because we didn't want to get in over our heads. We didn't want a huge order until our systems were in place.

We thought we were doing the right thing by focusing on small shops. But looking back, we weren't taking control of our company.

Wholesale buyers dictated sales to us. We would let customers pick and choose flavors, even splitting cases to fill orders. We even accepted terms at first, when customers asked us to bill them.

I was humble because I just wanted people to like the product and I wanted to make the sale. It's funny—in all the years that I was in sales before I became an entrepreneur, I never took rejection personally. This was different, though, because I made this product.

The way we operated caused more work and wasn't paying off with reorders. In the meantime, we were continually developing new products after talking to customers. Wine shop customers were buying our chips in bulk orders for wine tastings, but they were buying dips elsewhere—so we developed a line of wine dips. We also developed frappe vino, a mix that turns wine and water into a frozen drink.

We finally realized we were working stupid. We were working extremely hard—not smart. Everything changed when we took a step back and addressed the problem of reorders.

The first signal came from a snap decision made just before the Vintage Ohio retail show last August. Mark asked me what our package deal would be. I added up the cost of a frappe vino, a wine dip mix and a 6-ounce bag of Tuscan Triangles. Then I discounted $1.95, for a total of $20. Almost under my breath, I said, 'It's like a cocktail party in a bag.' He wrote "party in a bag" on a chalkboard, and we sold out.

The entire fourth quarter last year we did phenomenally well with "party in a bag" at consumer shows throughout the region. It's a unisex gift at a great price point. Everyone wants something new and different.

We started thinking about how we could transfer this success to our wholesale accounts. I thought about the decade I spent as a sales representative for various companies and I knew the importance of properly merchandising the product.

We came up with a display system for 108 items, enough to sell 36 "party in a bag" kits. My customers pay $465 for the display, signs, bags, all the products and some extra product for a sampling program. The key to selling any gourmet product is sampling. Before we came up with this system, the vast majority of retailers were not sampling.

Since January, when we introduced the display system, sales have climbed 60 percent. Because of this system, our average sale has doubled. My customers are enjoying higher sales, and empty slots in the display remind them to reorder. In retail, you never want to sell out. You want to sell through your inventory.

As we add products to our line, we're going to sell them using our merchandise display system. If our retailers are making sales, the products are a success for all of us.

Cleveland bakery owner discovers the only constant is change

Alma Sapia Alfonzo
Title: President
Company: Lelolai Bakery & Café
Founded: 2001
Headquarters: Cleveland
Employees: Nine

We opened Lelolai Bakery & Café in March 2001 when the economy was booming and Mayor Michael White's plans for Ohio City and the West Side Market were outstanding. We love being around so many different cultures in this area.

I decided to open a bakery after my husband and I both got laid off around the same time. I was working in hospital administration and he was in banking. By the time Francisco was offered a job in another city, I was already preparing for a grand opening.

We intended to serve the Hispanic population with Spanish pastries that include flan and polvorones. Soon after we opened, though, we quickly learned that 70 percent of our customers were non-Hispanic.

We changed our packaging. Next to the Spanish word "polvorones" we added the English version, "shortbread pastry."

We added a café to the bakery, offering Cuban sandwiches and beverages. The plan was eventually to expand into the wholesale market with money from the retail business. But after the Sept. 11 terrorist attacks, business fell drastically and we had to change our plans to try to enter the wholesale market sooner.

We were ill-prepared.

We wasted so much money and time traveling to Buffalo and Pennsylvania with our flan to visit major supermarket chains. When we told them our products had no preservatives, they frowned.

My biggest mistake was targeting large wholesale operations when we weren't willing to change our ingredients.

Our company is seven years old now and our macaroons and polvorones are sold in local grocery stores like Nature's Bin, Dave's Market, Marc's, West Point Market in Akron, Gibbs Butcher Block in Columbia Station and in specialty stores in Indianapolis and Michigan.

We found that family-owned markets have great customers who appreciate our products. At any given time we can talk directly to CEOs or owners, and decisions are made immediately.

But when we first tried to enter the wholesale market, we targeted much larger operations that couldn't handle the freshness of our products. Flan has a lot of calcium and protein in it because it's basically milk, eggs and sugar. Company officials who tasted our flan told us they enjoyed it and had never tasted anything like it.

We never thought about risks, like being required to grow at their pace by producing as much product as a chain wanted. But we had a much bigger problem. By the time our products would have made it to all of their distribution centers, they would be out of date. I had no interest in adding preservatives.

One reason we opened a bakery is because I first started making flan when a good friend of mine was battling cancer and had trouble swallowing. I wanted her to eat something nutritious that was rich in calcium and protein and was easy to swallow. Flan is a delicious alternative to Jell-O and pudding.

But it's also an upscale dessert. We weren't prepared for

spending so much time explaining the dessert. When we were trying to go wholesale with much larger distribution, we spent a lot of time educating buyers. Their knowledge of Spanish foods in general was limited to foods from Mexico and spicy foods. But there are all sorts of foods in various Spanish cultures.

Unfortunately, it took a while for me to realize that flan is considered a specialty food that calls for specialty marketing. It's a mainstream product where I come from in Puerto Rico, as well as in Latin America, Spain and some areas in Europe, but it's hard to find in the United States. It didn't click until I went to the Fancy Food Show in New York and it was treated as a specialty or fancy food.

The bottom line is that we weren't ready or willing to change any of our products in order to grow a wholesale business. We had several meetings with U.S. Foodservice about an opportunity to sell our cheesecakes to cruise lines, hotels and catering companies. Again, it would mean changing the formulation. I hated to close the door on that opportunity, but I didn't feel comfortable moving that fast and changing our fresh products.

That's when I decided to search for other distributors and venues that had a better understanding of and appreciation for freshness and quality. We're continually building the wholesale side of our business, but we're doing it at our own pace by targeting smaller markets and chains.

I've learned a lot in the last six years. My advice to any business owner is never to rest on your laurels. Keep your business plan handy and be ready to make changes.

PASSION

HOW MANY TIMES HAVE YOU DRIVEN DOWN A STREET or logged on a computer and wondered, "What happened to that business? It's gone."

Companies fail for different reasons. Sometimes it's unavoidable. But more often than not, it's because the owner didn't have what it takes to stick it out and jump over hurdles—Passion.

Running a small business isn't just about the numbers, goods, services, customers and employees. It takes a lot of heart, guts and determination to hang in there when naysayers are telling you to hang it up. And naysayers come in many forms, ranging from bankers to friends and family.

You've heard this story: two entrepreneurs start with the same resources, one builds a sucessful enterprise while the other one fails. Or the two entrepreneurs that lose everything, and one, once again is able to create success.

Both have challenges. Both make hard choices. Both probably felt like quitting at times. But the successful one has something the other one just doesn't have—passion. Without question it's the one factor that gave him or her the tenacity to push through hardships.

Sometimes the first step to getting through the most difficult times is remembering why you decided to go into business. What was it that used to make you jump out of bed and start your day? You need to call on that same drive to figure out a way to tackle tough issues. Then you can get back to doing what you love the most.

Only this time, you'll be even better and have much more fun.

Learn from your mistakes and vow not to ever go down that same path again.

By blindly expanding, couple was spread thin

Yvonne Sanderson
Title: Owner/Photographer
Company: Focal Plane Photography LLC
Founded: 1986
Headquarters: South Euclid
Employees: 2

When you run a small business, it's natural to want to expand. We expanded our aerial-photography business twice. But both times, we actually hurt the business.

Most of our customers are corporate clients. We're often hired for construction progress reports or by commercial real estate firms and developers who need photos of highway access and rooftops for real estate finance packages. Sometimes we're hired by individuals, usually for gift giving. If customers are moving and want to have a keepsake of their home, they need a view from the sky, especially if they want to include tennis courts, swimming pools and a lake.

Aviation has been in our blood for a long time. I met Mark Sanderson, my husband and business partner, in 1984 at a local club flying sailplanes. I started Focal Plane Photography two years later after studying photography in New York City. I fell into the business from referrals of local aviation contacts, but it's been a great opportunity to combine both of my passions.

About 10 years later, Mark got the idea to put the airplane to work at night with a second business, a lighted, computerized sign company. Messages scrolled on a digital board under the plane's wing. That business lasted three years.

Aerial photography is a thrilling business, but it's also a business with ebbs and flows, especially in the winter. Six years ago I decided to open a photography studio in Cleveland Heights, taking photos of people and pets. That business lasted four years.

Our biggest mistake was losing focus on our primary business—aerial photography.

Both the lighted sign and the photo studio businesses seemed like the right thing to do at the time. But they cost us a lot of money and time, with little payoff.

We opened Nighthawk signs at a time when Jacobs Field was always sold out. Clients ranged from politicians running for office to people celebrating anniversaries or proposing marriage.

Unfortunately, we didn't understand that that business had more to do with specialty advertising than with aviation. It required a different set of marketing skills in order to explain the business. And at $350 an hour, it wasn't cheap.

It also had to be dark enough for the lighted ads to be visible on the ground. During the long days of summer, baseball games and other events often ended before dark.

At the time, Mark was working full time as chief pilot for a Cleveland-based corporation, which meant I had to hire flight instructor pilots. We lost money on that venture.

Six years ago I decided to open a photography studio, thinking it was the perfect opportunity to use my photography skills in a different way. I thought I could take portraits during the slower periods and have space to show off large aerial prints to clients and prospective clients.

I enjoyed taking photos of individuals, families and pets. But I didn't have a clear understanding of how much competition there is for portraiture, including big-box retailers. And it wasn't easy dividing my time between two very different photo specialties. It was a constant juggling act. I tried to take care of aerial clients on good-weather days, but when a family spends time coordinating clothes for a family portrait, you don't want to have to reschedule because the sun is shining.

Sometimes cancellations were unavoidable. Other times I was dashing out to the airport while the weather was still good. And even when the weather was good, sometimes it was difficult finding a pilot.

The photography part of the business was fun. Everything else around it was stressful. In the end, it was financially frustrating. With all of the overhead expenses, we just broke even.

Two years ago I decided to return to my home-based office and focus exclusively on aerial photography. Last year we had a record year in business with a 25 percent increase in sales from the previous year. Sales are up 50 percent since we closed the studio.

Part of the increase had to do with timing. Even though we've had a web site for years, technology is faster now and people can find us quickly and see photos in seconds.

We've also gotten better at optimizing our web site since Mark retired and became my full-time technology professional. He spends a couple of hours each week ensuring that our company is among the top two aerial photography companies listed on search engines.

When we had the studio, about half our clients were out of state. Now those clients account for 80 percent of our business. We've never even met many customers. They find us on the internet. We negotiate the price and location by phone. After we take the photos, we put the proofs on the internet and take credit card numbers by phone.

Increasing our business has involved cold calling, subscribing to lead services and following leads in newspapers. We've gotten more active with the chamber of commerce and joined the Society for Marketing Professional Services, a group that specializes in marketing for architecture, engineering and construction.

We're working harder than ever, but we're also more productive and having more fun. It's true—if you do what you love and really apply yourself, the money will come.

Parma caterer has taste of trouble

Bill Rini
Title: President
Company: A Taste of Excellence
Founded: 1992
Headquarters: Parma
Employees: 50

When my sister, Michelle, got her first catering job, she locked her keys in the car before the event. I threw a brick through the window, calmed her down and then helped her pull off the event with style.

A Taste of Excellence was my sister's dream. I was a sophomore, with short-term plans of having fun in college and long-term plans of getting into broadcasting. She persuaded me to get a bachelor's degree in culinary arts and hospitality management in Miami, then return to Cleveland as her business partner in 1995.

She was a culinary artist. I was stronger in sales and marketing.

We were an awesome team. Sales tripled to $350,000 in a year. But she died unexpectedly a year later, right before we learned the company would finally turn a profit.

She was my best friend. Within a three-month period, six close relatives and a friend died. When you endure so much tragedy, it's difficult to concentrate on business. I wanted to hang it up. Two good friends motivated me to push forward. Then they helped me land a contract to cater a Welcome Back Browns Ball at the [team's] training facility in Berea. It was the beginning of my comeback.

I kept plugging away until we outgrew our space four years later. Instead of finding office and kitchen space, I got in over my head with a 40,000-square-foot building that included a 200-seat Italian restaurant and an 800-seat banquet facility.

My biggest mistake was trying to grow too quickly without having the proper team in place to manage growth.

People including my accountant and my father told me not to

do it. My attitude was, "I got this." I thought if it was a venture that involved food, I could do it. Never mind that I was underfinanced going into it. Eight months later, I pretty much lost everything.

I had an executive chef with no culinary degree. He couldn't manage food and labor costs. Nor could he manage a staff that tripled in size immediately.

Now, I don't hire anyone for executive positions without a degree. We have people who go far in this company without a degree. But for executive positions, it's a requirement.

My break-even point before turning a profit went from a half-million dollars to $600,000 to about $2 million. I bought the place in April. By August, I knew we weren't going to make it.

We were losing about $3,000 to $4,000 a week. I had a large payroll. Sales weren't coming in. Rent was too high. Utilities were three times what I had anticipated. I could go on and on.

We worked out the lease, but I had to sell all of my assets, including a rental property in Cleveland and my interest in a condo in downtown Chicago. I sold my stock portfolio. I had to bleed the business financially, borrow money from family and take out loans.

I was always successful as an off-premise caterer, so I started building out a new place to work from. I still had two salespeople booking parties, but sales dropped because my attention was somewhere else. I was depressed. Employees saw right through me. We were all so excited. To fail like that was tough.

After three months of spending a lot of time on my couch at home, my wife, Dawn, encouraged me in her own special way to get up and live up to my potential. She basically told me to get off my butt.

I knew that marketing would be key in building the business, so I spent a ton of money on our web site and other marketing channels. It paid off. I was invited to bid on a food service contract at Case Western Reserve University. We beat out a national company and other well-established food service operations by bringing a fresh approach to food preparation and service at the location.

After that, we grew by hiring a great corporate chef, a district manager, a general manager of special events and a director of retail operations. Now, contract dining services account for about 60 percent of revenues. Contracts include Crawford Auto Aviation Museum, Hale Farm and Village and Cleveland Museum of Natural History.

Now my break-even point is $1.4 million with sales projected at $5 million for 2008. Sales more than doubled in the last year, which put us on the Weatherhead 100 list for Northeast Ohio's fastest-growing companies for the first time.

Our team wants to grow. We have every intention of doubling our revenues in the next five years. But we're cautious because we take so much pride in the work we do. We recently turned down two major requests for proposals because we just entered a long-term agreement with a Fortune 500 company. It's tempting to grow fast. But when we commit to a customer, we want to give them undivided attention and the world-class food and service that we promised.

Recourse loans gone bad tanked thriving business

Sal Spagnola
Title: President and CEO
Company: OBM
Founded: 1975
Headquarters: Parma
Employees: 50

Find the prospective company. Find the right contact at the company. Arrange the demo. Build rapport. Do the demo. And then close.

It's a six-step sales process that helped build our company to as many as 450 employees at one point.

Recourse loans also helped us to build Ohio Business Machines. The positive side is that no customer who wanted a copy machine was ever turned down. Everybody got credit. The down side to recourse loans was that if a customer didn't pay up, we were stuck paying the bank.

Each year, we built about $200,000 into our budget to cover bad debt as a cost of doing business. At one point we were doing $2 million a month in leases, so it was OK.

We used to be the largest dealership in Ohio. After a reorganization, we had about 350 employees and $35 million in sales in 2000. Then in eight months, bad debt resulting from recourse loans increased to $3.7 million. We filed for Chapter 11 reorganization in 2002.

My biggest mistake was doing recourse loans.

I inherited this financial arrangement from my predecessor when I bought the company 20 years ago. Recourse loans were part of the company when it was founded in 1975. The loans were good for OBM for many years. In this business, about a third of sales don't close due to financing problems. Recourse loans guaranteed that all sales went through.

But in 2000, we had a lot of bad luck with big accounts. Several factors involving recourse loans led to the demise of the company.

LTV Steel went out of business and took a lot of after-market companies with them. One account was $450,000. The bank called the note the next day. A mortgage company went out of business, and we got stuck holding that note for $350,000.

When Credit General Life Insurance Co. went out of business because of fraud, the bank seized all the assets—including my copiers. The bank called the note for $1.3 million.

It was tough times with $20,000 in sales here and $30,000 there.

Then after the Sept. 11 terrorist attacks, sales declined overall by 10 to 15 percent. Softening in sales caused us to violate our covenants at the bank.

The bank started charging us $25,000 a month in fees in order for them not to call the loans. OBM was economically sound, but bad debt consumed us. We were so profitable that Konica Minolta Business Systems, our manufacturer, bought the company's assets in November 2002 and kept me in business in Toledo.

It wasn't an easy decision. I did it after I had exhausted every alternative. When you're in bankruptcy, everybody on the creditors committee has to vote for you to restructure your debt. The leasing companies and banks refused to negotiate. In essence, selling the company cleansed it of all bad debts. I signed a 3-year-non-compete clause to stay out of the Cleveland market. But the OBM name and Konika Minolta kept us in business, working as one of their authorized dealers.

Selling the company was extremely difficult for me. I was very depressed.

I started out as a salesman in 1982 and moved up through the ranks to president fairly quickly. When the founder died suddenly at a young age, I bought the company six years after I started working there. OBM was part of my fiber.

For two weeks after the sale, I kept my head in a pillow. Then bills, including college tuition, forced me to get up. That, and my fear of failure.

We already had a presence in Toledo with three employees and about 300 customers. That's nothing in the digital office solutions business. We worked hard to build the company by expanding in the Toledo and Michigan markets.

We also formed a relationship with another manufacturer, Panasonic. In three years, we became the dominant dealer in the Toledo area with customers including Toledo public schools, Campbell's Soup and Tenneco Inc. Our 25 employees moved into a 10,000-square-foot building.

As soon as our noncompete ended, we moved back to Cleveland, and we haven't looked back. We've been fortunate to renew old relationships as well as gain new relationships, including the Cleveland Municipal School District.

The OBM name is strong in this market, synonymous with office equipment. For 25 years, the company ran radio commercials. The future is looking bright again. Panasonic received the J.D. Power award in 2006 for its No. 1-ranked line of copiers and overall customer satisfaction. For the first quarter of 2007, OBM was ranked as the second-largest Panasonic dealer in the Midwest and the ninth-largest in the nation.

OBM is virtually debt free with no long-term finance loans or debt in general. We plan to stay that way. We will never do another recourse loan. We're growing every day with profits, not borrowed money.

Sculptor learned belatedly to believe in his own abilities

Woodrow Nash
Title: Owner
Company:The Rage Gallery
Founded: 1994
Headquarters: Akron
Employees: Four

I'm a sculptor. Each year I exhibit my work at art shows throughout the country at fine art venues, gallery exhibitions and about 10 international trade shows, including the New York International Art Expo. Working with stoneware, earthenware, terra cotta, porcelain and heat, I combine various styles and techniques to create an art form that I call "African Nouveau."

My work is collected internationally. Pieces range in price from a $350 figurative vase to a $20,000 life-size, full-figure statue. Collectors include working professionals, politicians, sports figures and entertainers.

Right now I'm at a relatively comfortable place. I feel that I've reached a degree of success that allows me the time needed to be more creative without worrying about paying bills. But I didn't start out this way. I got off to a slow start with an entirely different form of art before I discovered my niche. Early on, I participated in art and craft fairs in small towns throughout the country, selling vases I created that resembled large field stones.

My biggest mistake was not believing enough in my own

abilities to become a free-lance artist sooner.

Not having the confidence to overcome all of the challenges and hurdles that come along with leaving the security of a corporate job was also a mistake.

I have always been strong in art. But like a lot of people with artistic talent, I spent 20 years in corporate America working as a technical illustrator and artist.

Working at companies including Goodyear Aerospace, American Greetings and Widen Colour Graphics, my creativity was limited. I always felt I was only as good as my last assignment. And it was a tremendous amount of stress.

I left my last corporate job under duress. It was a blessing in disguise, though, because I probably still would be working for a company otherwise.

Art is not a career that is encouraged.

It's generally looked at as something that you do as a hobby. I was taught that you couldn't become successful as an artist. That's why most people who choose art as a career either become art teachers or go into commercial art fields.

In 1992, while I was working in Wisconsin, my wife and I were walking around a lake one day when we saw a lot of people gathered around the state capitol.

An art fair was going on, and I noticed that people were buying art. They were pulling out credit cards and cash, and I was taking it all in. I thought, "I could do this."

I immediately rented a studio the size of a closet and started working with clay. I spent about a year creating vases before I was ready to participate in a craft fair.

In Wisconsin, field stones are everywhere—remnants of the state's glacial past—so I created vases that looked like stones. I made $3,000 in one weekend, and that was enough encouragement for me.

The problem was, the vases were not universally accepted. I went to many shows where I made just enough money to keep me going. It wasn't an easy decision to leave corporate America.

I no longer had the security of a regular paycheck and

benefits, and I had to stay motivated. I put a sign in my studio that said, "The safety net is gone." That sign kept me grounded and motivated.

About a year into working as a free-lance artist, I realized that nothing about my work said anything about me. I was trying to be all things to all people, and it wasn't working. I changed my strategy, defined a customer base and started selling work at African festivals and professional conferences.

Then I spent $10,000 that I didn't have to self-publish a black and white paperback photo book about my work. I wasn't known to anyone at the time, so the $15 book helped to legitimize me as an artist and also served as a business card.

Initially, my goal at the shows became selling my book. People who were serious contacted me later to make purchases.

It wasn't an overnight fix, though. I had to work odd jobs. At one point I had three part-time jobs while spending hours and hours at my studio.

At the same time, I used skills gained as a former art director and production supervisor to promote my work.

As an artist, defining your customer is key. It's common to find only 10 potential customers at a trade show with 5,000 participants.

Becoming a free-lance artist is the best decision that I've ever made. Now, I'm limited only by my ability to create.

Photographer in business took time to get the picture

Cheryl DeBono
Title: Owner/photographer
Company: Michaelangelo's Art Photography & Framing
Founded: 1985
Headquarters: Strongsville
Employees: 4

I see photos everywhere I go. It's all about instinct and timing when it comes to capturing a memorable expression.

My love for photography started when I was a teenager, always snapping pictures of family and friends. After I graduated from high school, I spent a couple years taking pictures at retail stores throughout Ohio, Pennsylvania, New York and West Virginia.

I started my business on a fluke. I took photos of my nephew in a makeshift home studio and started getting customers when people saw the pictures posted at the custom photo lab where I worked.

My experience runs the gamut from family portraits and weddings to industrial photography and even close-up shots of flowers. Today my husband and I operate an art gallery and photo studio, and I've never been happier taking photos the way I want.

I wish I could say that I've always been on the right path. My biggest mistake was spending way too many years not taking pictures from my heart. I was shooting what people believed they wanted, which is the same thing that they saw at other places.

I'm no different from any other professional who wants to continually grow. But when I look back at much of my portfolio, I see dozens of families and children in photographs similar to what's offered at chain photographic studios—complete with props and seasonal things like bunnies.

Those are not fine-art portraits. My clients wanted photos where subjects were centered with the perfect smile. I wanted to focus more on the subject and not use distracting props and backgrounds. You want to be able to look at a portrait and really see the subject.

About 10 years ago, I started taking extra photos the way I wanted. But my clients didn't get it, so they hardly bought those extra shots.

I'd hear things like, "Why is the baby's head or foot cut off?" And I didn't exactly work hard to persuade clients to try something different. For many years, I was not only a business owner but also a single mother raising two girls. I just wanted a happy client because I had to pay bills.

I also knew I wasn't the only photographer who felt that way. I'd hear other wedding photographers say that they weren't going to waste time shooting anything artistic, like an angle from the back of a bride's dress, because they had to please the customer.

I knew I could do a better job. A couple years ago I finally decided to follow my passion and change the way I took pictures.

I had built up a big enough following and enough confidence to realize I could find customers who appreciated my style. You can deviate from the mainstream with lighting, poses and angles and capture something incredible.

Business has improved since we moved to our location in Strongsville. Maybe it's because the business attracts more art lovers and people who expect something different from an attached photography studio. Customers walk in and see all sorts of eclectic art from local and national artists made from pewter, glass, wood and metal.

I believe portraits should say something about a person. I love close-ups because they capture a personality. Some of my favorite works are a collage of head shots of a little girl showing her happy, frustrated and mad. Basically it captures a typical toddler's many moods. Another favorite shows a sleeping newborn cupped in the palm of her father's hand.

Don't get me wrong, I know that one of the golden rules of business is that the customer is always right. But after my experience, I firmly believe that in a creative industry where you're selling a product that you've made, you also have to evolve.

Another one of my favorites is a shot of 3-year-old toddler twins. I got it when they were preparing to leave the studio after their mother had changed their clothes from elegant dresses to a casual denim outfit. They were just standing there, and, without being told, they wrapped their arms around one another. As one tilted her head onto the other's shoulder, I snapped the picture. That fleeting moment was priceless.